Moralizing the Market

Moralizing the Market

How Gaullist France Embraced the US Model
of Securities Regulation

YVES-MARIE PÉRÉON

Johns Hopkins University Press
Baltimore

Johns Hopkins University Press
2715 North Charles Street
Baltimore, Maryland 21218-4363
www.press.jhu.edu

Cataloging-in-Publication Data is available from the Library of Congress.

A catalog record for this book is available from the British Library.

ISBN-13: 978-1-4214-2485-9 (hardcover : alk. paper)
ISBN-10: 1-4214-2485-1 (hardcover : alk. paper)
ISBN-13: 978-1-4214-2486-6 (electronic)
ISBN-10: 1-4214-2486-X (electronic)

*Special discounts are available for bulk purchases of this book. For more information,
please contact Special Sales at 410-516-6936 or specialsales@press.jhu.edu.*

Johns Hopkins University Press uses environmentally friendly book materials,
including recycled text paper that is composed of at least 30 percent post-consumer
waste, whenever possible.

To the memory of Marie-Louise Gilles,
who did not live to see the book completed

CONTENTS

Many people helped me tell this story.

Mr. Jean-Yves Haberer agreed to be interviewed and to share his invaluable and remarkably precise recollections of the events surrounding the creation of the Commission des Opérations de Bourse; his personal papers, deposited with the archives of the French Ministry for the Economy and Finance, proved a treasure trove of information.

Mrs. Jean-Jacques Burgard graciously gave me access to the personal papers of her late husband.

Mrs. Françoise Buisson, director of the European and International Affairs Division at the Autorité des Marchés Financiers, was kind enough to shed a more contemporary light on the relationship between the French and foreign securities regulators.

Several archival repositories were essential to my research. I wish to thank the directors and archivists at the Centre d'histoire de Sciences Po (Paris), the Institut pour la Gestion Publique et le Développement Économique (Montreuil), and the Institut Georges Pompidou; and the archives of the Banque de France (Paris), of the French Ministry for the Economy and Finance (Savigny-le-Temple), of the French presidency (Pierrefitte-sur-Seine), of French banks Crédit Agricole and BNP-Paribas (Paris), of French industrial conglomerate Pechiney at the Institut pour l'Histoire de l'Aluminium (Clichy), and of the Hoover Institution Library (Stanford University) for their assistance on site and via e-mail. At Stanford, I was lucky to have had the help of a diligent researcher, Jenny Fischmann.

The idea for this book emerged from a seminar organized in 2012 in Lagardelle, France, by Robert Frank, professor of the History of International Relations at the Sorbonne. It took shape in a series of conversations with Vincent Michelot, professor of American Politics at Sciences Po (Lyon).

Olivier Feiertag, professor of Modern Economic History at the University of Rouen, was a source of ideas and support throughout the process of writing this book. Olivier; Michel Margairaz, professor of Modern Economic History at the University of Paris I Panthéon-Sorbonne; and Laure Quennouëlle-Corre, directrice de recherche at the Centre National de la Recherche Scientifique

(CNRS), generously opened their address books and pointed me in the right directions. I had the opportunity to present and discuss some of my early assumptions during an international conference entitled "Money, Power, Representations in the Americas and in Europe" at the University of Paris Ouest Nanterre La Défense in November 2014. Conversations and e-mail exchanges with friends and colleagues on both sides of the Atlantic Ocean helped me delineate the scope of my investigations.

In focusing on a brief period in the history of the Paris Bourse, I have necessarily relied on the existing scholarship of the French and American securities markets. A special mention must be made of Laure Quennouëlle-Corre's *La place financière de Paris au XXe siècle*, Pierre-Henri Conac's *La régulation des marchés boursiers par la Commission des Opérations de Bourse (COB) et la Securities and Exchange Commission (SEC)*, Michael E. Parrish's *Securities Regulation and the New Deal*, Joel Seligman's *The Transformation of Wall Street*, and Michael Perino's *The Hellhound of Wall Street*.

Marie-Elizabeth Rosenzweig and Michel Barnoud offered valuable help to identify and locate out-of-print articles and decades-old government documents. Jean Boissinot, himself not unaware of the dilemmas facing market regulators, lent an understanding ear to my questions.

Writing books is a struggle, but writing books in a foreign language is an even harder one. I am fortunate to have been able to rely on the thoughtful reading and advice of Dina Goldfinger, Geraldine Vaughan, Éléonore Chinetti, Anne-Laure Tissut, and Jean-Marc Agostini, whose suggestions significantly improved the manuscript. To them all, my sincere thanks.

I am also grateful for the support offered by the University of Rouen in the form of a sabbatical. Miguel Olmos and Marc Martinez, then co-heads of our research group, helped me gain the time I needed to make progress in my project.

Colleagues from the Department of English Studies have always remained aware of the challenge posed by writing a book while fulfilling other academic requirements. I am especially obliged to Alain Lauzanne and Luc Benoît à La Guillaume, co-chairs of the department at the time.

At Johns Hopkins University Press, Elizabeth Sherburn Demers believed in this book from an early stage. Andre Barnett offered guidance through the editing process. Anonymous reviewers also must be acknowledged for their contribution.

Finally, I owe a great debt to my friends and my family, who gave me support and much-needed encouragement.

Any mistakes are mine.

Moralizing the Market

Introduction

Honest, austere, and hardworking, Bernard Tricot was the quintessential French *haut fonctionnaire* (high-ranking civil servant). He served as general secretary of the Élysée Palace under President Charles de Gaulle between 1967 and 1969 and was later, between 1980 and 1984, to chair the Commission des Opérations de Bourse (COB). In *Mémoires* published in 1994, Tricot briefly described the origins of the institution in charge of regulating the Paris Stock Exchange:

> As Pierre Chatenet [the COB's first chairman] told me, the COB is indeed one of those institutions at the crossroads of government and civil society, often inspired by Anglo-Saxon models; Franklin Roosevelt's American SEC had been established at a time when the 1930s crisis made it urgent to restore investors' confidence. Michel Debré, Georges Pompidou and General de Gaulle (in an order that is not hierarchical but reflects the path followed, in that particular instance, by thought and initiative) had wanted to redirect savings towards the needs of a modern economy and, first and foremost, towards industrial activities; this would be achieved by giving the general public better information and a higher level of security.[1]

In this short paragraph, Tricot expressed his and his predecessor's perception of the COB's origins, missions, and administrative status. He dutifully acknowledged what was owed to the three men who embodied the Fifth Republic during the first decade of its existence—President Charles de Gaulle, Prime Minister Michel Debré, and Prime Minister Georges Pompidou, whom de Gaulle successively appointed to head the French government—and celebrated their successful effort to modernize the French economy. Tricot also matter-of-factly stated that the "Anglo-Saxon" Securities and Exchange Commission (SEC) had been their source of inspiration. In doing so, he was not unveiling a shameful secret: Pierre Chatenet; Debré, then the minister of finance in his successor's government; and others who played a decisive part in the foundation of the COB in 1967–1968 routinely referred to the SEC, President Franklin D. Roosevelt, and the 1930s.[2] General histories of the French securities market, along with research monographs on the COB, mention the

American institution that had inspired its promoters,[3] and comparative law scholars have demonstrated the extent to which American securities law influenced the COB's own philosophy.[4] The creation of the COB, however, has not been investigated thoroughly by historians.[5]

It is all the more surprising that the decision made by Gaullist authorities in the late 1960s is highly paradoxical. Debré, strident apostle of French sovereignty that he was, chose to imitate an American institution that had been established more than thirty years earlier in a very different environment. What were his other options, if any, when he set out to reform the securities market? What events, or series of events, prompted his decision? Did American regulators attempt to "export" their model? In his memoirs, the former prime minister pointed at an insider trading case in France that had angered investors and had made it necessary to take immediate action. It is unlikely, though, that the 1966 Ugine-Kuhlmann scandal had been the first one and that market professionals had always been above reproach. Debré and others frequently used the words *moral, morality*, and *moralization* in their public statements and administrative correspondence. This was no novelty: a decade earlier, the moral fight against expensive debt and "swindlers" had legitimized government regulation of consumer credit.[6] What purpose was being served by the solemn call to morality? The antiquated Paris Stock Exchange of the 1960s had little in common with the Wall Street of the Roaring Twenties. While the French stock market had been going through a period of protracted decline since the beginning of the decade,[7] there was no spectacular crash and no Pecora Commission to bring speculators' wrongdoings to the attention of the French public. Yet, beyond the obvious differences between the American and the French scenarios, is it possible to discern a pattern in the political process that led from public outrage to reform? At some point, *la moralisation des marchés* became *la régulation des marchés*—in that context, a neologism in French. How did the Brandeisian concept of investor protection through the disclosure of information translate into a very different legal culture? Independent governmental agencies (*autorités administratives indépendantes*) are common in France today, but in the 1960s, they were unheard of. Faced with skepticism, if not open hostility, from a centuries-old civil service system, how did the COB build its legitimacy? In this administrative tug of war, Chatenet used the prestigious, yet ambiguous, American model and, despite significant differences between the two institutions, tried to position the COB as the French SEC. How did American regulators perceive his efforts?

Rather than a comparative history of securities regulation in France and the United States, this book is an investigation of the dynamics of policy transfer in the field of securities regulation—a subject that has rarely been considered from a strictly historical perspective.[8] Far from the abstract mechanisms presented in economic models, it is an attempt to show how regulation worked in practice in the late 1960s. The actions of individuals—statesmen, bureaucrats, market professionals, large and small investors, bankers, lawyers, diplomats, journalists, and so on—and the impact of impersonal forces—the opening of European borders, heightened international competition among exchanges, nascent globalization—all must be considered in the analysis and interpretation of the sequence of events.

The story of the creation of the COB took place in Paris and, to a much lesser extent, in New York and in Washington, DC. In the late 1960s, the French presidency, the ministries, the central bank, and the Bourse (the Paris Stock Exchange) were all located within a tight perimeter, the limits of which more or less matched the medieval city walls. One of the most symbolic decisions made by Chatenet in 1967 was to settle in La Défense, the newly built business district west of the capital, at a safe distance from the traditional seats of power. Since then, the Parisian geography of money and politics has changed significantly. Much to the delight of museum curators and art lovers, the Ministry for the Economy and Finance has vacated the northern wing of Musée du Louvre to relocate in a massive building overlooking the Seine in out-of-the way Bercy. The Banque de France is still housed in the magnificent Hôtel de Toulouse, but monetary policy is conducted from Frankfurt, Germany, where the European Central Bank is headquartered. The securities market transformed into a network of interconnected computers; trading no longer takes place on the floor of the Palais Brongniart, the venerable building that had accommodated the Bourse since the 1820s:[9] abandoned by the noisy crowd of stockbrokers, it has become "a leading, international Event and Conference Center" housing "offices, reception and event spaces, public services, as well as an organic, fast-food restaurant open to the general public."[10] La Défense's skyline now rivals that of Midtown Manhattan or the City of London; many banks and insurance companies have migrated there. Ironically, though, the successor entity to the COB, the Autorité des Marchés Financiers (AMF), has returned to the Bourse district.

An examination of archival records shows that a multitude of stakeholders were involved in the process. Yet it also confirms Tricot's assessment of the role played by Debré, Pompidou, and, to a lesser extent, de Gaulle. An attempt had to be made to understand their perceptions of money and market mechanisms. The scope of this inquiry includes a brief presentation of their political and personal backgrounds, as well as of the circumstances that presided over the formation of this unlikely trio of financial reformers. During the early years of the Fifth Republic, the French government was highly centralized; decision making was concentrated in the hands of a small number of individuals at the highest level of the executive. Particular care has been paid to reconstituting, when relevant, the personal connections between the key characters; at the risk of sounding anecdotal at times, petty skirmishes on the front lines of bureaucratic wars have not been neglected: painstaking attention to such details is the best way to avoid the peril of teleology in the presentation and analysis of macro forces.

During the early stages of the COB's life some of the most decisive steps were taken; it is also the moment when the dynamics of policy transfer unfolded in all their complexity and revealed their many ambiguities. This investigation, therefore, has been focused on a six-year period, from the beginning of Debré's tenure at the Ministry of Finances in 1966 to the end of Chatenet's chairmanship of the COB in 1972. In plowing this rather narrow field, one did not expect to unearth intangible truths about the nature of Western capitalism. More modestly, the ambition of this study in microhistory was to carve out one of the building blocks of a still-to-be-written worldwide history of financial regulation. Along the way, the enterprise was likely to reveal a few things about French and American perceptions of morality and capitalism but also, more generally, about the exercise of political power in modern democracies, the interaction between business and government, and the mechanisms of institutional innovation.

Cross-border influence has been a major topic of the political science literature on financial regulation; it has been reinvigorated by the financial crisis that began in 2007–2008. Although a significant portion of this literature focused traditionally on the definition of international capital adequacy ratios for international banks, more recent scholarship has moved beyond banking to the securities and insurance industries.[11] Current debates about global governance, however, are unhelpful in understanding the origins of the COB. In the late 1960s, the Cold War was far from over and the notion of a global economy encompassing the whole world had yet to emerge; Eurodollar trading had been developing for some time, but the demise of the Bretton Woods system did not happen until the end of Chatenet's chairmanship; international capital flows had not reached the magnitude and volatility of later decades; derivative instruments were still to come; policy makers were not acquainted with the rapid succession of international episodes of financial instability. The short period under study (1966–1972), therefore, predates the era of globalization and the creation of "the complex network of institutions and practices,"[12] which characterizes global finance today.[13]

To meticulously historicize the creation of the COB, a chronological approach, if a bit traditional, has been considered the most adequate. Between 1966 and 1972, a number of dramatic events—May 1968, the resignation and death of de Gaulle—reverberated throughout French society. These events were never out of the minds of individuals who played a role in the process that led to the creation of the COB; to that extent, they are part of the story.

Chapter 1 establishes the major people and events in the early years of the Fifth Republic. In January 1966, Debré was appointed minister of finances in Pompidou's government. In that position, the former prime minister distinguished himself for his zeal for action. Following the March 1967 legislative elections, the Gaullist majority shrank to 244 seats out of 487. To regain the initiative, Debré convinced de Gaulle and Pompidou to launch a broad reform plan intended to modernize the French economy. They resorted to the *ordonnance* mechanism, a constitutional procedure that gave the executive considerable freedom of action. The French Parliament was not involved in, and did not even discuss, the eminently political decision to create a market regulator. That there was a conspicuous contradiction between the ordonnance procedure and the ideal of transparency that the COB was intended to promote was apparently ignored by Debré, Pompidou, and de Gaulle.

There were very good circumstantial reasons to add the creation of a market regulator to the already long list of reforms proposed by Debré. In May to June 1966, an insider trading scandal had revealed the failure of existing stock market rules or lack thereof. People had shouted, "Thieves!" in the Palais Brongniart; small investors had protested vocally against decisions made by a managerial elite oblivious to the legitimate rights of small shareholders. A former banker, Pompidou had felt compelled to publicly declare that the market "had to be moralized." One year later, Debré seized the opportunity to take action (chapter 2).

For most of the 1960s, the Paris Stock Exchange was in a state of stagnation. Compared to the banking system, then largely controlled by government, its role in the allocation of capital remained relatively marginal. Ensconced in traditions going back to the eighteenth century, the Bourse was paradoxically underregulated, which opened the door to unsavory characters and practices.

Investor protection was not a priority: financial statements were primarily used to calculate taxes to be paid by corporations, not to provide information to shareholders. Ten years after the Treaty of Rome was signed, the opening of European borders challenged the status quo: government and business were aware of the need to prepare for the resulting heightened competition (chapter 3).

Débré wrote in his memoirs that, having learned of the SEC's existence in an American newspaper, he immediately saw it as a source of inspiration. Whatever the truth in this retrospective statement, French politicians and businessmen of the postwar decades were fascinated by US economic leadership. It was common practice to send the most promising civil servants of the Ministry of Finances on a study trip to the United States. Among other distinctive features of the US market, the SEC came across as one of the most efficient tools of modernity (chapter 4).

Jean-Yves Haberer, a young member of Débré's staff who had spent several months in New York and Washington, DC, was instrumental in drafting the constituting documents of the COB. He relied on a thorough analysis of the powers and missions of the SEC prepared by the French Embassy in Washington, DC. The constituting documents were issued on September 28, 1967. In characteristic administrative lingo, they provided for the creation of an independent commission "in charge of controlling information [disclosed] to security holders and the general public, about publicly traded companies and the securities issued by them, and of watching over the proper functioning of the stock exchanges"[14] (chapter 5).

The French were aware of the controversy caused by Roosevelt's choice of Joseph P. Kennedy as the SEC's first chairman. Débré appointed his old friend Chatenet, a seasoned and highly respected politician, as the COB's first chairman. Although Chatenet faced opposition from market insiders, the Banque de France, and the Ministry of Finances, he received unconditional support from Débré. Chatenet also surrounded himself with a small team of skilled, dedicated professionals (chapter 6).

The echo of the Ugine-Kuhlmann scandal was limited to the narrow world of small investors; it had little in common with the public outrage ignited by the Pecora Commission in the United States three decades earlier. Yet a few weeks after the COB began to operate, the events of May 1968 shook the nation. During the night of May 24, demonstrators attempted to set the Palais Brongniart on fire. They failed, but their action was symptomatic of the contempt in which large segments of the French population held capitalism and its symbols. Gaullist authorities used market moralization as a rhetorical weapon to defend free markets against their opponents. They were also trying to increase the number of small shareholders and promote employee participation in the benefits of company growth (chapter 7).

The COB survived Debré's departure from the Ministry of Finances following the May 1968 events. Having lost the support of his main political ally, Chatenet nevertheless successfully asserted his independence and legitimacy. He also positioned the COB as the promoter of mass investment and the protector of small shareholders (chapter 8).

As a young diplomat in the late 1940s, Chatenet had spent about a year in the New York headquarters of the United Nations. Immediately after he had been appointed chairman of the COB, he decided to travel to the United States. During his chairmanship, he met with all successive SEC chairmen: Manuel F. Cohen (1964–1969), Hamer H. Budge (1969–1971), and William J. Casey (1971–1973). COB employees were invited to attend training sessions in Washington. In a series of detailed reports, Chatenet developed his vision of an America-inspired capitalist utopia. His meetings with his SEC counterparts marked the beginning of a much wider multilateral cooperation in the field of securities regulation (chapter 9).

As happened with the SEC in the 1930s, several high-profile cases contributed to building the credibility of the recently established French regulator. When Chatenet left office in 1972, the COB had become a respected agency of the French government. Since then, the principle of investor protection through the disclosure of accounting information has gained widespread acceptance; other *autorités administratives indépendantes* have been established; the word *régulation* is now used very frequently in French. Yet it took a long time for the COB and its successor entity, the AMF, to be granted full jurisdiction over the Paris Stock Exchange. In the 1970s and 1980s, other European nations established an independent securities regulator modeled after the SEC—ironically, for all the limitations of the COB, France played a pioneering part in the spreading of a very American idea (chapter 10).

It is in the rather unengaging environment of administrative archival records that the actions of reformers, their motives, and their feelings of frustration or satisfaction can be identified and analyzed. This book is based on investigations conducted in French and, to a much lesser extent, American archives. French archives included the Debré and Chatenet papers at the Centre d'histoire de Sciences Po (Paris); the private papers of Jean-Jacques Burgard, the first general secretary of the COB (Paris); the Banque de France (Paris); the Compagnie des agents de change (Savigny-le-Temple); the French Ministry for the Economy and Finances (Savigny-le-Temple); the French presidency (Pierrefitte-sur-Seine); French banks Crédit Agricole and BNP-Paribas (Paris); and the French industrial conglomerate Pechiney at the Institut pour l'Histoire de l'Aluminium (Clichy). A special mention must be made of the personal papers of Jean-Yves Haberer, a former member of Debré's staff and the driving force behind the writing of the COB's constituting documents. This collection has been deposited in the archives of the Ministry for the Economy and Finance at Savigny-le-Temple; Haberer's personal testimony, recorded during an April 2014 interview, also proved illuminating. Unless otherwise indicated, all translations are my own.

To the extent that the French and American press were used by politicians and professionals to explain and justify their decisions, it fell within the scope of this inquiry. Newspapers and magazines provided information on the broader political, economic, and social context; along with excerpts from novels by such giants of French literature as Balzac or Stendhal, they also revealed enduring stereotypes that were part of the conventional wisdom of the period.

This book also uses many autobiographies, memoirs, and testimonies. While these documents must be approached with the required caution, they help to understand the intentions and perceptions of policy makers of the postwar era.

French archives, if at times patchy, were invaluable to assess the French "reception" of an American idea. One of the original ambitions of this investigation was to find out whether Americans had deliberately tried to export this idea. The reader will see, at greater length, that this question was answered negatively. This conclusion, which resulted from the examination of French records, was confirmed by investigations carried out in the remarkably rich papers of William J. Casey, the third chairman of the SEC during Chatenet's own chairmanship of the COB, at the Hoover Institution Library (Stanford). Neither the reading of articles and editorials from American newspapers nor a targeted probing of available American diplomatic records contradicted this conclusion. The attempt to locate COB-related documents within the administrative records of the SEC at the National Archives and Records Administration proved fruitless. As evidence accumulated from investigations in French archives, it became clearer that such documents, if they existed, were unlikely to add much value to this book or significantly alter its substance. A cost-benefit calculation, a familiar tool for financial analysts, led to the frustrating, if logical, decision to abandon that quest.

In perusing the voluminous records left behind by individuals and institutions, I have endeavored to apply the standards of the historical profession. They are not so different, after all, from those of accountants, auditors, and regulators. They are all engaged in the quixotic, yet rewarding, pursuit of truth and fairness.

Although this book is primarily the work of a historian, I am not totally foreign to the world of finance. My interest in this rather abstruse subject was aroused during the years I spent writing a biography of Franklin D. Roosevelt. Along with Social Security or the Tennessee Valley Authority, the reform of the securities market is part and parcel of New Deal mythology. Yet the technicality of the subject made it impossible to do it sufficient justice. While I experienced great satisfaction in telling the saga of de Gaulle's troubled relationship with Roosevelt and the "Anglo-Saxons," I could not help but feel a bit frustrated in that respect. By chance, I opened Debré's memoirs to check for a late de Gaulle quotation on Roosevelt and found the passage about the creation of the COB. Debré explicitly referred to the SEC as his source of inspiration. At that moment, I did not think much about it; yet, it stuck in my memory. When time came to move to another historical project, I felt the need to focus on a narrower, more specific subject. Friends and colleagues had long encouraged me to weave together the variegated threads of a rather erratic professional destiny: finance and history; France and the United States; New York, Washington, DC, and Paris; the Great Depression and the then still unfolding economic crisis, which is viewed by many as a consequence of a failed international regulatory system. Indeed, my interest also owed much to the fifteen years I spent in a large French bank, first in the Paris headquarters as an auditor and then in the New York office as a member of the team in charge of structuring and selling securitization transactions. In these very different environments, I have had numerous opportunities to observe how innovation—financial, academic, or otherwise—challenges established "regulation" systems.

CHAPTER ONE

A Minister on a Mission

Following President Charles de Gaulle's contentious reelection on December 19, 1965, Georges Pompidou was reappointed prime minister of France. While Pompidou had been heading the French government for almost four years, he was not the first statesman to serve in this position under de Gaulle. In April 1962, he had succeeded Michel Debré, the first prime minister of the Fifth Republic and the chief architect of its 1958 constitution.

By the beginning of 1958, the Fourth Republic was moribund, paralyzed by institutional gridlock and the colonial war that had been raging for almost four years in Algeria. In May, French Army generals and colonists staged a coup d'état in Algiers and proclaimed their allegiance to de Gaulle, the former leader of the Free French, who had headed the provisional government of liberated France in 1944–1946. After several years in retirement, de Gaulle did not want his newly restored authority to be tainted by suspicion of illegitimacy. Respectful of the expiring Fourth Republic's still valid constitution, he formed a perfectly legal government and obtained emergency powers from the National Assembly.

De Gaulle chose Debré to be minister of justice in the last government of the Fourth Republic. He was fully qualified for the office. Debré, born in 1912, was the son of a well-known professor of medicine. He studied law and political science, and, at age twenty-three, he entered the prestigious Conseil d'État (Council of State), France's highest court for administrative justice, also in charge of providing legal advice to the French government. During the war, he joined the Resistance against German occupation and played a key role in the preparation of postwar administrative structures. When the country was liberated, de Gaulle entrusted him to reform the French Civil Service. Debré created the École Nationale d'Administration (ÉNA), which produced generation after generation of highly skilled hauts fonctionnaires. After de Gaulle's dramatic resignation from the presidency of the provisional government in January 1946, Debré remained in contact with the man whom he regarded as the political savior of France.

In de Gaulle's 1958 government, Debré was responsible for heading a group of experts in charge of drafting a new constitution; the group comprised constitutional lawyers and seasoned politicians, including former heads of Fourth Republic governments. He brought considerable knowledge and energy to the task. The opinionated minister of justice espoused the theory of rationalized parliamentarism; he pushed for inserting a series of technical provisions designed to ensure government stability. Compared to the situation that prevailed during the Third and Fourth Republics, the balance of power between the branches of government was decisively tilted in favor of the executive. On September 28, 1958, an overwhelming majority of the French people approved the Constitution of the Fifth Republic. Elected by a large college, de Gaulle was inaugurated as president of France on January 8, 1959. His already considerable powers were further strengthened by the October 28, 1962, referendum, which provided for the direct election of the president by the French people.

President de Gaulle's choice of Debré as his first prime minister was interpreted as a sign of goodwill toward the partisans of French Algeria: the "Father of the Constitution" of the Fifth Republic had indeed been one of the most vociferous adversaries of decolonization. In a time of crisis, Debré's energy and attention to detail worked wonders. President and prime minister made full use of the powers at their disposal, including the emergency powers defined in article 16 of the 1958 constitution, to maintain law and order. Resolutely and, at times, callously, the police fought against the OAS (Organisation de l'Armée Secrète), which gathered diehard partisans of French Algeria; in October 1961, a demonstration of pro-independence Algerians was brutally repressed in the streets of Paris. The newborn republic survived another coup d'état in April 1961 and several assassination attempts against de Gaulle. Eventually, the president outmaneuvered the OAS; he came to accept the principle of self-determination and started a negotiation with the Algerian rebels of the Front de libération nationale (FLN). For all his qualms about abandoning Algeria, Debré's allegiance to de Gaulle remained unshakable: "He was a cardinal who had lost his faith," said a critic, "but who had to feign the mystical ardor, at least out of loyalty."[1]

The Evian agreements between the French government and the FLN were massively ratified by the French people in an April 8, 1962, referendum. A few days later, an exhausted Debré was replaced by Georges Pompidou, then a relatively unknown adviser to the president, at the helm of the French government.

Freed from the burden of the Algerian war, a regal de Gaulle was able to conduct a foreign policy of national independence and speed up modernization of the economy. This was not the end of democratic life in France, though, as evidenced by the unexpectedly strong performance of his opponent, François Mitterrand, the leader of a coalition of left-wing parties, in the 1965 presidential election.

In the context of the Cold War, France's adherence to the Western alliance was never in doubt, but her president made sure that it would not be taken for granted. De Gaulle was haunted by the memory of the fall of France in 1940—never again would this proud nation suffer the humiliation of defeat. In his *Memoires de guerre*, published before he came back to power, the former leader of the Free French had taken particular care—and obvious delight—in telling of his heroic fight against Franklin D. Roosevelt and lesser "Anglo-Saxon" evildoers.[2] Rhetorical pyrotechnics, targeted at all manifestations of American imperialism, real or imagined, became part of that nebulous ideology, "Gaullism."[3] Shortly after he won reelection in 1965, the *New York Times* commented on his priorities for his second term in office:

> Informed sources predicted today that the general would make no major changes in his basic foreign policy.
>
> They expected him to remain adamant in his decision to end political integration—which he calls "subordination"—within the North Atlantic Treaty Organization. They said that there was as yet no timetable for a French initiative in this sense. The initiative is not expected before spring.
>
> On the issue of the European Common Market the new Government is expected to remain equally firm in its opposition to further political integration while at the same time probably striking a more moderate tone in the forthcoming foreign ministers' meeting in Luxembourg. [. . .]
>
> [Outgoing finance minister] Valéry Giscard d'Estaing's austerity measures have given France a stable currency and permitted her to pile up large surpluses in her international payments and hence to increase her gold reserves. This financial policy is an essential part of General de Gaulle's concept of "national independence" and of his challenge to United States "Hegemony."[4]

While the president was draping himself in the flag of French glory, Pompidou was proving to be a shrewd political operative in his management of day-to-day domestic affairs. His predecessor as prime minister was less fortunate: after his abrupt dismissal, Debré suffered a rather humiliating defeat when he failed to win a seat in the National Assembly in the November 1962 legislative elections.

The following year, however, Debré was elected *député* by Réunion Island, an overseas *département*. He took his new role seriously and remained a powerful presence in parliamentary politics. On the eve of the president's second term, both de Gaulle and Pompidou wanted to rescue Debré from semioblivion. Debré, who missed executive responsibilities, had not lost all hope to return to the Hôtel de Matignon, the official residence of the French prime minister. Reluctantly, he accepted Pompidou's offer to join a reshuffled cabinet as minister for the economy and finances.

On January 8, 1966, Debré entered the grand ministerial office located within the Richelieu wing of le Louvre—since the last decades of the nineteenth century, the most powerful department of the French government had been known as the Rue de Rivoli, after the street that ran along the imposing palace of kings and emperors.[5] French and foreign journalists joked about the "vice-Prime Minister." The *New York Times* reported: "His thinking follows closely that of General de Gaulle, the only man, perhaps, whose intellectual authority he recognizes."

So said the newspaper *Paris-Presse* of Michel Debré, then minister of justice, shortly after he triumphantly helped to bring General de Gaulle back to power in 1958. Few other leading Frenchmen had been so loyal for so long to the seventy-five-year-old general. Michel Debré, discarded as premier four years before, had his reward and was brought back into the government as a Gaullist "super-minister."[6]

A slight change in Debré's official title reflected his ambitions. While his predecessor had been ministre des Finances et des Affaires économiques, he would be ministre de l'Économie et des Finances. All cabinet members in charge of economic affairs were to report to him—social affairs, too, or so he thought: his colleague Jean-Marcel Jeanneney, the minister for social affairs, would at times have to assert the independence of his department.

On Wednesday mornings, when the cabinet gathered at the Élysée Palace, Debré was seated to the immediate left of de Gaulle—the punctilious president wanted to show his consideration for his former prime minister but did not want to deprive André Malraux, the adventurer-turned-writer-turned-minister of cultural affairs, from the privilege of occupying the seat to his right. De Gaulle and Debré had frequent meetings, which took place in a trusting and friendly atmosphere—to the extent that it was possible to be on friendly terms with the always courteous, yet so intimidating general. At the beginning, the two men scrupulously limited their conversations to economic and social questions. Progressively, topics under discussion exceeded the wide territory under the minister's stewardship—de Gaulle, never an economics enthusiast, was keen on hearing Debré's opinion on current issues. It is not surprising that an irritated Pompidou sometimes took offense on what he considered an encroachment on his prime ministerial prerogatives. Shortly after Debré's return to government, the *New York Times* shared with its readers what was conventional wisdom among Parisian political analysts: "When the day comes," observed a pundit for the newspaper *Le Monde*, "he will, if he can swing it, become the faithful candidate to succeed General de Gaulle."[7]

Both Pompidou and Debré were considered potential successors to de Gaulle;[8] they were also very different human beings. In his memoirs, Debré was later to admit: "Our relationship suffered from the difference in our personalities. [Pompidou] sometimes thought that I was too much of a rigorist, and sometimes that I was too passionate."[9]

In spite of ongoing, subdued tensions and the occasional open disagreement, however, the prime minister never opposed the many reforms promoted by his ebullient minister for the economy and finances.

Debré believed that "the legitimacy of a government does not reside exclusively in the source of its power, but also in its ability to take effective action."[10] Effective action he did take and without delay. The second part of the fourth volume of his voluminous memoirs is entirely devoted to the two years he spent in the Rue de Rivoli (January 1966 to May 1968). At the beginning, he boldly, if rather awkwardly, described his state of mind when he took office:

> [. . .] my ambition is part of a larger, long-term effort: to carry out an economic evolution, the effects of which would be similar to those of the [political] evolution I was able to complete in constitutional matters with support from General de Gaulle. The challenge facing France and the French people in the years to come is of an economic, social, political and military nature. It is my intention to leave my mark on my time at the helm of the [Ministry] of the Economy and Finances by [conducting] real reforms aiming at the same objective: to give the Republic the power to assert itself and triumph.[11]

Debré had succeeded Valéry Giscard d'Estaing, an ally of de Gaulle but not a member of the UNR (Union pour la Nouvelle République), the Gaullist party. In his memoirs, therefore, Debré could rightfully present himself as the first Gaullist to head the Ministry for the Economy and Finance. He was Gaullist in his desire to cast himself as the heir to a prestigious tradition of statesmanship. Audaciously stepping over two centuries of French history, he claimed the conflicting legacies of two of his most illustrious predecessors: Colbert, the "interventionist" minister of Louis XIV, and Turgot, the "liberal" reformist of late eighteenth century whose efforts to modernize the Old Regime met with fierce opposition from privileged groups. Along with other postwar policy makers, Debré the memoirist was not shy about presenting himself as an isolated hero fighting against powerful establishments.[12] Having invoked the spirits of Colbert and Turgot, he went on to state his approach to the dilemmas of economic policy in more contemporary terms:

> Republican government has three economic duties: to establish a set of moral rules in the name of the common good so that money does not become the only benchmark for moral values; to ensure solidarity among French citizens, consistent with our tradition of equality, with respect to both the law but also the hazards of life; and finally to direct and stimulate the key sectors of our economy, such as space, the arms industry, and, more generally, cutting-edge technologies. It is all the more necessary to refuse extreme liberalism, and for government [to refuse] to give up action, that foreign domination must be avoided: nationalization would then be the only solution in the eyes of an outraged citizenry! Liberating the French economy while not losing sight of national responsibilities: it is the duty of a Republican government to reconcile these two obligations. Against those who lean towards socialism, I defend the laws of the market, therefore I am regarded as a liberal. Against those who lean towards liberalism, I defend the rights of government, therefore I am regarded as a socialist.[13]

For all the retrospective ruminations he developed in his memoirs, Debré was not losing sight of more mundane and immediate duties. If de Gaulle and Pompidou had wanted him back in government, it was not only to acknowledge publicly the merits of a distinguished former prime minister. They also intended to turn the page on a disappointing three-year experiment in economic stabilization, a government-engineered slowdown that had damaged their popularity.

The effects of the economic stabilization plan, however, were only temporary and must be put in perspective. Debré's stewardship of the French economy started in the middle of an impressive growth cycle. In a country saturated by history, the three decades separating the end of World War II and the oil shock of 1973–1974 are still known today as *les trente glorieuses*, the thirty glorious years—a reference to the three glorious days of July 1830, when King Charles X was overthrown by the Parisians. By 1966, the French economy had recovered from the destructions of the World War II, and economic performance had been sustained and spectacular; between 1949 and 1969, the gross domestic product had grown at an average annual rate of 4.6 percent.[14]

While Gaullists in power claimed that the national economy, along with political institutions, had been reorganized on a sounder basis in 1958, there was a great deal of continuity between the Fourth and the Fifth Republics. In 1945–1946, the provisional government headed by de Gaulle had laid the foundations of the French welfare state and established the Commissariat général du plan in charge of national economic planning. A large state-owned sector had been created by the nationalization of utilities, banks, insurance companies, and Renault, a car manufacturer. Keynesianism, mitigated by the occasional input of dissenting domestic thinkers, such as Jacques Rueff, provided the intellectual framework for the macroeconomic policy pursued by successive governments.

The state played a decisive role in modernizing the French economy during the trente glorieuses. More than by the changing faces of rotating ministers sitting briefly in the Rue de Rivoli office, government action was embodied by a new generation of civil servants graduating from the ÉNA—another institution created in the immediate aftermath of the war, and which owed much to Debré's initiative. The most brilliant among them flocked toward the prestigious Direction du Trésor, "the sanctuary inside the temple of the Ministry of Finance, the economic apex in a centralized state."[15] Within the Ministry of Finance, the Trésor was in charge of managing the French national debt. It relied on a complex administrative structure, the Treasury circuit (*circuit du Trésor*), to funnel credit to the modernization of the economy[16]—as detailed in chapters 2 and 3, the stock market, then, played a very minor role.

American aid, in the form of the Marshall Plan, provided key assistance in rebuilding war-damaged infrastructures. Long protected by trade barriers, France progressively opened its borders. In 1950, the Schuman Declaration paved the way to European economic and political cooperation. The European Coal and Steel Community (established in 1951) was followed by the signature of the Treaty of Rome (in 1957), which established a Common Market among six European nations: France, Germany, Italy, Belgium, the Netherlands, and Luxembourg. The price-support mechanisms of the Common Agricultural Policy (1962) benefited French farmers, still a significant proportion of the workforce. This was changing, though, as industrialization and urbanization were rapidly transforming the landscape and the economy. Demographic growth and societal change provided the background for the trente glorieuses. As a result of an increase in life expectancy and the postwar baby boom, population rose from approximately 40 million in 1945 to approximately 50 million in 1970. A new *classe moyenne* emerged, more educated, eager to enjoy the pleasures of a freer society and to buy a growing variety of consumer goods—and willing, increasingly, to invest their savings on the securities market. All across Europe, the ascent of a prosperous middle class sharing the characteristics of its American counterpart—enjoying comfortable standards of living, individualistic yet integrated in "large organizations," competitive and seeking professional success—was perceived as essential to political stability.[17]

France, however, was not immune from financial and monetary troubles. The Fourth Republic had been plagued by recurring inflation and trade deficits. Following de Gaulle's return to power, the "New Franc" had replaced the old one—in reality a devaluation inspired by Rueff, by then one of de Gaulle's principal financial advisers. Apparent monetary stability had followed, which gave credibility to Gaullist claims of economic restoration. After a significant slowdown in 1958–1959, economic growth accelerated. The fourth National Plan was launched in 1962, with an expected average annual growth rate of 5.5 percent. Early results were encouraging—ambitious infrastructure projects, in particular, benefited from the influx of foreign capital.

Tensions on the labor market, however, put pressure on domestic prices. To eradicate inflation and eliminate a resurgent trade deficit, the French government devised and implemented the economic stabilization plan: prices were frozen, bank loans were strictly restricted, efforts were made to compress wages. The economic stabilization plan was a half-success—at best: inflation went down, but growth deteriorated and unemployment reached unprecedented levels. It also proved very unpopular:

> [. . .] the stabilization plan, as it curbed inflation, also exacted its own price: a slowdown in national economic growth in 1965. The gross national product went up only 2.5 per cent, compared with more than 6 per cent in previous years. [. . .]
>
> In December [of 1965], the big Paris retailers blamed "the stabilization" for a meager increase in Christmas sales.
>
> "In the old days," said the manager of a department store, "we used to register a 15 per cent boost from year to year. This year it's running around 5 per cent."
>
> There were more basic indicators. Auto production dropped slightly. So did coal and steel. New construction starts eased, partly because despite a continuing shortage of low-priced housing, high and medium-rent apartments glutted the market. [. . .]
>
> If the average factory worker's purchasing power went up 3 per cent, he was

apparently spending it on rent or food instead of television and home appliances. Sales of those consumer items dropped slightly or stayed the same.[18]

Many analysts pointed at the economic stabilization plan—and at the minister in charge of enforcing it—to explain the less than impressive performance of de Gaulle in the 1965 presidential election. When Pompidou announced the reshuffle of his government at the beginning of 1966, the *New York Times* identified several "important changes." Among them, the comeback of Debré and "the departure from the Government of Valéry Giscard d'Estaing, the outgoing Finance Minister, whose austerity policies of price controls and tight credits had been a political liability to General de Gaulle in last month's presidential election. Mr. Debré is identified in the public mind with more liberal policies."[19]

A skillful lawyer and, arguably, a consistent political thinker, Debré was not an economist, and he had absolutely no business experience. However, a short stint on the team of Finance Minister Paul Reynaud in 1938–1939 had familiarized him with the dilemmas of economic policy making. When he was put in charge of the French economy, he asked Antoine Dupont-Fauville, who had been one of his closest aides when he was heading the French government, to be his *directeur de cabinet* (chief of staff). He also surrounded himself with a group of young technocrats from the Inspection Générale des Finances, the auditing department of the Ministry for the Economy and Finance—many were ÉNA graduates. Among them, thirty-three-year-old Jean-Yves Haberer became his trusted *conseiller technique* (technical adviser). Contrasting with his curmudgeonly public persona, Debré was considerate with and supportive of the members of his inner circle in the Rue de Rivoli. Adding to the respect they felt for their minister was an appreciation for the rapidity and thoroughness with which he reviewed, annotated, and sent back memoranda, reports, and drafts. Former members of his cabinet would later fondly remember their time at his side.[20]

Debré, who did not share de Gaulle's rather detached approach to economic issues, confronted the economic slowdown with head-on determination. At a cabinet meeting on February 16, 1966, he unveiled a comprehensive—and rather haphazard—set of measures, immediately dubbed "plan Debré" by journalists.

The minister's ambitions, however, exceeded the short-term objectives assigned to him by Pompidou. It was his intention to prepare for the coming into force of the Treaty of Rome, scheduled in 1968 and, along the way, to leave a durable imprint on the French economy; political stability, therefore, was of the essence.[21] A little more than one year after Debré took office in the Rue de Rivoli, legislative elections were planned. The results were disappointing: on March 5 and 12, 1967, the majority supporting the Pompidou government in the National Assembly shrank to 244 seats out of a total of 487. Renamed UDR (Union des Démocrates pour la République), the Gaullist party was reduced to a mere 200 seats. Support from its traditional ally, the Républicains Indépendants (RI), became all the more necessary. Analysts speculated on the possibility of a left-dominated coalition government, but the conservative RI group was unlikely to side with the Left and form an alternative majority in the assembly.[22] Yet the task of the prime minister and his government would be made more difficult, as RI lawmakers, very much aware of the leverage gained in the electoral booth, were expected to raise the stakes for their support. Their leader was none other than Giscard d'Estaing, Debré's predecessor in the Rue de Rivoli. The young and ambitious politician was still brooding over his departure from the Pompidou government in January 1966: he felt that he had been scapegoated for the failure of the 1963 economic stabilization plan and complained that he had been "dismissed like a lackey."[23] After the new National Assembly gathered in the Palais Bourbon, a resentful Giscard d'Estaing was elected chairman of the powerful Committee on Finance. Debré rightfully feared that his plan to reform the French economy was threatened: he anticipated a "war of attrition, bill under discussion after bill under discussion."[24]

The outcome of the 1967 elections was another test, if not for the stability, at least for the efficiency of the Fifth Republic. The nation was not being invaded by a foreign army, as in 1940, and the regime was not in danger of being overthrown by factious generals, as had again been the case in 1961. Neither "the institutions of the Republic, the independence of the Nation, the integrity of its territory or the fulfillment of its international commitments" were "under serious or immediate threat": article 16 of the 1958 constitution was limited to very exceptional situations, which was not the case in 1967, and de Gaulle did not contemplate using the emergency powers that had proved so helpful to resolve the Algerian crisis—and which had given some legitimacy to the arguments of those who, like Mitterrand, his challenger in the 1965 election, had accused the new regime of operating under the conditions of a "permanent coup d'état." While article 16 did not apply, however, other constitutional provisions had been designed, or inspired, by Debré to avoid the risk of political stalemate. Article 49, paragraph 3, was to be used again and again by prime ministers who doubted their ability to gather a sufficient number of supporters in the National Assembly: it gave them the ability to request a vote of no-confidence on a specific bill and, provided no majority rallied against it, the bill was adopted. The scope of article 49, paragraph 3, was later to be restricted by a constitutional amendment, but it remained a powerful weapon in the hands of the French executive. In March 1967, however, Debré had much more in mind than a single bill: his ambition to enhance French economic power in Europe required that several bills be passed simultaneously in the French Parliament. Article 38 of the constitution, another tool of "rationalized parliamentarism," allowed him to proceed with his plan.

Article 38 reads as follows:

> In order to implement its program, the Government may ask Parliament for authorization, for a limited period, to take measures by Ordinance that are normally the preserve of statute law.
>
> Ordinances shall be issued in the Council of Ministers, after consultation with the Conseil d'État. They shall come into force upon publication, but shall lapse in the event of failure to table before Parliament the Bill to ratify them by the date set by the Enabling Act. They may only be ratified in explicit terms.
>
> At the end of the period referred to in the first paragraph hereinabove Ordinances may be amended solely by an Act of Parliament in those areas governed by statute law.[25]

This quoted translation emanates from the Conseil Constitutionnel, the French constitutional court. To avoid confusion with other meanings of the English word *ordinance*, from this point on, "ordinances" shall be referred to as *ordonnances*.

Debré seized the opportunity to reenter the good graces of de Gaulle. Three days after the second run in the legislative elections, he met with him at the Élysée Palace and suggested that article 38 be used. Never shy about exercising his powers, the president listened favorably. Pompidou, whose position had been temporarily weakened by the results of the elections, overcame his initial reservations and approved his minister's initiative. The ordonnance project was presented formally during a meeting of the Council of Ministers on April 26, 1967. According to the testimony of Education Minister Alain Peyrefitte, who recorded his impressions in his diary, de Gaulle and Pompidou had no qualms about calling the ordonnance procedure an *astuce* (a trick) made available to them by the Fifth Republic constitution. In 1958, de Gaulle observed, these astuces had had no better advocates than the former heads of

Fourth Republic governments who had been associated with the drafting of the constitution[26]—an argument that was used repeatedly by Pompidou during the parliamentary debates.

Alone among the members of Pompidou's government, Edgard Pisani, the minister of public works, expressed his frustration openly and resigned. In his memoirs, Pisani was later to justify his decision: "I [questioned] a political decision which [meant] that a recently elected majority [was] being ignored and I [expressed] my fear of a possible general strike since Social Security, in particular, [would] be under attack."[27]

Columnist François Mauriac, a Nobel Prize winner and an ardent Gaullist, was not far from sharing Pisani's concerns:

> [. . .] of all the criticisms attracted by the *ordonnances*, the only one which really affects me is the criticism formulated by resigning Minister Edgard Pisani in *Le Monde*. Having praised de Gaulle for his inflexibility, his passion, his desire for greatness, and for the fact that he gave us political mores and institutions in conformity with the modern world, Edgard Pisani added: "It is precisely these political, institutional, and diplomatic achievements that are being jeopardized by the request for special powers. They [the special powers] are causing a shock wave in which everything can be washed away." Were this fear legitimate, then I would be adamant against the *ordonnances*. But I cannot believe that Pompidou would have deliberately incurred such a risk.[28]

On May 5, the president of the National Assembly was officially informed, by the prime minister, of the "urgency" of "a bill authorizing the French government, as per Article 38 of the Constitution, to take economic and social measures." In the National Assembly, *députés* from opposition parties were numerous enough to reach the 10 percent quorum necessary to petition for a no-confidence vote; pursuant to article 49 paragraph 3, the bill would be considered passed in the National Assembly unless the resolution of no-confidence would be voted by a majority of députés. The Senate, the upper chamber of the French Parliament, was dominated by opposition parties. A negative vote in the Senate, however, would not result in the final rejection of the bill. It would just make it necessary for the députés to vote a second and then a third time. After three votes, the National Assembly would prevail over the Senate. De Gaulle, Pompidou, and Debré were convinced that Gaullist supporters and their allies would reject the no-confidence resolution, even if reluctantly.

In a press conference on May 16, de Gaulle warned the members of the newly elected majority: "Under these circumstances, any attempt, coming from the ranks of the majority, which would tend to divide it in order to weaken it, at the very moment when it has just been elected under one and only one banner, by voters who are convinced that this majority had gathered in order to support one and only one policy, such an attempt, I tell you, would obviously be against political morality and the general interest."[29]

Parliamentary debates, which started officially on May 18, lasted until the end of June. Even if their outcome was predictable, they were extremely tense. Pompidou defended the ordonnances procedure in speeches at the National Assembly. This was not the first time, he argued, that the French government was resorting to special powers. He did concede, however, that article 38 had never been applied in the context of an economic reform plan:

> Why is it different today? Is it because we are in an alarming situation, [a situation] requiring serious measures? Absolutely not. [. . .] But we find ourselves on the eve of a new and major mutation of our economy, which we must not only anticipate, but also prepare: the last step of the Common Market. [. . .]
>
> July 1, 1968 will be a crucial date. Up until 1958, our economy had lived in isolation. Since 1958, we have restored our currency, suppressed inflation, and provided for the expansion of the economy in a stable monetary environment, at a time when tariff protection was eroding.
>
> However, between lowered tariffs and no tariff at all, there is a big gap! When we face, resolutely, competition from our five partners, the powerful German industry in particular, when we accept that our protection with respect to third-parties be significantly lowered by the implementation of the common tariff, as well as the consequences of the G.A.T.T. negotiations which have just come to a happy conclusion in Geneva, we are making a critical decision. *We do accept the constraints and the risks of a free market economy on an international scale.* How could we not draw the conclusions domestically? It means not only making a big investment and modernization effort, but also encouraging financial and industrial concentration, renovating the retail sector as well as the agricultural sector, acknowledging that the very idea of profit is not an idea to be ashamed of but an absolute necessity which applies to all, employees as well as employers.[30]

The prime minister went on to highlight three priorities: (1) employment, (2) social security, and (3) the participation of workers in corporate profits (*la Participation*). He stopped short, however, of offering a detailed agenda or a list of the projected ordonnances.

Lawmakers from the opposition pointed out that the request for special powers originated in the divisions of the conservative majority. Communist député Waldeck-Rochet highlighted the contradiction between the recent electoral campaign and the request for special powers:

> Ladies, gentlemen, yesterday the Prime Minister attempted to justify his request for special powers by putting forward the urgency of the problems that need to be solved; however, during the whole electoral campaign, representatives of the Fifth Republic had a completely different discourse; they were happy, then, to sing their own praises and paint an idyllic picture of the state of public affairs. No allusion was made to the difficulties which are discovered today. The coffers were full. The situation of France was excellent. The Prime Minister was trumpeting national prosperity. [. . .]
>
> The urgency became apparent overnight. One cites, in particular, the suppression, as of July 1, 1968, of the last customs barriers among the six countries within the Common Market, and the resulting necessary adaptations. But why having waited for the deadline to draw so near?[31]

Jacques Médecin, then a member of Progrès et démocratie moderne, a centrist group, added cruelly: "As the leader of the parliamentary majority, Mr. Prime Minister, you should have indicated, during the electoral campaign, that your candidates had no other program but to win the election and then immediately give up their powers."[32]

Pierre Mendès France, who had headed an inordinately successful, if short-lived, government in 1954 and remained one of the Left's most influential leaders, attacked Pompidou for what he considered a violation of the rights of parliament.[33] Giscard d'Estaing, dutifully informed by the prime minister in person, did not ignore that the use of article 38 was meant to curtail his newly won political capital. In an interview with *L'Express*, a weekly magazine, he declared: "During and after the electoral campaign, we have publicly taken several commitments. [. . .] An exceptional situation has never been mentioned. Much to the contrary, everybody, including the Prime Minister, emphasized the need for dialogue. Yet suddenly public opinion discovers an exceptional procedure which was not announced by any warning sign during a period—the electoral campaign—meant specifically to inform the public."[34]

Giscard d'Estaing, however, did not want to provoke a political crisis: he and the RI eventually sided with the Gaullists—which did not prevent him from vehemently criticizing Debré during the meetings of the Committee on Finance.[35] During the debates in plenary session, he mocked his successor in the Rue de Rivoli—without even mentioning his name:

> As I was listening to the most important orators who spoke yesterday, I have been struck by the fact that many among them looked at [our] modern economy as lawyers and not as economists. Yet a modern economy is not made up of [legal] documents; it is made up of flows and realities. If one is to know if France will or will not be ready to enter the Common Market on July 1ˢᵗ [1968], a close look at price levels, tariffs, government expenses, interest rates, savings, growth rate is much more important than the list of administrative documents which will be issued between now and then.[36]

As debates were approaching their conclusion, députés were growing increasingly exasperated by the lack of transparency of the French government. On June 16, Jacques Maroselli, a member of the center-left Parti radical-socialiste, took the prime minister to task:

> Mr. Prime Minister, when you first requested special powers, you looked both ignorant of the content of your *ordonnances*, and surprised at the bad political and economic situation.
>
> But as of today, it is not possible that you might still ignore the provisions which they will include. And yet you continue to refuse to inform Parliament.
>
> In brief, you ask from us a vote in a state of ignorance. You keep asking from us to sign a paper in blank. You do not answer questions from elected representatives of the people, thus weakening the role of Parliament.[37]

Centrist Franck Cazenave, who joined the no-confidence vote, asked the question: "Do you think it wise to treat behind closed doors, in *Rivoli* or in *Matignon*, the endemic diseases which exhaust our economy and jeopardize social progress?"[38]

French lawmakers eventually voted the Enabling Act, which was promulgated by the president under reference number 67-482 on June 22, 1967. The authority to issue ordonnances was set to expire on October 31, 1967, and ratification bills were to be submitted to parliament before December 31, 1967.[39] The Enabling Act outlined five objectives:

1. To better ensure full employment and the professional reorientation of workers, to adapt working conditions, to improve or extend guarantees benefiting workers who have lost their jobs or might lose their jobs [. . .], to facilitate

the training of both the young and the adults in order to permit their adaptation to the evolution of the economy;

2. To ensure employee participation in the benefits of company growth, while facilitating the build-up of [personal] savings and the development of investments;

3. To amend or unify the scope of the various social security and insurance schemes and institutions, to adapt their structure and ensure their financial stability;

4. To encourage the adaptation of companies to the [new] competitive environment resulting from the enforcement of the treaty instituting the European Economic Community and, more specifically, the elimination of customs duties among member states as of July 1, 1968;

5. To facilitate the modernization or the restructuring of industries or regions the economic structures of which are obsolete.[40]

These objectives were sufficiently general to accommodate a wide variety of social and economic reforms. Much to the irritation of lawmakers, it is only after the vote of the Enabling Act that they were brought to their knowledge. At the end of August, the *New York Times*, while echoing the rationale formulated by Pompidou and Debré, also indicated that some of the reforms were inspired by US models: "The announced aim of the measures, *some of them based on United States experience*, was to prepare French business for the end of trade barriers within the European Common Market next July, and the subsequent lowering of worldwide tariffs as a result of the Tariff-Cutting agreement of the recent Kennedy Round."[41]

Thirty-four ordonnances were to be signed by de Gaulle between August 1 and October 31—three months that had very little in common with Roosevelt's Hundred Days. While the grandiose, yet ultimately doomed, Participation scheme would live on in Gaullist mythology, the legacy of the other ordonnances would be more durable: Social Security was reorganized; the Agence Nationale pour l'Emploi (ANPE, National Employment Agency) was established to provide jobs and training opportunities to the unemployed; a new form of legal entity, the Groupement d'Intérêt Économique (GIE, Economic Interest Grouping) was created.

During the parliamentary debates of May–June 1967, lawmakers complained about the French government's lack of transparency. While this might have been interpreted as the sign of insufficient preparation, archival records indicate the opposite: Debré and his team left little to improvisation. On April 1,

1967, before the ordonnance project was even discussed by the government in a formal Council of Ministers, Haberer, Debré's *conseiller technique*, had written a memorandum made up of thirty-three detailed notes, each of which summarized a proposed reform in the field of banking and finance.[42]

Financial reform had long been debated by French politicians, bureaucrats, and professionals. During the 1950s and 1960s, a number of ad hoc committees had recommended that the banking sector and the financial markets be liberalized. The Debré archives in Sciences Po (Paris) include an undated, unsigned document entitled "*Ordonnances* about Credit, Savings and the Financial Market." It is very likely a summary of the arguments used by the minister for the economy and finances to defend his program. It refers in broad terms to those recommendations of the Fifth National Plan, which had not yet been implemented. More pointedly, it insists on "the necessity to adapt the financial market to its mission as a supplier of capital, and to its increasingly international role."[43] These objectives had been shared by Giscard d'Estaing; they illustrated the continuity between Debré and his immediate predecessor. As early as September 1965, administrative controls on banks' lending operations, which had been part of the economic stabilization plan, had been made more flexible. The Debré plan of 1966 had included a number of measures designed to make access to credit easier for corporations.

Note number 32 in Haberer's April 1 memorandum contemplated the creation of a "new entity, inspired by the Securities and Exchange Commission." Alone in dealing specifically with the organization of the securities market, the penultimate item in the memorandum appeared a little bit out of place. There were very good circumstantial reasons, though, to add it to Debré's reform agenda.

CHAPTER TWO

"Thieves!"

Time and again, in his many public speeches and later in his memoirs, an anxious Michel Debré would remind his audience and readership of the necessity "to face competition inside and outside the Common Market."[1] His return to government in 1966 marked the beginning of a new phase in national industrial policy.[2] Both Debré and Georges Pompidou agreed that French industry had to be strengthened against foreign competitors. As bigger corporations were believed to have greater chances of survival in an increasingly open environment, they actively encouraged mergers among them. The Fifth National Plan (1966–1970) recommended that there only be a small number of conglomerates of international dimension; in some industrial sectors, it was even suggested that their number should be restricted to one or two.[3]

By the mid-1960s, the French chemical industry—arguably one of the most strategic—was thought to be extremely fragmented. In a report written at the request of Pompidou, experts estimated that no less than seventy different corporations accounted for 75 percent of the aggregate sales of the industry.[4] It was dominated by the Big Five: Pechiney, Rhône-Poulenc, Saint-Gobain, Kuhlmann, and Ugine. Even though they were large corporations by French standards, they were dwarfed in comparison by their American competitors (DuPont de Nemours, Union Carbide, Olin Matheson, Dow Chemical, etc.).[5] The already long history of the Big Five testified not only to the industrial achievements of the nation but also to the many challenges French industry had encountered during its takeoff.

The Société Kuhlmann, named after its founder chemistry professor Frédéric Kuhlmann, had been created in 1825. Based originally in Northern France, with strong ties to the raw materials–producing regions of the French colonial empire, Kuhlmann had developed an expertise in the production of fertilizers. By the mid-1960s, however, the company did not have a clear strategy; it was considered poorly managed, with obsolete production facilities.[6]

The Société d'électrochimie, d'électrométallurgie et des aciéries électriques d'Ugine was known as "Ugine," a small town in the Savoie *département* where its largest facilities had historically been located. It had resulted from the merger, in the immediate aftermath of World War I, of several steel manufacturers based in the Alps region. Making full use of the hydroelectric potential of its surroundings, Ugine had specialized in the production of stainless steel and aluminum.

The first step in the long-term consolidation of the French chemical industry was the merger between two of the Big Five, Kuhlmann and Ugine (along with a much smaller company, Produits Azotés, an affiliate of Ugine). With aggregate sales of approximately 3.7 billion French francs, the resulting entity was expected to reach a critical size, in the same category as its largest European competitors (Rhône-Poulenc, Bayer, Hoechst, BASF, Montecatini); however, it was still outdistanced by British Imperial Chemical Industries and American DuPont de Nemours.[7]

	Kuhlmann	Ugine	Produits Azotés
Equity	258,479,775 FRF (3,446,397 shares of 75 FRF each)	388,299,000 FRF (5,177,320 shares of 75 FRF each)	32,262,750 FRF (430,170 shares of 75 FRF each)

FRF = French francs. *Source:* Rapport des Commissaires aux apports à l'Assemblée générale extraordinaire à forme constitutive du 7 décembre 1966. Rio Tinto France, Archives Pechiney—Collection historique, Secrétariat général: Box 072-2-24974: Société des Produits Azotés—Fusion Ugine Kuhlmann / SPA

	Kuhlmann	Ugine	Produits Azotés
Consolidated sales	1,500 million FRF	1,960 million FRF	214 million FRF
Maximum share price in 1966	237 FRF	294.50 FRF	500 FRF
Minimum share price in 1966	193 FRF	241.5 FRF	390 FRF

Source: "La Bourse croit à une fusion Ugine-Kuhlmann," *Les Échos*, May 25, 1966.

The negotiations between the two companies resulted in an exchange transaction engineered by their bankers. The circumstances of the transaction, however, did not bode well for the future of the new entity—nor, for that matter, for the success of other mergers in the chemical industry. During the May 26 trading session at the Paris Bourse, news of the exchange transaction caused a brutal collapse in the market price of Ugine shares. One month later, Maurice Pérouse, who held the key position of directeur du Trésor within the Ministry of Finances, stated mildly that "some observers judged severely the behavior of the management of the two companies involved [in the merger]."[8] This was typical administrative euphemism: according to Jean-Yves Haberer's testimony, corroborated by *Le Monde*, people had shouted "Thieves!" (*Aux voleurs!*) in the Palais Brongniart.[9]

Newspapers gave voice to the outrage of small investors. On the cover page of its May 25 edition, *Les Échos*, a daily financial newspaper, reported that "the

Bourse believes that a merger between Ugine and Kuhlmann is going to happen." The apparent neutrality of the title was slightly misleading: "For twelve days now, Kuhlmann shares have been among the most actively traded securities at the Paris *Bourse*, closely followed by Ugine shares. Financial circles believe that they have good reasons to think that these two large companies have decided to unite their destinies [. . .]. It is urgent to inform investors and shareholders, otherwise small investors, who too often feel that they are given late notice of events, will be discouraged. In a difficult market environment, timely information is essential if one is to bring back hesitating investors to the securities market."[10]

The relatively tame presentation of the rumors was accompanied by a much more forceful editorial signed by Alain Vernay, also in the May 25 edition of *Les Échos*. The journalist was putting the merger in the broader context of public disaffection for the securities market: "Maximum fairness, apparent as well as real, is indispensable if one is to mobilize successfully the increasing amount of liquid savings, which is moving away from the securities market, and if one is to stop the downward trend in stock prices [. . .]."[11] The French government, according to Vernay, had to take some of the blame—in 1964, the Ministry of Finances had been criticized for interfering in the reorganization of the debt and capital structure of La Compagnie des Machines Bull, a computer company:[12] "Nobody can point the finger at any given company, and certainly not political authorities, who concealed their intentions long after they had made their decisions in cases as important as that of the Machines Bull in 1964, or who condemned to an almost certain death the launching of real estate investment-trusts when they modified conditions that had previously been agreed upon."[13]

The journalist pointed at the Securities and Exchange Commission (SEC) for a potential source of inspiration: "It is pointless, however, to multiply examples of the past wrongdoings of each and everyone. On the other hand, it is urgent to set clearer and stricter rules, which can be modeled after the American Securities [and] Exchange Commission. Such a tidying up effort was done recently by major professionals of the banking sector and of the stock market with respect to the narrow, yet vital subject of take-over-bids. Yet it is not sufficient at a time when the Minister of the Economy and Finances, in his turn, is looking into the operations of the *Bourse*."[14]

Interestingly, Vernay did not feel the need to justify his use of the SEC as an example of good practices and a source of inspiration. He ended his editorial with an impassioned plea for "market democracy." The future of the capitalist system was at stake: "Given the current state of world financial markets, which can hardly be called bullish, reformers have little time at their disposal. When an army retreats, doesn't the rumor spread that it has not been defeated, but betrayed? When prices go down, when investors lose money—at least in the short run—because of the laws of the market, it is even more essential that their natural discontent have no motive, no excuse to transform itself into mistrust or resentment."[15]

Two days later, *La Vie Française*, a weekly newspaper specializing in the securities market, complained about the "turmoil in stock prices" and gave specific indications about the conditions of the merger:

> The "KUHLMANN mystery," at last, is clarified. Confirming the rumors which circulated in the market, and which we reported [in a previous edition], a press release, published Wednesday evening, announced the merger of KUHLMANN, UGINE and PRODUITS AZOTÉS (a UGINE subsidiary), [resulting] in a new company, UGINE-KUHLMANN.
>
> Breaking the code of silence was long overdue, because rumors about this spectacular merger gave free rein to speculation. At the *Bourse* on Wednesday, the exchange ratio (one UGINE-KUHLMANN share for one KUHLMANN share) had become an open secret, even though a more favorable exchange ratio had been mentioned earlier.
>
> This situation explains the diverging evolution of the two securities. In a very active market (31,000 securities traded in four trading sessions), Kuhlmann shares rose as high as 234 on Tuesday, and then came back at 224.90 [. . .] on Thursday. One can recall that the price was less than 200 three weeks ago.
>
> On the other hand, Ugine, also very active (15,400 securities traded), weakened from 249 to 226, its lowest level this year. During the only trading session on Thursday, the stock went down by 26 French Francs.
>
> Ugine shareholders will observe, not without some bitterness, that the first consequence of the merger has been . . . the fall in the price of the shares they owned. This results from the terms of the exchange transaction, which boil down to giving Kuhlmann a "weight" equivalent to two-thirds of Ugine. This proportion is more or less consistent with the difference between the respective balance-sheets, turnovers and net profits of the two companies, but it does not take into consideration the fact that Ugine has always been valued more favorably by the *Bourse* because of the very nature of its activities.[16]

On June 6, Henri Jolivet, the chairman and chief executive officer of Ugine, sent a four-page letter to all of the company shareholders.[17] He reiterated the need to prepare for the opening of French borders and explained that the merger was perceived favorably by the French government. The letter also included a brief allusion to the May 26 incident: "At the *Bourse*, the exchange ratio between Ugine and Kuhlmann shares has given rise to varied reactions. A very objective examination [of the situation] shows that the ratio is absolutely justified."[18]

In subsequent public statements, the chairmen of Ugine and Kuhlmann attempted to play down the concerns of investors, emphasizing instead the business rationale of the merger.[19]

Confidentially, the prime minister ordered an inquiry. It was conducted by the Direction du Trésor. Maurice Pérouse, the directeur, summarized the findings in a memorandum dated July 6.[20] Three days later, Haberer transmitted the memorandum to Debré, suggesting that it be forwarded to Matignon—in other words to the prime minister's office. Debré's answer was an emphatic "yes" on Haberer's cover note. Pérouse's memorandum, to which a detailed schedule was attached, included a postmortem analysis of the Ugine-Kuhlmann scandal.

On May 25, on the eve of the infamous trading session, the boards of Ugine, Kuhlmann, and Produits Azotés had informed their shareholders of the merger. It was to take place under the following conditions: "Kuhlmann shareholders were to receive one Ugine-Kuhlmann share for each Kuhlmann share they already owned; Produits Azotés shareholders were to receive nine Ugine-Kuhlmann shares for five Produits Azotés shares."[21]

The Produits Azotés component of the transaction was not controversial and was not discussed further in the memo. The analysis focused on the market prices, both current and forward, of Ugine and Kuhlmann shares:

In French Francs	Ugine–Current	Ugine–Forward	Kuhlmann–Current	Kuhlmann–Forward
May 2	260.50–263	262.50–263	198	201.50
May 11	254	257–257.80	197–198	201–200
May 25	250–245	252–245	224.50	229–227.50
May 26	225	223–226	216.50–222	219–224.90

At the beginning of May, the price of Ugine shares was well above the price of Kuhlmann's: approximately 260 against approximately 200. Market conditions, therefore, were not consistent with the proposed terms of the merger.

According to Pérouse, the boards of the two companies had concluded that the difference in market prices was not justified and that the exchange had to take place at par. In the case of Kuhlmann, dividing the net asset value of the company by the number of shares outstanding resulted in a value of 200 French francs, which was close to the market price as of early May. In the case of Ugine, however, the calculated value amounted to significantly less than the May 2 current market price of approximately 260 French francs.[22] Dividends per share were, respectively, 7.50 French francs (Kuhlmann) and 6.98 French francs (Ugine).

Between May 11 and May 25, the market price of Ugine shares remained stable, whereas the price of Kuhlmann shares increased significantly. Meanwhile, an analysis of the number of Kuhlmann shares traded daily showed a suspicious increase after May 12:

Number of Kuhlmann Shares Traded Daily	Current	Forward
Daily Average—May 2 to May 11 (8 trading days)	671.75	668.75
May 12	1,436	2,400
May 13	1,041	2,975
May 16	1,262	4,675
May 17	511	3,550
May 18	540	3,500
May 20	1,330	5,100
May 23	1,073	4,750
May 24	2,358	16,300
May 25	1,054	4,850
May 26	876	9,225
May 27	1,028	10,375
May 31	546	4,700

During the nine trading days between May 12 and May 25, 32,205, Ugine shares were traded, that is, 0.62 percent of the total number of Ugine shares. This compared to 63,767 Kuhlmann shares traded, that is, 1.85 percent of the total number of Kuhlmann shares. Most of the Kuhlmann transactions resulted from purchase orders, which led to an increase in the market price.

The directeur du Trésor tried to explain this unusual trading activity: "The number of additional transactions likely due to information which might have leaked before the official announcement of the merger, even if not very significant compared to the total number of shares, is however not negligible."[23]

In his memo, Pérouse seemed to be at a loss for words to describe what was indeed an insider trading case. Besides, his rather euphemistic treatment of the whole affair might have reflected his embarrassment—after all, as detailed in chapter 3, it was the Trésor's responsibility, if an indirect one, to supervise the securities market.

On May 26, the news of the merger caused the market price of Ugine shares to drop dramatically, by approximately 10 percent in one day. Meanwhile, the price of Kuhlmann shares eroded only marginally. Ugine shareholders, smaller ones in particular, had some reason to feel cheated. During the December 29 general meeting of shareholders convened to ratify the merger, one of them was to complain bitterly about having lost 8 percent of his holdings in one single trading session.[24]

At the end of his analysis, Pérouse concluded that the bankers had not prepared the merger with sufficient care. The consequences were highly regrettable: "If it is unlikely that this merger gave rise to speculative transactions of a significant size, one cannot exclude that, for some shareholders who had been informed at the beginning of the month of the exchange ratio, [the merger] was an opportunity to execute speculative buy or sell orders. In any event, it is certain that the conditions under which the merger took place contributed to exacerbating the disturbing aspect that, too often, market transactions have in the eyes of the general public."[25]

The outrage of investors was such that the French government could not remain silent. On June 9, one month before he would receive a copy of Perouse's memorandum, Pompidou was the guest of the Syndicat de la Presse économique et financière (Guild of Economic Journalists) at Ledoyen, one of Paris's best restaurants.[26] In the interview, he attempted to reassure public opinion about the state of the French economy. The prime minister commented on the rise in interest rates and indicated that the French government would probably issue another large *emprunt* (public loan) in 1966. He said he was confident in the outlook for economic growth: emerging from the economic stabilization plan, French industrial production had been growing at an annualized rate of 7 to 8 percent over the first four months of 1966. While he declared that he was favorable to ending the price freeze, he reiterated his determination to keep inflation under control. He also distanced himself from an initiative supported by the most left-wing members of the Gaullist party and which had caused much irritation among investors large and small. The Vallon amendment, which asserted "the right of workers to benefit from the increase in the company's assets resulting from self-financing,"[27] was being discussed in Parliament. To assuage the concerns of the investing public, the prime minister affirmed two principles: first, managerial authority would not be diminished; second, the ability of French corporations to generate cash flows would be protected.

Had they remained limited to the overall economic environment, Pompidou's remarks at Ledoyen would not have attracted much attention. The prime minister, however, decided to add a few words on the Bourse. *La Vie Française* quoted them in its June 10 edition: "A lot remains to be done in order to create, in France, a *Bourse* that would be worthy of its name (which demands a sufficient number of listed securities, an informed public, and an active market). Reforms are being conducted. The minister for the Economy and Finances has been asked to put together a 'moralization plan,' in particular with respect to the fair valuation of securities."[28]

Les Échos also reported Pompidou's merciless appreciation of the Paris Bourse, adding that "the stock market would need to be sufficiently active in order to not be distorted by irrational interventions"[29]—an allusion to the recent Ugine-Kuhlmann incident. According to the newspaper, the prime minister wished that accounting information published by the listed corporations be made more comprehensive. The "effort in favor of the moralization of the *Bourse*" was not mentioned by *Les Échos* in connection with the state of the market or the need to improve the quality of investor information, but in the context of the Vallon amendment, "Money, the Prime Minister emphasized, will have to remain within the companies, in order to be reinvested. This is a serious problem, which raises a legitimate social issue, but also shows practical difficulties: the rise of the revenues of those who are not owners [of stocks]. It will be interesting to know what the [Prime] Minister means by that, and what he means when he speaks of an upcoming effort in favor of the moralization of the *Bourse*."[30]

While *La Vie Française* and *Les Échos* differed slightly in their transcription of the prime minister's remarks, neither of them omitted the word "moralization," which resulted in a long-lasting commotion among politicians, professionals, and investors. Their echo was such that they were still quoted in administrative correspondence six months later.[31]

The use of the word "moralization" by Pompidou seems to have been unpremeditated; archival records do not indicate that there was a concerted effort by the prime minister and the minister for the economy and finances to direct the attention of public opinion on the need to "moralize the market." Pompidou, however, frequently commented on the protracted stagnation of the Paris Bourse; the lunch at Ledoyen would not be the last time that he expressed his misgivings publicly. A few weeks later, he was interviewed on TV by French journalist Roger Priouret. He ad-libbed on the subject of the securities market:

Ah! The *Bourse* . . . You spoke to me of an almost dead *Bourse*, alas, yes! Our stock market is indeed almost dead. Since April of 1962, I believe that market capitalization for French securities has declined, in average, by 40%. It is obviously very bad with respect to the ability of [French] corporations to raise capital. Here as well, we are trying to make an effort to enlarge this financial market, to give it more substance, and the Minister of the Economy and Finances, upon my request, is currently preparing a plan on this subject. Above all, what would be needed is that the French people regain confidence, if not in the stock market, at least in the companies that are listed there. I believe that the present situation should allow them to regain confidence; but I will stop here because some will say that I want to speculate in the stock market.[32]

This kind of warning was not unexpected of an acting prime minister, but Pompidou's professional background gave them special weight; his emphatic determination to "moralize the market" and his not-too subtle denial of being a speculator might also have resulted from his desire to atone for his background: for several years, he had worked for Rothschild, the famed investment bank.

Before heading the French government, Pompidou's career had followed a meandering path. His and Debré's credentials in the eyes of de Gaulle were very different. Born in 1911, one year earlier than his predecessor in the Hôtel de Matignon, Pompidou graduated from the École Normale Supérieure, the *grande école* which attracted France's most brilliant students of humanities. The former teacher of literature, Greek, and Latin was to retain a lifelong love of poetry and contemporary art. Shortly after the liberation of Paris, in 1944, he joined de Gaulle's staff and was put in charge of writing reports. More than his rather undistinguished attitude during the German occupation of France, his writing skills and organizational abilities ingratiated him to the leader of the provisional government. After de Gaulle's resignation in January 1946, Pompidou did not go back to his teaching job and remained one of his most trusted advisers.

In 1954, however, Pompidou was hired by Guy de Rothschild, head of the French branch of the banking dynasty. This unexpected career move shaped his public persona. In an obituary published by the *New York Times* at the time of his death, American journalist Albin Krebs offered an apt summary of his several-year stint in banking: "The hard-working Mr. Pompidou plunged with zest in his new undertaking, which was to help rouse the Rothschild empire out of the torpor into which it had sunk during the war years. He travelled widely, to Senegal, Gabon, Guinea and other African territories, compiling reports on investment opportunities for the Rothschilds. In less than two years he became director general of the banking house and second in command to Guy de Rothschild himself."[33]

According to testimonies from his former colleagues, Pompidou never transformed completely into an operational banker.[34] However, his analytical mind enabled him to gain a quick and thorough understanding of investment banking transactions; besides, his relative lack of creativity was more than compensated for by his solid common sense. He did, in the end, make a significant contribution to the development of Rothschild.

In May 1958, when de Gaulle became the head of the last government of the Fourth Republic, he asked Pompidou to serve as his directeur de cabinet. After de Gaulle had officially been inaugurated as president of the Fifth Republic, in January 1959, Pompidou returned to Rothschild. His appointment as prime minister, following the ratification of Algerian independence in the April 8, 1962, referendum, surprised politicians and journalists. His professional background did not go uncommented on: "There was criticism then, and it continued, that he had never been elected to office and to the effect that he was a 'technician' rather than a seasoned political animal. [. . .] Mr. Pompidou's appointment was also criticized because of his banking connections. 'The Rothschilds' man,' as the leftists press dubbed him, was never fully able to free himself of that yoke."[35]

For all the consideration that they might have had for a former "Rothschilds' man," market professionals did not condone the prime minister's choice of words: that he had declared publicly that the Bourse needed to be moralized cast a shadow on the morality of all market professionals. One week after the lunch at Ledoyen, *La Vie Française* editorialized somewhat skeptically on the moralization of the stock exchange:

> As we had announced last week, Mr. Pompidou asked the Minister of the Economy and Finances that a "moralization" plan for the *Bourse* be prepared. Obviously, the ideal measure would be to put an end to the bear market. In order to achieve this, there is no miracle: buyers must have good stocks to buy. If one is to believe Mr. Pompidou: "current price levels can be considered, if not as low, at least as reasonable"; this is also our opinion. We have already said it many times. But the problem is: buyers are missing in action! The solution to the crisis of the *Bourse*, therefore, is not to "moralize" investors, but to reassure them. And that is another issue: the issue of trust.[36]

La Vie Française conceded that, "on specific points, certain initiatives are certainly desirable." But while the author of the editorial reminded his readers that the newspaper had always been in favor of a large disclosure of accounting information, he did not suggest any improvement in the existing obligations of publicly traded companies.

Ironically, it fell to Debré to smooth the feathers ruffled by the usually more diplomatic Pompidou. Speaking to an audience of *agents de change* (stockbrokers) one month later, he explained: "The phrase 'moralization' of the stock exchange was used by the Prime Minister in circumstances of which all who are present here [today] are aware. Obviously it does not apply to market professionals. More than anybody else, you know that the Paris *Bourse* and its *agents de change* enjoy a flattering and justified reputation of respectability and honesty."[37]

In his capacity as *syndic* de la Compagnie nationale des agents de change (head of the national organization of stockbrokers), Pierre Bottmer was the official representative of market professionals. In an interview with a journalist from *Fortune française*, another business newspaper, he offered a quaint interpretation of Debré's declaration: "A question was asked by one of my fellow stockbrokers about the statements on the 'moralization of the *Bourse*.' Mr. DEBRÉ confirmed that the problem was not to moralize the *Compagnie des agents de change*, but to give 'a good morale' to the *Bourse*. I then added that in order for the *Bourse* to have a good morale, it had to offer investors securities of well-known quality. The big problem, therefore, is that of public information about listed companies, [information] on their assets, their activities, their results."[38]

Bottmer went on to enumerate the many efforts undertaken by the compagnie to improve the quality of investor information. However, there was some disingenuity in the confusion between "morale" and "morality"; the syndic's rather lame efforts to deflect Debré's veiled criticism proved ineffectual.

The memory of the scandal did not fade quickly. During the months that followed, the press continued to refer to the "turmoil" caused by the merger:[39] in a series of four articles published in November, *Le Monde* was to remind its readers of the "Aux voleurs!" catcalls shouted during the May 26 trading session at the Palais Brongniart.[40]

Ugine shareholders, of course, were the first concerned. Three general meetings took place between the announcement of the merger and its formal approval at the end of the year: on June 22 (ordinary annual general meeting) and on November 14 and December 29 (extraordinary general meetings). The historical archives of the Pechiney Group include detailed shorthand minutes of these meetings. The following excerpts offer a glimpse into the outraged feelings of small investors.

At the June 22 meeting, Mr. Delcassé, a shareholder, took to the floor after a fifteen-minute presentation delivered by Jolivet, chairman and CEO of Ugine. Delcassé immediately quoted Pompidou's remarks on the "moralization of the *Bourse*": "When Mr. Georges Pompidou uttered those words ten days ago, at the end of a lunch where he had been the guest of honor, he brutally awoke quite a number of people: since then, bankers, market professionals, the business community as a whole have kept wondering about the intentions of the Prime Minister. It is the best kept secret in Paris!

"In the dismal state where the *Bourse* finds itself, this "mystery-plan," however, has given rise to a fragile hope."[41]

Delcassé went on to deplore the "black hours" of the stock market since 1962. He observed that the categories of the French population with a capacity to invest had little appetite for securities, "an investment vehicle of which they no longer expect anything." According to him, they looked at the Bourse with mistrust, and a number of recent transactions had seemed to prove them right. When he mentioned the merger between Ugine and Kuhlmann, he was interrupted by an uproar of protests. Undaunted, Delcassé continued his accusation: "Insiders (*des initiés*) very close to the company have made big profits without taking any risks: they knew that one Kuhlmann share would be exchanged against one Ugine share, even though the price of Ugine shares exceeded the price of Kuhlmann shares by 25%."[42]

In more colorful language, another shareholder added that it was unacceptable that the chairman and the managers of a company had "torpedoed their own shareholders."

Delcassé regretted that, "contrary to the situation that [prevailed] in the United States," the French government had been powerless to prevent such a "scandal"—a "theft," he was to call it later during the meeting. The Ministry of Finances did not allocate sufficient resources to the surveillance of market transactions—another striking contrast with the United States: "In France, mergers happen again and again. Are the shareholders of the companies involved informed or consulted? Never. They are faced with a *fait accompli*, they can either submit or resign. This, either, does not happen in the United States."[43]

Delcassé deplored that the French press, dependent on advertising revenues, did not provide objective information on economic issues.

Another shareholder, Mr. Mauvoisin, shared Delcassé's somber assessment of the French securities market: "Let us remember what was the state of the economy in the age of our parents and our grandparents, and let us look at the situation today. Do you want to try to convert your children to the *Bourse*, to investing, to securities? I tried . . . and I wasted my time. No matter how large the profits you are making, Mr. Chairman, [. . .] one has to admit that the dividend we will receive will enable us to buy first-class subway tickets (laughter) . . . [. . .] How do you want to trust anything or anyone? This is not possible anymore."[44]

Mauvoisin, however, did not support Pompidou's moralization plan, in which he saw another attempt to restrict liberties; he added that, in so many years of presence on the stock market, he had never witnessed a single criminal act perpetrated by an agent de change.

Mr. Texier complained about the lack of information: negotiations between Ugine and Kuhlmann had remained secret; management had neglected the opinion of employees and small shareholders; along with the rest of the population, shareholders had heard about the merger on television. Texier blamed the French government, which had supported, if not masterminded, the merger. He did not believe in the moralization plan and went as far as to question Pompidou's professional skills—if not his honesty: prior to heading the French government, the angry investor reminded his audience, the prime minister had been managing a corporation that had seen its share price fall to face value.

Mr. Duchesne corrected Texier when he said that the negotiations between Ugine and Kuhlmann, kept secret at the beginning, ended up being not so secret—at least for some. He did, however, agree with him on the conditions of the merger: "The opinion of the investing public was, more or less, that one Ugine share was worth 1.2 or 1.25 Kuhlmann share. And in that projected merger, Mr. Chairman, you have substituted your own judgment to that of the *Bourse*, of shareholders, of public opinion."[45]

Mr. Partridge questioned the competence of auditors and criticized the delay with which accounting information had been sent to shareholders.

Against all evidence, Jolivet vehemently denied that the announcement of Pompidou's moralization plan had anything to do with the merger. His attempted justification of the exchange ratio was not supported by a detailed analysis of the accounting data.

The infamous May 26 trading session was still very much at the center of the discussion during the November 14 extraordinary general meeting. Angry shareholders did not fail to mention the article published in *Le Monde* two days earlier.[46] Said Mr. Beaucaire: "In that particular instance, however, I am amazed that this board of directors had permitted, for I do not know what reason, maybe as a result of leaks, maybe as a result of carelessness, something that a newspaper as serious as *Le Monde* considers a scandal."[47]

Mr. Blin read an excerpt from the May 26 edition of *La Cote Desfossés*, a financial newspaper, in which a market professional was quoted as saying that Ugine shares had been "thrown away." He also referred to a statement by Debré in *Le Figaro*: three weeks after the incident, the minister for the economy and finances had declared that he wanted to avoid "the tricks which happened recently in the context of mergers between corporations." Many shareholders, shocked that the reputation of the company had been tarnished, announced that they would vote against the ratification of the merger. Mauvoisin, who had already expressed his disagreement in June, put the consequences of the transaction "plotted by" the chairman in historical perspective:

> The result, you know what it is. Your method pertains to what certain events which took place one hundred and seventy five years ago could not eliminate completely—and by that I mean government fiat. I told you and I tell you again, this is not acceptable to public opinion anymore and, believe me, if the regrettable example you gave were followed by others, the lost confidence—because confidence in the financial market is lost. Don't people here know some who said: "I threw overboard all my securities"? These days I had a conversation with a major provincial *notaire* who told me: "In all the estate cases that I happen to handle, I consider it my duty to get rid of all securities."[48]

If provincial *notaires* had lost faith in the Bourse, the seriousness of the situation could not be underestimated. Mauvoisin dreaded the perspective of a market narrowed down to only forty or fifty large corporations. All of them could easily be nationalized by government decree: "And who, then, would go to the barricades? Certainly not you, Mr. Chairman."[49]

In a similar political vein, Delcassé quoted François Mitterrand, one of the leaders of the opposition: "The *Bourse* is being conducted from within company boards of directors": small investors did not have a say in strategic decisions, which nevertheless affected their interests directly.

Pressed by questions from smaller investors, a representative of the Société Nationale d'Investissements (SNI), a major shareholder of Ugine, confessed that the SNI had started to reduce its exposure on Ugine and Kuhlmann securities prior to the official announcement of the merger. This admission triggered cries of "that's disgusting!"

Eventually, though, shareholders ratified the merger. By July 1967, the price of Ugine-Kuhlmann shares had fallen to 158 French francs.[50] From an industrial standpoint, the transaction was not a success: there were little operational synergies between the two companies; the two former chairmen, who shared the management of the resulting entity's operations, did not get along well.[51] In October 1969, a senior executive of the company admitted in an internal document: "The merger between UGINE and KUHLMANN was the juxtaposition of two corporations rather than an industrial reorganization and, besides, the merger was practically not done." Tellingly, the memorandum was entitled: *L'impasse d'UGINE-KUHLMANN* ("The Ugine-Kuhlmann Deadlock").[52]

This did not deter the French government from actively promoting industrial mergers to improve the international competitiveness of French corporations. In April 1971, Ugine-Kuhlmann merged with Pechiney to form Pechiney-Ugine-Kuhlmann (PUK).[53] Four years later, the new "French giant" became the subject of an influential book written by economist Michel Beaud, civil servant Pierre Danjou, and financial analyst Jean David.[54] They concluded their scathing analysis of PUK's strategy with a fervent call to nationalization and *autogestion* (direct management by the workers of the company).

As early as August 1966, Gaston Défossé, a highly respected banker, acknowledged that the Ugine-Kuhlmann transaction had been a technical failure. In a presentation to the board of directors of Banque Nationale de Paris (BNP), he voiced his concern about the negative consequences of mega-mergers on public opinion: "People wonder [. . .] whether the excessive size of the [resulting] corporations will make them more prone to being nationalized, or, conversely, whether smaller corporations have any chance to survive European competition [. . .]."[55]

Défossé's prediction—and Debré's fear of a backlash against "extreme liberalism"—were to be vindicated by history: in 1982, one year after Mitterrand's election to the French presidency, PUK was indeed nationalized.

By mid-1966, however, for all the outrage generated by the Ugine-Kuhlmann scandal, nationalization was not an option. If the prime minister had felt compelled to proclaim his determination to moralize the Bourse, he had not questioned the legitimacy of private ownership of large corporations. De Gaulle had not commented publicly on the scandal—much more was needed to attract the attention of the Olympian president of the French Republic. Yet he would memorably mention the securities market in a press conference a few weeks after the incident.

CHAPTER THREE

The Paris *Bourse* in the 1960s:
A Basket Case?

President de Gaulle's press conferences live in collective memory. They took place in a heavily decorated room of the Élysée Palace, crowded with journalists and members of the French government. Seated behind a draped table in a stately armchair, the president never failed to deliver impressive performances. Old age had not impaired his intellectual alertness, obvious in his command of the most technical issues. He also knew how to stage a good show: his sense of humor, ferocious at times, would delight his audience. As a man born in the nineteenth century, the general had a taste for old-fashioned, sophisticated words that he combined with popular phrases for dramatic effect. One of his most celebrated witticisms was uttered on October 28, 1966: "Well, now that you mention it . . . The market, in 1962, was exceedingly good. In 1966, it is exceedingly bad. But you know, France is not ruled from the *corbeille*."

Located in the middle of the stock exchange's main hall, the corbeille (literally, the basket) was a circular banister over which only the most senior agents de change were authorized to lean while trading—and smoking: cigarette butts were aimed at the pile of white sand situated at the center of the circle. This picturesque contraption stood as a symbol of the esoteric traditions of the Paris securities market.

De Gaulle's choice of words and his body language—the smirk, the arched eyebrows, the inflections of the voice, the movement of the hands, the confident expectation of audience applause—expressed his contempt for the petty corbeille. The general shared the prejudices that were not infrequent among the French Catholic, provincial gentry. The son of a history teacher in a Jesuit college, he did not opt for the military career to satisfy a need for money. His devout wife belonged to a family of prosperous industrialists from Northern France, but the couple was never wealthy. Their estate in Colombey-les-Deux-Églises had been purchased in return for a life annuity, and they had been fortunate that the seller died a couple of years after the transaction had been signed.[1]

Drawn into public life by the disaster of French defeat in 1940, de Gaulle was more at ease in the rarefied atmosphere of international politics than among the more mundane contingencies of economic life. In December 1965, the perception by the French electorate that their president was not paying sufficient attention to the consequences on their daily lives of the "economic stabilization plan" contributed to the humiliating second ballot in the presidential election. Grudgingly, the embattled General consented to a televised interview during which he had to deny having uttered another aphorism, apocryphal this time: "L'intendance suivra!" ("Logistics will always follow!"). Contrary to Pompidou, he never sought, nor particularly enjoyed, the company of financiers and entrepreneurs; in the pantheon of French statesmen, he chose his heroes among cardinal-ministers, men-of-letters, military commanders, diplomats, or even orators of the Revolutionary period, rather than among the bankers and the industrialists who engineered France's take-off during the nineteenth century.

Political and economic institutions, however, had not developed along parallel, never intersecting lines; the French Government and the *Bourse* had cooperated, and clashed, on numerous occasions over the centuries. This legacy was a heavy burden to carry: in its second annual report, published on March 11, 1970, the COB) would inventory, in the course of 170 years, no less than "46 laws, 57 decrees and 19 ministerial orders of some importance."[2]

The history of the complicated—and at times contentious—relationship between power and money was present in the minds of both politicians and market professionals, who frequently reminisced over its most colorful episodes. A good example is given by Yves Meunier, Pierre Bottmer's successor as syndic de la Compagnie nationale des agents de change, in a lecture delivered on April 20, 1967. While Meunier was addressing a topical question—*Où va la Bourse?* ("Where Is the *Bourse* Going?")—he mentioned several incidents in the history of the Paris securities market. At some point in the lecture, he felt it necessary to set the 1807 *Code du Commerce* (commercial code) in its historical context: "The philosophy of these institutions can be explained, above anything else, by the year 1807: the [Napoleonic] regime was essentially authoritarian and willing to reorganize the nation; oblivion operates quickly, but not to the point of having erased the disastrous memories of the financial turmoil of the Revolution; the elders could still remember the stories told by their fathers about the mad adventures of the Regency and about the first among the great financial illusionists."[3]

It was not uncommon, among journalists and politicians of the 1960s, to compare de Gaulle with Napoleon. *Mutatis mutandis*, Meunier's remarks about the agents de change of the early nineteenth century still applied to their successors: the specter of "the first among the great financial illusionists" was still haunting the narrow streets of the Bourse district; "the mad adventures of the Regency"—the Roaring Twenties of another era—continued to resonate across the centuries.

When Louis XIV died in 1715, the prolonged wars of the last decades of his reign had depleted the royal treasury. Scottish-born John Law, a gambler and an economist, believed in the virtue of paper money to stimulate an ailing economy and write off government debt. In 1716, he convinced the regent Philippe d'Orléans to give him the authorization to open the Banque Générale, a privately owned bank issuing notes against deposits of gold or government bills. Law's venture was a success. In 1718, it became the Banque Royale, with the French government as its sole shareholder and no limit on the quantity of banknotes it could issue. Meanwhile, Law took over several trading companies specializing in the commerce of colonial products; the resulting conglomerate was known as the Compagnie du Mississippi. Lured by an orchestrated advertising campaign, investors were persuaded to purchase Mississippi shares in exchange for government bills. In the absence of a stock exchange, transactions took place on rue Quincampoix, in the vicinity of Les Halles, the main marketplace for fresh products in Paris. In 1720, the compagnie merged with the Banque Royale and received permission to issue additional shares. At the height of its prosperity, it combined the activities of a deposit bank, a merchant bank, a central bank, a trade monopoly, and a tax collector.[4] Law himself was appointed controller-general of French finances by the regent. Mississippi shares "became the object of frenzied speculation":[5] the narrow rue Quincampoix was obstructed by hysterical speculators of all conditions, sexes, and ages— British investors even joined the crowd.[6] In 1720, however, smarter—or better-informed—investors began to liquidate their holdings. The Mississippi bubble burst, along with the equally infamous South Sea bubble in London. Several people died and thousands were ruined in the ensuing bank run; Law was ignominiously dismissed from his post and left the kingdom—he resumed his gambling career and died in obscurity in 1729.

In the eyes of contemporaries—and of many a latter-day novelist or film-maker—the Mississippi bubble epitomized the moral laxity associated with the Regency period: wild speculation had gone along with impiety, licentiousness, and political corruption. This stereotyped and moralizing interpretation has repeatedly and successfully been challenged by historians. Yet the trauma was real and had lasting effects on French finance: from then on, bankers carefully avoided the name *banque*, preferring instead the less toxic *caisse*, *crédit*, *comptoir*, or *société*;[7] paper money was discredited for decades; and the Banque de France was not to be established until 1800.

In the name of law and order, the royal government endeavored to reorganize the market for negotiable securities—which were then almost exclusively government securities. On September 24, 1724, a decision of the king's council established the Bourse de Paris. It was housed in a single building, the Hôtel de Nevers, where securities were auctioned publicly. Until the construction of the Palais Brongniart in the 1820s, the Bourse de Paris was to move to different locations, but it never left a very tight perimeter on the Right Bank of the Seine. Women were banned from the Hôtel de Nevers—the Bourse remained an exclusively male community until 1967, when it was decided that this form of discrimination could no longer be tolerated.

Police informers routinely reported on the market, but of course their presence was of little use to prevent recurring waves of speculation. In an attempt to control the trading in government securities, a legal monopoly was established in favor of the guild of agents de change. The profession had existed since medieval times—money changers had given its name to the Pont au Change, the covered bridge where they had their shops. The guild had been formed in the seventeenth century; by then, the activities of money changers had extended from the exchange of coins to that of promissory notes. The 1724 edict limited the number of agents de change to sixty.[8] Sworn to professional secrecy, the agents de change were intermediaries: they were prohibited from engaging in proprietary trading and banking activities.

All guilds were dissolved in 1791 during the early stages of the French Revolution, and the agents de change were no exception. The securities market, however, was not liberalized completely. In a war context, the embattled Republic had to liquidate the colossal national debt it had inherited from the old regime. To quench speculation, strict restrictions were imposed on trading, and the Bourse was closed temporarily. In 1795, it reopened in a deconsecrated church, with twenty-five registered agents de change. Meanwhile, illegal transactions were still being conducted in the gardens of the Palais Royal, the Regent's former residence.[9]

Inaugurated by the coup of Brumaire in 1799, Bonaparte's consulate restored financial stability: the tax system was reorganized, the Banque de France was created, and the franc Germinal, which perpetuated until 1914, was established. While the Banque de France had a monopoly on the issuance of the French currency, it was owned by a small number of banking houses; its shares were traded on the stock exchange. Along with government securities, these shares represented the bulk of the Paris market capitalization.

Logically, the Bourse, too, had to be reformed. Between 1801 and 1816, a series of laws, edicts, and ordonnances enshrined a number of principles that endured for almost two centuries. These principles, rooted in history, shaped the hybrid status of the agents de change. Their number was limited under the *numerus clausus* system. They were appointed or, as the case may be, removed from office, by the minister of finances. Yet they were not government employees but *officiers ministériels* (literally, ministerial officers). An 1816 ordonnance confirmed that they "owned" their office and that they could "transmit" it to their successor. While the profession was not without risks and experienced many spectacular bankruptcies, Parisian dynasties remained active on the market for generations. However, proud as they were of their privileged status and traditions, they were looked down on by members of the *haute banque*, the prestigious banking houses with representatives sitting on the board of the Banque de France—the Parisian branch of the Rothschild family, which was later to hire Pompidou, was one of them.

The agents de change could not engage in banking activities, but they had a monopoly on securities transactions, and they were liable for the good execution of orders—a solidarity fund was created in order to come to the rescue of the less fortunate among them. Together, they constituted the Compagnie des agents de change de la Bourse de Paris—other compagnies were formed in Lyon, Marseille, Lille, Bordeaux, Nantes, Toulouse, and Nancy. Compagnie members were given the right to elect a board of representatives, the *chambre syndicale*, comprising the syndic (chairman of the board) and six other members. In addition to being the official representative of the agents de change, the chambre syndicale supervised their activities and could take disciplinary action against them, either out of its own authority or upon request from the minister of finances. It mediated potential conflicts between agents de change, or between agents de change and third parties; it also administered the solidarity fund. Competition was restricted by the numerus clausus system and the rules enacted by the chambre syndicale. Agents de change, however, were challenged by unofficial brokers, who were prohibited from entering the Bourse and had to operate under the colonnade of the Palais Brongniart. Despite numerous attempts, the chambre syndicale failed to eradicate these competitors, who were to survive under various names (*coulissiers, banquiers en valeurs*, etc.) until the 1960s.

During the course of the nineteenth century, total market capitalization increased and diversified. As was the case in the United States, the construction of railways required enormous sums of money. In addition to banking facilities, industrial companies began to raise funds on the stock and bond markets; foreign securities were admitted to trading. Speculation went along with the development of market activity. A series of resounding scandals marked the century: speculation on *sociétés en commandite* (a local version of limited partnerships) in the 1840s, the bankruptcy of the French bank Union Générale (1882), the Panama scandal (1893), and so forth. That these scandals had little repercussions abroad does not mean that they were easily forgotten in France. Novels by Balzac, Stendhal, Zola, Barrès, and others abound with minute descriptions of insider cases and fraudulent bankruptcies.[10] They gave credence to the claim that the Bourse dominated the economic, social, and political life of the nation: "A government cannot undo the *Bourse*, but the *Bourse* can undo a government,"[11] Stendhal wrote in *Lucien Leuwen*—a statement with which de Gaulle, in all likelihood, would have taken issue.

The number of investors rose steadily. Effective control of the day-to-day operations on the stock exchange was essential to their safety. In practice, government had delegated this responsibility to the agents de change. Little attention was paid, though, to another aspect of investor protection: the completeness and accuracy of the information available on publicly traded companies. Along with the louche intermediary and the unscrupulous robber baron, the gullible investor became a stereotypical character in French literature. In *La Maison Nucingen*, Balzac marveled at the audacity of his hero, a shameless speculator, and the complacency of his victims:

> At the time, this great man was thinking of paying his creditors with fictitious securities, while keeping their money. [. . .] That kind of transaction is equivalent to giving a little pâté against a *louis d'or* [a gold coin] to big kids who, like the little kids of old, would rather have a single pâté than the coin with which they could buy two hundred of them.
>
> —What is it, then, that you're saying here, Bixiou? Couture exclaimed. Nothing is more straightforward; these days, not a single week passes when people are not offered pâtés for their *louis d'or*. Are people forced to give away their money? Is it not their right to be enlightened?[12]

Rabid speculators of the Nucingen type prospered in the unstable legal environment of the first decades of the nineteenth century. It took a long time for French company law and accounting practices to mature. The origins of the auditing profession can be traced back to the May 23, 1863, law, which made it an obligation, for publicly traded companies, to designate *commissaires de surveillance* (statutory auditors).[13] On July 24, 1867, a comprehensive Company Act provided a stable legal framework for the creation of publicly traded companies: the *société anonyme*. Shareholders benefited from some of its provisions: auditors were to be designated by the general assembly; the directors of the société anonyme had to present to the general assembly the balance sheet, the profit-and-loss statement, and the inventory of assets and liabilities; prior to the general assembly, auditors had to prepare a report on the financial statements of the société anonyme.[14] Nothing was said, however, about the independence of auditors or the professional requirements they had to meet.[15]

In 1907, the *Bulletin des Annonces Légales et Obligatoires* (*BALO*) was created. An addition to the *Journal Officiel*, the official gazette of the French Republic, the bulletin gave official notice of all upcoming transactions (initial public offerings, additional issuances of shares and bonds) on the securities market. Information thus made public, however, was primarily legal in its nature—financial statements were not disclosed in the *BALO*. The primary use of accounting information remained for the calculation of the taxes to be paid by corporations. In his book on "governance by numbers," French law scholar Alain Supiot emphasized this point: "Anglo-American accounting standards (which are prevalent today) have always put forward the point of view of investors. It is first and foremost to their attention that accounting is geared, with the objective to arouse their trust and permit their control [of corporations]. However, in the tradition of continental Europe, it is the point of view of government, more specifically the point of view of the tax administration, which came first."[16]

Several reasons explained this apparent lack of interest in disclosing and disseminating accounting information. French investors were attracted to bonds, more specifically government bonds, rather than to shares. Defiant of "tax inquisition" the business community defended its traditions of secrecy. Trading on insider information was not necessarily perceived as criminal or even unethical—politicians and civil servants, including employees of the Trésor, could occasionally benefit from their position at the intersection of business and government.

With the benefit of hindsight, the last decades of the nineteenth century appeared as the golden age of the French securities market. In 1914, the Paris Bourse ranked second to London as supplier of international capital.[17] World War I, however, had very disruptive effects on the Bourse, which never recovered its prewar status. After 1918, cross-border capital flows gravitated toward

New York and, to a lesser extent, London, while French corporations turned to banks for an increasing share of their financing. During the 1920s, the intensity of speculation in the Bourse never remotely approached that of Wall Street. Yet a number of spectacular swindles (the Hanau, Oustric and Stavisky *affaires*) cast an unflattering light on the practices of market professionals and poisoned the political atmosphere of the interwar years: in February 1934, the Third Republic almost succumbed to the furor provoked by the affaire Stavisky.[18] The October 1929 Wall Street crash resonated strongly across the Atlantic; in France, however, its consequences were not as traumatic as in the United States. Minor changes to the organization of the Bourse did not result in a reform comparable to the 1933 Securities Act and the 1934 Securities Exchange Acts, two landmark pieces of legislation of the New Deal era. As to the disclosure of financial information, French lawmakers simply added specific provisions to existing requirements.[19]

The outbreak of World War II in 1939 and the fall of France in 1940 had dramatic consequences on the French economy. For all its pretension of being a shield protecting the French population, the Vichy government headed by Marshall Pétain repeatedly caved in to German demands for the shipment to Germany of agricultural and industrial goods and the implementation of a system of forced labor. Yet Pétain and his associates did not view themselves as mere caretakers; rather, they harbored the ambition to regenerate all aspects of French national life. Inspired in part by the regime's corporatist ideology, a number of professional organizations were established. The accounting profession was no exception: a 1942 law created the Ordre des experts comptables et des comptables agréés (OECCA), a professional organization of certified accountants supervised by the Ministry of Finances.[20]

The Bourse did not escape Vichy legislative activism: the Vichy authorities not only purged the agents de change profession of its Jewish members but also attempted to reinforce government control on the stock market. According to Yves Bouthillier, minister of finances from July 1940 to April 1942, "these measures aimed at establishing market discipline and at limiting, or cutting down, capital gains."[21] The February 14, 1942, law established the Comité des Bourses de Valeurs (Securities Exchange Committee), which was to survive until the creation of the COB in 1967.[22] The *comité* was chaired by the governor of the Banque de France (or, in his absence, by a deputy governor). Its vice chairman was the syndic of the Compagnie des agents de change de Paris. In the early 1960s, it also included two other agents de change, two representatives of banks and financial institutions, two representatives of investment funds and French investors, and one employee of the Compagnie des agents de change. Also sitting in the comité, the directeur du Trésor held the title of *commissaire du gouvernement* (government commissioner).

The comité was not independent. Its composition reflected the supervision exercised by France's central bank and, through the directeur du Trésor, by the minister of finances. Government control of the comité was made even tighter by the fact that, with the exception of its ex officio members, all other members were appointed by the minister of finances. Resources allocated to the comité were scarce. Secretarial duties were performed by employees from the Banque de France on a temporary posting. Employees of the Compagnie des agents de change and the Banque de France were asked to provide assistance on an ad hoc basis. Expenses were shared between the Compagnie des agents de change and the Banque de France. In 1965, they reached the modest amount of 195,000 French francs.[23]

The comité could make proposals to modify laws and rules applicable to the operations of the stock exchange; these proposals, however, were not necessarily implemented. It was entitled to take "individual decisions," disciplinary in their nature, concerning specific agents de change or securities. "General decisions," the scope of which might have affected the stock exchange as a whole (fees, forward transactions, etc.) had to be approved by the minister of finances. All decisions could be vetoed by the directeur du Trésor in his capacity as government commissioner. The comité's investigative powers were strictly limited—never did it verify the accuracy of the information disseminated by issuers, underwriters, or brokers. Investigations were conducted by auditors from the Compagnie des agents de change or inspectors from the Banque de France. The comité was not a court of justice: it could not prosecute, much less condemn an agent de change who had engaged in criminal activities.

Kept on a short leash by the French government, the comité had to share its responsibilities with the chambre syndicale, which had significant powers over its members, and other supervisory bodies. Banks and financial institutions were supervised by the Commission de Contrôle des Banques, another entity established by the Vichy government. Along with the comité, the commission was chaired by the governor of the Banque de France and relied on its personnel for secretarial purposes.[24]

World War II accentuated the relative decline of the Paris securities market, largely outdistanced by New York and London. In the immediate aftermath of the war, the Bourse did not play a significant role in financing the French economy. While the concept of "overdraft economy" was to be developed by

British economist John Hicks in the 1970s, it best characterizes the state of the French economy of the postwar decades.[25] In his discussion of the concept and how it applied to the French situation, historian Michael Loriaux identifies "some of the unusual characteristics of France's political economy—its high degree of indebtedness vis-à-vis banks and other lending institutions, the high level of bank indebtedness vis-à-vis the Banque de France, the comparative narrowness of the French financial market, and the comparative difficulty of defining and implementing monetary policy."[26] The implications in terms of monetary policy lie beyond the scope of this investigation; suffice it to say that French corporations of the 1950s and 1960s had come to rely on the banking sector and a network of public and parapublic institutions to access capital. Policy makers treated the stock market with benign neglect—or worse, according to Loriaux: "The financial market, victimized by continual inflation and political uncertainty, was abandoned to its fate of death by starvation. On the other hand, the banking sector became the object of structural reforms designed to render it a willing and able partner in the government's expansionist policy orientation by giving banks the means to supply industry with capital that was no longer forthcoming from the financial market."[27]

In comparison to the United Kingdom and the United States, France distinguished itself with a narrower stock ownership and a lower stock market capitalization to gross domestic product.[28] Less than a decade after the creation of the COB in 1976 the financial market would still account for only 15 percent of all sources of credit to the French economy, compared with 85 percent for all institutional lenders. In the United Kingdom and the United States, the numbers were, respectively, 42 percent and 49 percent for the financial market, and 58 percent and 51 percent for institutional lenders.[29]

Not only was the Bourse of the postwar decades playing a minor role in the financing of the French economy, it was also isolated from the international financial market. Fewer foreign shares were being listed in Paris; the portion they represented of the nominal capitalization of the stock market was declining; transactions in foreign shares and transactions originated by foreigners remained at a low level.[30]

Consistent with historical tradition, French investors preferred to invest in government bonds rather than in shares issued by publicly traded companies. Had demand for shares been stronger, however, it is unlikely that it would have met sufficient supply: the nationalization of Renault, utilities, banks, and insurance companies had reduced the presence of a significant number of potential issuers in the stock market—a large portion of listed companies were in fact nationalized companies or state credit institutions. Finally, the establishment of the French social security system did not encourage the constitution of securities portfolios by investors seeking to build a retirement fund.

In 1952, Georges Lutfalla, a businessman and an economist, was commissioned by the Conseil Économique et Social (Economic and Social Council, a consultative body advising lawmakers on social and economic issues) to write "a report on the financial market, its economic role, its current situation and the reforms that this situation demands."[31] Presented on November 14, 1952, the report started with an emotional defense of the French investor: "Mothers have inculcated upon their children the belief that excessive consumption was unseemly. Schoolteachers have taught us that saving money was a virtue. We learnt from the rest of the world that this was a French virtue. History reminds us that this French virtue gave France an eminent rank in the concert of nations during the nineteenth century."[32]

To explain the reasons of the "worrying languor of the financial market," Lutfalla blamed the moral and material destructions left behind by two wars, currency depreciation, along with more specific causes: an impoverishment of the middle classes, who traditionally save and invest a lot, loss of anonymity, obsessive fear of tax inquisition, and the government's suspicion of the wealthy.

Foreign investors were very much aware of the French Bourse's shortcomings. Francis Auboyneau, a seasoned member of the Compagnie des agents de change de Paris, reached out to them in an article published by the *American Banker* in March 1965. In the process, he offered a somber diagnosis of the French securities market:

> [. . .] the elements of a reliable accounting analysis are badly lacking. The serious investor has neither the time required nor the complete information which is indispensable.
>
> A market dominated by the spirit of speculation, insufficiently supplied and inadequately informed, produces the evils which have caused the price excesses for which the Paris market is paying so dearly at this time. Remedies can and must be found.
>
> *For a long time now the American market has pointed in the direction of the road to be followed.*[33]

There was more than base flattery of his American readers in Auboyneau's praise of the American market. The agent de change had given serious thought to the ways in which investor education could be improved:

Recently undertaken studies on motivation as well as personal experience in this field prove abundantly that the elite elements of our population and the class of people who make a practice of saving are totally ignorant on the subject of investments.

They do not see any connection between securities with a variable income and the economy of the country.

Neither are they aware of the comparatively simple methods of operation of the stock exchange. That institution is for them principally an object of curiosity—and mistrust.

This indicates the direction in which a psychological attack on the problem should be initiated.

Such action should not fail to stress the ties between growth and investment, as well as the idea of making investments on the basis of long-term appreciation.

If by these means the rather widespread anti-profit prejudice prevalent here could be combatted, this would be to the good. [. . .]

Finally, much remains to be done as regards offering reliable and frequent reports to the public, with facts and figures on the life of various enterprises.[34]

Incremental progress was indeed being made to improve the disclosure and dissemination of accurate financial information with ordonnance no. 59-247, dated February 4, 1959, and decree 65-999, dated November 29, 1965. *Le Monde*, however, noted wearily: "French corporations are known for their discretion. In most cases they inform their shareholders tardily and incompletely. [. . .] The provisions [of the November 1965 decree] are a significant progress, but they should be completed."[35]

The Conseil National de la Comptabilité, the organization in charge of setting accounting standards, made a number of recommendations with respect to the presentation of accounting documents and the publication of consolidated data. But the most important step was the July 24, 1966, Company Act, which reformed the auditing profession.[36] On August 12, 1969, an application decree established the Compagnie nationale des commissaires aux comptes, a nationwide professional organization of auditors; from then on, external auditors were legally required to certify the "regularity" and "fairness" of financial statements.[37]

Improving the quantity and quality of information made available to the public, however, was not sufficient. There was a consensus among market experts and government officials that investor education had to be upgraded.

Many considered the French financial press mediocre and corrupt.[38] In the analysis he presented to the board of Banque Nationale de Paris in August 1966, Gaston Défossé commented wryly: "Investors [. . .] see that profit is considered a shameful disease and that it is more honorable to win at the Sunday races than to make money on the stock exchange. It is fair to add that the daily papers give more information on racehorses than on securities."[39]

In Paris, no paper existed that could be compared to the British *Financial Times*. The interest of the general public in the Bourse was growing, though, as indicated by the introduction of market news on television in 1964.[40] Increasingly, banks' retail networks were becoming aware of the potential offered by the savings of their growing middle-class customer base.[41]

Regulation of the securities market had not been part of the immediate postwar reform agenda—another indication of the perception that the Bourse was to play a minor role in the financing of the French economy. Both the Commission de Contrôle des Banques and the Comité des Bourses de Valeurs survived the Liberation of France and the demise of the Vichy regime. While the commission progressively gained strength and recognition, the role of the comité remained marginal. It did, however, offer a forum for discussion where market professionals and supervisory authorities (the Banque de France, the Trésor) met on a regular basis.[42] In 1966, the comité convened seven times (February 2, May 9, June 9, October 10, October 25, November 22, and December 6). The minutes of the meeting, while very detailed, do not include any reference to the Ugine-Kuhlmann scandal.[43] When Pompidou ordered an inquiry, it was conducted by the Trésor—in other words, only the Trésor and, to a lesser extent, the Banque de France, were held accountable for that failure of market surveillance.

Valéry Giscard d'Estaing, Debré's predecessor in the Rue de Rivoli, implemented a number of the recommendations included in the *rapport Lorain*, a report on the liberalization of financial channels.[44] Tax incentives encouraged investments on the securities market, and a new investment vehicle was created, the SICAVs (sociétés d'investissement à capital variable, open-ended collective investment funds).

The organization of the agent de change profession underwent significant changes. By the mid-1960s, eight stock exchanges still existed in France. The Paris Bourse, however, attracted 97 percent of the volume of orders, while the seven bourses de province shared the remaining 3 percent.[45] As per the July 29, 1961, act, securities had to be listed on a single exchange, but the rule was not implemented fairly: many securities were delisted from provincial bourses, but very few securities were transferred from Paris to the smaller exchanges. The French government considered their survival a component of its national spatial planning policy (*aménagement du territoire*); moreover, the network made up of the forty-seven provincial agents de change was viewed as an instrument to enlarge the national investor base. In 1966, the Compagnie nationale des agents de change was created out of the merger of the former eight compagnies; nationwide coordination and mergers among agents de change were encouraged, but the seven provincial bourses remained independent.

Between 1959 and 1962, stock indices had been going up: by 53.7 percent in 1959, 2.2 percent in 1960, and 20.6 percent in 1961.[46] In her 1973 study of the Bourse, Françoise Marnata noted that in three years, between February 1959 and April 1962, stock prices had been multiplied by two, while industrial production had been going up by 26 percent and the general level of prices by 13 percent.[47]

The boomlet of the early Fifth Republic, however, proved short-lived. In May 1962, after a spectacular first quarter (plus 15%), stock prices had started to go down. Coordinated action by the syndic and two large French banks (Crédit Lyonnais and Banque Nationale de Paris) had not succeeded in reverting the trend. Prices had stabilized somehow, but very little trading was being done. Numbers showed that de Gaulle had been right when he had complained about the market being "exceedingly bad" in 1966:

Index of French Securities Traded in the Paris Stock Exchange (December 29, 1961 = 100)	
Year-end 1962	99.9
Year-end 1963	85.5
Year-end 1964	79.8
Year-end 1965	73.4
Year-end 1966	65.5
Year-end 1967	64.3

Source: Commission des opérations de Bourse, "Rapport annuel 1968," *Journal officiel de la République française* (April 7, 1969): 54.

Confounding policy makers, analysts, and common wisdom, the French stock market crisis of the 1960s took place amid the golden age of postwar economic growth.[48] According to Françoise Marnata, stock prices decreased by an average 46 percent between May 1962 and August 1967, while the general level of prices went up by 16 percent. She calculated that investors lost more than 60 percent of their capital.[49]

By the end of the decade, French authorities had become seriously preoccupied by the stagnation of the Bourse. In February 1967, Pompidou was interviewed by French popular newspaper *L'Aurore*—interestingly, the question asked by the journalist referred to de Gaulle's disparaging comments about the corbeille:

> *L'Aurore*—The market continues to be bad. The reasons of that situation are many. Admittedly, the French government is not responsible for all of them. However, declarations by the President of the Republic and some members of government about the usefulness of the financial market certainly contributed to weakening it further. In your opinion, what role should the Bourse play in the French economy? According to you, does government have the power to stimulate the market? What practical measures do you intend to take to reach that goal?
>
> Pompidou—The *Bourse* should mirror our economic situation while simultaneously being a stimulating factor. To achieve that goal, companies must disclose complete information to investors; the investing public must give up on speculation and turn to solid and sustainable investments; investment companies, mutual funds of all kinds must exercise their responsibilities fully; finally, investors must become aware of all the decisions that have been made in their favor as well as of the obvious undervaluation of most blue-chip stocks.
>
> However, it is not the responsibility of the French government to stimulate the stock market. Of course, it can contribute to improving information requirements and even force companies to abide by them. It can help to widen the stock market, as it just did when it put an end to exchange controls. It can—and it did—reduce almost by half the tax to be paid on dividends; it can—and it did— encourage investment funds or, [more specifically], the *sociétés d'investissement à capital variable*. But it cannot carry out an artificial stimulation which, by the way, would be to the exclusive benefit of short-term speculators. It is up to the financial press, to banks, to all entities collecting funds to play their part and highlight the excessively low level of present market prices.[50]

A few months after Pompidou's interview, on June 15, a meeting was held at the Ministry of Finances on "the present problems of the *Bourse*." Echoing the observation attributed to a "major provincial *notaire*" by a Ugine shareholder a few months earlier, participants lamented investors' lack of appetite for French securities:

> The customers [of agents de change] are "traumatized." Disillusion, apathy and a form of resentment have succeeded excessive market gains. In spite of the high

returns offered by certain shares, many shares are sold in order to buy bonds. Investors of the roaring years got severely hurt and are not going to return to the market until long years have passed. "Old" customers sit on shrunken portfolios and do not react any more. Potential customers are not being sufficiently and intelligently canvassed. The permanent weaknesses of the Paris market (insufficient shareholder information, laziness of intermediaries, lack of entities in charge of regulating prices) make it very difficult to react [to this situation].[51]

The memorandum written after the June 15 meeting at the ministry went beyond this grim diagnosis. It also pointed at the necessity of "a true 'policy' of the financial market," articulated along three axes: (1) the "moralization" of the market, (2) the broadening of the investor base, and (3) the implementation of a number "technical measures." Among the initiatives that could contribute to the moralization of the market, participants discussed "the creation of a surveillance body similar to the American Security Exchange Commission [*sic*]"—Auboyneau was not alone in thinking that "the American market [had] pointed in the direction of the road to be followed."

CHAPTER FOUR

France Looks at America

Shortly after Michel Debré's appointment as minister for the economy and finances, an apparently minor decision signaled a dramatic shift in the attitude of the French government toward foreign investment. The ministry let it be known that Motorola, a multinational corporation based in the United States, would be authorized to set up a plant in Toulouse. American bankers and businessmen promptly noticed this change in policy: "The Government has officially renounced the hostility that drove away potential major investments by such companies as General Motors, Ford and Phillips Petroleum, and countless smaller projects. The doors are not wide open now—hardly. But the Government's inclination is no longer to say 'no.' It is to say 'yes,' with exceptions."[1]

A new paradigm was in the making: the French government had converted to the necessity of attracting foreign capital. The *New York Times* attributed this welcome—and rather surprising—development to the new minister in person:

> The turn-around is a direct result of the change in command at the ministry at the start of President Charles de Gaulle's second term in January. It had been expected that the new minister, Michel Debré, would be at least as tough on this point as his predecessor, Valéry Giscard d'Estaing. But the expectation turns out to have been wrong.
>
> Mr. Debré, in effect admitting that the old policy was self-defeating, has several times publicly cited the advantages of letting investment in and the disadvantages of freezing it out. But he also is known to be adamant on the development of wholly independent French strength in some sectors that are the mark of modern industrial prowess, such as atomic energy and some areas of electronics.[2]

Debré's turnaround was all the more surprising that he was known to be de Gaulle's most faithful disciple.[3] Interestingly, he later described his early conversion to Gaullism as an almost instinctive reaction against US interference in French politics. In the first volume of his memoirs, he recalled "three events which led [him] to change [his] life."[4] One of these epiphanies was set in French North Africa, where he lived from May to September 1941. A young haut fonctionnaire involved in Résistance activities, he met with American diplomat Robert Murphy, personal representative of President Franklin D. Roosevelt, and supplied Murphy and his network of vice consuls with strategic information. He warmly referred to one of them, Frank Canfield, with whom he remained lifelong friends. One morning in Fez, Morocco, he had to give him a brief note containing information on the state of mind of the French population if Americans were to land in Casablanca—operation Torch was to take place more than one year later, in November 1942: "I gave the document to my friend. This would be the last one. I became a Gaullist."[5]

For most of the 1960s, French foreign policy was conducted by de Gaulle himself, with the assistance of Maurice Couve de Murville, the minister of foreign affairs.[6] In his position as minister for the economy and finances in Pompidou's government between 1966 and 1968, however, it fell upon Debré to defend France's national interest in the French-American monetary conflict. In addition to pursuing his ambitious agenda of domestic reforms, he dedicated a good part of his energy to international monetary negotiations. He met several times with Henry H. Fowler, President Lyndon B. Johnson's secretary of the treasury, and the detailed story of his trips to Washington, DC, looms large in his memoirs. This offered him an opportunity to express his views of America and the Americans: "Behind the monetary problem, it is easy to discover the political one. The American people are a great people. The world, and us Frenchmen, owe them a lot. However, we cannot but be suspicious of their desire for domination."[7]

The nod to the "greatness" of the American people, the reluctant admission of gratitude, and the inevitability of suspicion are several components of de Gaulle's conflicted feelings toward the United States. There was no little irony, therefore, in Debré's efforts to lure American investors into France. In the French edition of the *American Banker* published on April 20, 1966, he tried rather painstakingly to explain "the philosophy behind the policy of independence applied to economics [*sic*] and finance":

> Neither autarky nor nationalism, this policy of independence is the expression of the feeling that there is no liberty for citizens if autonomous action and thought are not constantly asserted at the national scale so as to achieve, taking into account the French people's resources and work, the best possible balance of their economy and also its development so as to realize at once its greatest political potential, social progress and a high cultural standard. [. . .]
>   Let us take a good look at the efforts undertaken, and most often carried out

successfully—since General de Gaulle's return—to turn the French economy in the opposite direction from autarky and to establish it firmly in the midst of international competition. The recovery of the public finances in 1958 made it possible to follow up trade liberation and to apply the Common Market treaty. If domestic recovery of the French financial structure had failed, the Common Market treaty would have remained a dead letter.[8]

While sounding a bit sycophantic, Debré nevertheless expressed one of the core tenets of Gaullism: France, freed from the burden of her colonial empire and standing firm on sound economic foundations, was ready to open her borders and exercise her international responsibilities—as long as the rest of the world, her continental neighbors in particular, acknowledged her leadership: "Consequently, despite a justified reluctance to accept the ideology of political integration, France was a leader in the policy that led to accelerating the process of lowering customs barriers with the Europe of the 'Six.' She looks favorably upon opening her frontiers to world trade. At the same time, France has welcomed foreign investment and hopes herself to invest outside her frontiers."[9]

There was, however, an apparent contradiction between de Gaulle's foreign policy and Debré's attempt at seducing American investors. Alluding to France's recent withdrawal from NATO's integrated military command, the *New York Times* published a tongue-in-cheek article at the beginning of 1967: "The French Government opened the door last year to let United States armed forces out and to let United States investment capital in [. . .] The turn to military isolationism captured the headlines, but the turn toward economic liberalism was a more complete and unexpected reversal of policy—so much so that *L'Express*, the popular new weekly, recently accused General de Gaulle of selling out to the Americans."[10]

L'Express, the magazine mentioned in the article, had been cofounded in 1953 by Jean-Jacques Servan-Schreiber. Inspired by the American *Time*, the journalist-publisher had turned it into an influential newsmagazine with a large audience among the rising French middle class. A few months after the Motorola announcement, in September 1967, Servan-Schreiber published *Le Défi américain* (*The American Challenge*), an instant best seller.[11] The starting point of the book was an investigation of American investments in Europe—the scope of Servan-Schreiber's inquiry was indeed "Western Europe" rather than just France. The incoming flow of US dollars was compared to an overwhelming invasion, "the first great war without weapons and armors." Yet rather than a xenophobic, anti-American diatribe, *Le Défi américain* resonated as a call to arms for Europeans:

1. The American challenge is not essentially industrial or financial in nature. It involves, above all, *our intellectual fertility, our capacity to transform ideas into reality.* Let us be bold enough to admit that it is our political [institutions] and mental structures, indeed our culture, that are yielding to outside pressure.

2. Today's America still resembles Europe, yet with a fifteen year head start. It belongs to the same system; both are part of the same "industrial society." In 1980, however, the United States will have entered a different world. If we are not able to reach that world on our own, *the United States will be holding a monopoly in technology, science and power.*[12]

In admiring terms, Servan-Schreiber analyzed American creativity and management skills; instead of pleading for protectionism, he promoted the American way of doing business. The success of his book was a testimony to the attractiveness of America as an example of economic performance. While the essential part of Servan-Schreiber's analysis revolved around the superiority of American corporations, American politics was not completely absent. A partisan of European federalism, he believed that Europeans were standing at a critical crossroads of history, which could legitimately be compared to the circumstances of Franklin Roosevelt's dramatic victory over Herbert Hoover:

In 1932, faced with the greatest crisis in the development of his country and in the confidence of his people, the reformer who had just been elected to the presidency of the United States uttered his famous cry: "This generation of Americans has a rendez-vous with destiny." Americans shouldered their responsibilities and, through an immediate and popular movement supporting the New Deal, they irreversibly engaged America on the way to power at the very moment when it was in danger of losing all ambition.

Almost fifty years later, this generation of Europeans also has a rendez-vous with destiny.[13]

Servan-Schreiber, who was a flamboyant, if a bit erratic, figure of the non-communist Left, was no Gaullist—after all, he could have quoted de Gaulle's much-celebrated *Appel* of June 18, 1940, rather than Roosevelt's "rendez-vous with destiny." In his book, the reference to the thirty-second president of the United States was not followed by a detailed presentation, or even a brief summary, of his action in the White House. Not only was it not the objective of the book, but it might as well have been superfluous: in postwar France, many viewed the New Deal as an unambiguous success and a source of inspiration—the transformation of the federal government, the creation of the American welfare state, the conversion to Keynesian macroeconomic policies were all considered major achievements.

The establishment of the Securities and Exchange Commission (SEC) figured prominently in Roosevelt's legacy. During his presidency, public outrage generated by the so-called excesses of Wall Street in the 1920s was channeled into a complex, enduring piece of legislation. In that process, the role played by presidential rhetoric testified to the very political nature of the reform of the securities market. *Mutatis mutandis*, Rooseveltian America and Gaullist France were both characterized by the assertion of the executive over other branches of government, and of politics over the economy. The story of the interaction between Wall Street and Washington, however, was very different from that of the Bourse and successive French political regimes—be they Royal, Imperial, or Republican.

Along with his clarion call against "fear itself," Roosevelt's denunciation of "money changers" in his first inaugural address had a profound echo among his listeners: many Americans of the Depression era blamed Wall Street for the collapse of industrial production and the ensuing rise in unemployment. Shortly before Roosevelt's inauguration, Ferdinand Pecora, a pugnacious lawyer from New York, had been appointed chief counsel of the Senate Banking and Currency Committee, soon to be dubbed the "Pecora Commission" by journalists. In a series of dramatic hearings, he exposed the wrongdoings of major Wall Street executives; these disclosures "suggested a market in which the favored few had unerodible advantages over the ordinary investor."[14] The newly elected Roosevelt did not need to be spurred into action, but the public outrage ignited by Pecora emboldened lawmakers and gave them a lot of leeway in their drafting of the 1933 and 1934 Securities Acts. These two laws marked a shift in the history of the securities market.

During the nineteenth century, the principle of self-regulation by market professionals had prevailed. Meanwhile, the New York Stock Exchange had played an increasing role in the economic development of the nation, providing much-needed capital to railway companies and industrial corporations. Long-term growth, however, had been repeatedly slowed down by spectacular crashes; fortunes had been made or lost by investors; the history of Wall Street had been enlivened by the rise and fall of picturesque robber barons. By the end of the century, the denunciation of money power had become a key component of progressive thought. In a 1911 speech, future President Woodrow Wilson attacked "the money monopoly": "The growth of the nation [. . .] and all our activities are in the hands of a few men, who, even if their actions be honest and intended for the public interest, are necessarily concentrated upon the great undertakings in which their own money is involved and who, necessarily, by every reason of their own limitations, chill and check and destroy genuine economic freedom. This is the greatest question of all; and to this, statesmen must address themselves with an earnest determination to serve the long future and the true liberties of men."[15]

Justice Louis Brandeis, appointed to the Supreme Court by Wilson in 1916, articulated a legal philosophy aimed at defending "small" investors against the "Money Trust"—Wall Street investment bankers, in whose hands capital supply was concentrated, were the object of his virulent denunciations. In *Other People's Money and How the Bankers Use It*, he argued forcefully in favor of the restoration of a free market through the disclosure of financial information to all investors: "Publicity is justly commended as a remedy for social and industrial diseases. Sunlight is said to be the best of disinfectants; electric light the most efficient policeman. And publicity has already played an important part in the struggle against the Money Trust. [. . .] That potent force must, in the impending struggle, be utilized in many ways as a continual remedial measure."[16]

It took some time for Brandeis's views to prevail in the United States. While a number of state legislatures had endeavored to protect investors by passing the so-called blue-sky laws, the Republican administrations of the interwar era abstained from interfering with the stock market.[17] Industrial growth gave traction to a spectacular ascent of the stock market: the Dow Jones Industrial Average soared from sixty to almost four hundred. Stock distributors promoted mass investment, promising that "the stock market would universalize property-ownership, democratize corporations, provide security in old age or unemployment, and liberate the innate entrepreneurialism of the American male."[18] Speculators were purchasing stocks on margin, exposing themselves to the danger of magnified losses in case of a downturn. Ill-prepared for a rapidly changing environment, many investment bankers, stockbrokers, and other intermediaries were unwilling to exercise the role that was theirs in a system based on self-regulation. With the benefit of hindsight, former President Hoover denounced in his memoirs "the orgy of speculation" and acknowledged the illusions of the 1920s: "A contribution to optimism and the belief in the 'New Era' was the illusion that the economic system was [. . .] completely immune from financial crises."[19] For all the efforts of Brandeis and other Wall Street reformers, very little had been accomplished when the Twenties stopped roaring. The Dow Jones Industrial Average, which had reached a record high of above 380 at the beginning of September 1929, eroded slowly in the weeks that followed and collapsed brutally on October 24 and 29. By November 13, it had fallen to less than 200 and would drop farther as the Great Depression engulfed America and the rest of the world. The stock market was not to recover until the 1950s.

Notwithstanding his reassuring declarations about the imminence of recovery, Hoover proved incapable of stopping the economic slowdown, which reached a dramatic nadir in the winter of 1932–1933: by then, the gross domestic product had contracted by 44 percent, unemployment had risen to an estimated 25 percent of the workforce, and the banking sector, seriously weakened by a series of bankruptcies, was almost paralyzed. After their success at the 1930 midterm elections, Democrats sensed that the White House would be within reach of their candidate. The stock market crash reinvigorated their zeal for reform, which transpired in the 1932 party platform:

> We advocate protection of the investing public by requiring to be filed with the government and carried in advertisements of all offerings of foreign and domestic stocks and bonds true information as to bonuses, commissions, principal invested, and interests of the sellers.
>
> Regulation to the full extent of federal power, of:
>
> (a) Holding companies which sell securities in interstate commerce;
>
> (b) Rates of utilities companies operating across State lines;
>
> (c) Exchanges in securities and commodities. We advocate quicker methods of realizing on assets for the relief of depositors of suspended banks, and a more rigid supervision of national banks for the protection of depositors and the prevention of the use of their moneys in speculation to the detriment of local credits.
>
> The severance of affiliated security companies from, and the divorce of the investment banking business from, commercial banks, and further restriction of federal reserve banks in permitting the use of federal reserve facilities for speculative purposes.[20]

During his spirited 1932 campaign, Democratic candidate Franklin Roosevelt blamed the Hoover administration for its inaction—incidentally, his choice of historical precedents reveals that Americans were very much aware of the "mad adventures of the Regency":

One of the major causes of the 1929 smash could have been prevented by our national administration. This was the flotation of a twentieth-century "Mississippi Bubble" on a sea of popular ignorance. Three forms of this scandalously unsound speculation could and should have been instantly suppressed by straightforward comment from Washington. [. . .] The government must protect its citizens against financial buccaneering. No federal administration can prevent individuals from being suckers, but our government has the right as well as the positive duty to dissect, for the benefit of the public, every new form of financial action.[21]

Roosevelt did not intend to abolish the stock market and start a revolution but, rather, to "restore [the temple of civilization] to the ancient truths."[22] He took immediate and decisive action to end the banking crisis—reminiscing triumphantly on the success of the National Bank Holiday, his adviser Raymond Moley later claimed in his memoirs: "Capitalism was saved in eight days [. . .]."[23] It took a little longer for the Glass-Steagall Act to be voted and signed into law by the president on June 16, 1933: from then on, commercial and investment banking activities were to be strictly separated, and the federal government was to guarantee deposits through an independent agency, the Federal Deposit Insurance Corporation (FDIC). Two years later, the Banking Act of 1935 strengthened and enlarged the powers of the Federal Reserve Board.

At the time of Roosevelt's first inauguration, Brandeis was still sitting on the Supreme Court. His disciple Felix Frankfurter, a Harvard law professor who became an associate justice of the Court in 1939, successfully promoted his and Brandeis's views on financial reform. Frankfurter's former students James M. Landis and Benjamin V. Cohen played a key role in drafting and subsequently implementing the 1933 and 1934 Securities Acts. Landis and Cohen joined forces with seasoned politician Sam Rayburn, US representative from Texas, to overcome opposition from market professionals and their supporters in Congress. The Truth in Securities Act was signed by Roosevelt on May 27, 1933. While the act did not eliminate the risks inherent in the acquisition and holding of securities, it did protect investors through the regulation of the offering and sale process. Among other provisions, issuers of securities were required to disclose detailed information in a prospectus or offering circular. Lawyer William O. Douglas, who later chaired the SEC, pointed at the political nature of the act in a 1934 article published in the *Yale Review*:

The current battle on the Securities Act is being waged on political lines. [. . .] Therefore, curiously enough, what the Act contains, what it actually does, the soundness of its method of protecting investors are not particularly important.

The nature and quality of the arguments mean only that the Act is significant politically. It is symbolic of a shift of political power. That shift is from the bankers to the masses; from the promoter to the investor. It means that the government is taking the side of the helpless, the suckers, the underdogs. It signifies that the money-changers are being driven from the temples.[24]

The 1933 act, however, did not regulate the exchanges; another act, therefore, was needed. Largely discredited in 1933, investment bankers and other market professionals had regained some strength and were able to make their voices heard in Congress: "The stock exchange bill, which Roosevelt signed into law on June 6, 1934, provided the first real confrontation between his administration and important segments of the business community on the issues of domestic financial reform and stability."[25]

Declining to monitor the stock exchange directly, the federal government established the SEC, an independent federal agency headquartered in Washington, DC—as opposed to New York, the financial center of the nation. The SEC comprised five commissioners appointed by the president of the United States, with the advice and consent of the Senate, and their terms were set for five years. All US stock exchanges were to be registered with the SEC.

The decision by elected leaders to delegate the authority to regulate and supervise the financial industry to an independent agency presented several political advantages: "financial regulation requires a level of expertise not commonly found in elected bodies. Moreover, legislatures themselves are not able to devote enough time to supervise the financial sector, given their other policy priorities and the exigencies of electoral politics. In addition, legislatures may have incentives to delegate responsibility as a means of shifting blame in the event of a financial crisis."[26]

The newly established regulator was to become the chief protector of the investing public and the enforcer of US securities regulation: "With the creation of the SEC, the proponents of securities law reform had secured an ongoing agency to enforce the new statute and to continue studying the need for further corporate law reforms."[27]

During his September 30, 1934, fireside chat, Roosevelt blandly declared:

> The country now enjoys the safety of bank savings under the new banking laws, the careful checking of new securities under the Securities Act, and the curtailment of rank stock speculation through the Securities Exchange Act. I sincerely hope that as a result [of the Securities Exchange Act] people will be discouraged in unhappy efforts to get rich quick by speculating in securities. For the average

person almost always loses. Only a very small minority of the people of this country believe in gambling as a substitute for the old philosophy of Benjamin Franklin that the way to wealth is through work.[28]

Roosevelt's selection of Joseph P. Kennedy, a man of dubious reputation, to be the first chairman of the SEC, seemed to contradict the president's proclaimed intention to eradicate speculation.[29] Kennedy, however, proved an efficient administrator; in 1935, he was succeeded by none other than Landis, "the prophet of regulation."[30] In 1940, the Investment Company Act and the Investment Advisers Act further extended the protection of the investing public. Through a series of landmark cases, the SEC built up its reputation as one of the most efficient New Deal agencies.

When he published his memoirs in 1960, Wall Street legend Bernard Baruch reminisced over the events of the 1920s and 1930s. He asked the most relevant of questions: "When one recalls the boom of the twenties and the ensuing crash, one is haunted by the question: Can it happen again?"[31] The exceptionally long and varied career of the former adviser to Presidents Wilson and Roosevelt gave him a long-term perspective on the reform of Wall Street:

> From time to time, more recently in 1958, our economy has faltered badly, and a shudder of fear that we were about to plunge into another depression has spread through the land. But each time, with the help of safeguards built into our economy since 1929, we have regained our equilibrium. Such programs as unemployment insurance, bank deposit insurance, social security and a host of regulatory measures to prevent economic abuses, have helped maintain stability in time of stress. The investor in the stock market is protected today, as he was not in 1929, by a watchful SEC. He has the benefit of a vast amount of information that companies are required to divulge. He can also seek the advice of professional, disinterested investment analysts.
>
> Nevertheless, the measures have not yet been devised which can permanently protect men from their folly.[32]

Three decades after its creation, it was indeed generally believed that the "watchful SEC" was doing a good job protecting men "from their folly." Its reputation extended beyond the borders of the United States. The influential report written by Georges Lutfalla in 1952 on the state of the French securities market included a detailed analysis of the US market. Under the headline "The Lessons of the 1929 Crash," the report offered a presentation of the American regulatory system. Understandably, the SEC played a prominent role in the narrative: "Among all the legacies of the New Deal, the SEC is assuredly one of the most remarkable."[33]

Based on the Lutfalla report, a 1959 internal memorandum of the Banque de France told the edifying story of securities regulation in America:

> It is not necessary to go far back in the past to learn some lessons from the American securities market. In many respects, the October 29, 1929 crash was a beginning. On the New York Stock Exchange that day, a market cataclysm broke out, unprecedented with respect to suddenness and magnitude. In the following years, a deep and extended institutional regulatory system (*une régle-mentation institutionnelle étendue et profonde*) replaced the earlier freedom-based organization. Established July 2, 1934, the Securities and Exchange Commission was put in charge of enforcing the new laws, of which the most important were:
> - The May 27, 1933 *Securities Act*, which made the issuance of new securities subject to prior registration with the SEC.
> - The April 23, 1934 *Securities and Exchange Act*, which made it mandatory for all exchanges to register with the SEC, and regulated securities trans-actions.
>
> This twofold regulation (*double réglementation*)—regulation of the issuance of securities and of transactions—slowed economic recovery significantly [. . .], but it also permitted the emergence of small investors, who took a bigger part in the financing of the American industry, taking over progressively from the wealthiest investors, who were hit by the progressivity of direct taxation. At the same time, market psychology was modified profoundly: the speculator gave way to the investor.[34]

This simplistic version of the story, blessed with a happy ending, was pleasant to read: the horrendous 1929 crash had resulted in the creation of an admirable regulatory system; combined with progressive taxation, the 1933–1934 secu-rities reforms had eradicated speculation and transformed the New York Stock Exchange into a paradise for small investors.

In his memoirs, Debré's account of the creation of the Commission des Opérations de Bourse (COB) indicates that he adhered to conventional wisdom about the SEC—to the extent that he knew about it. His version of the story began rather strangely with his recollection of having read an American news-paper: "In the fall of 1966, I remember having learnt in an American newspaper the existence of a commission, the Securities and Exchange Commission (SEC), which rules over the New York stock exchange and is endowed with extended powers to enforce some morality in purchase and sell transactions."[35]

Debré added that he went on to ask his staff for more detailed information.[36] In response to his inquiry, he was told of the importance of the SEC and of the flaws in the surveillance system of the Paris Bourse: the "police of the financial market" was divided among the Treasury, the Banque de France, and the Compagnie des agents de change; neither of these institutions had adequate resources to fulfill their missions. It is only after this dim assessment of the situation that Debré mentioned in his memoirs the "commotion" brought about by the merger between Ugine and Kuhlmann.[37]

Interestingly, Debré wrote "the merger between Pechiney and Ugine-Kuhlmann": the acquisition of Ugine-Kuhlmann by Pechiney would take place at a later date, in 1971; at the end of the 1980s, during Mitterrand's presidency, the resulting entity, known as Pechiney-Ugine-Kuhlmann, would be at the center of another much-publicized insider trading case. This coincidence might be the cause of this lapse in the otherwise precise memory of the former minister for the Economy and Finances.

Having mentioned the Ugine-Kuhlmann case and the unflattering light it shed on the shortcomings of the French surveillance system, Debré concluded that "it was necessary, for the reputation of the Paris Stock Exchange, to modify that state of things."[38] Without further details on the sequence of events, he then mentioned ordonnance 67-833, dated September 28, 1967, which established the COB.

Archival records confirm the gist of the story told by Debré in his memoirs, albeit with a slightly different chronology. Yet they also reveal what the minister did not share with his readers: the resistance he had to overcome to achieve his objective. During the more than twelve months that separated the Ugine-Kuhlmann scandal and the signature by de Gaulle of the ordonnance, a member of his staff played a decisive role: Jean-Yves Haberer.

Born in 1932, thirty-three-year-old Haberer had been one of the most brilliant students of his class at the École Nationale d'Administration.[39] His ranking at graduation enabled him to join the prestigious Inspection Générale des Finances, the auditing department of the Ministry for the Economy and Finance. In 1963, the young *inspecteur* spent several months in the United States. He was not the first promising recruit of the ministry to be sent on a study trip abroad—many a directeur du Trésor was a former *conseiller financier* in the French Embassy in Washington.

Haberer's mission was not part of the famed *missions de productivité* (productivity missions), studied in detail by, among others, French sociologist Luc Boltanski and American historian Richard Kuisel.[40] His study trip in America, however, can be put in the larger perspective of the discovery, by French policy makers, businessmen, and workers, of postwar America's prosperity. During the first half of the 1950s, the *missions* had indeed contributed to the diffusion, in France, of such American values as "the spirit of productivity," "management," "human engineering," and so forth; in the field of banking, they had played a significant role in the later development of consumer credit in France.[41]

While Haberer was in the United States, he investigated "maturity transformation" in the American banking system—the recycling, by American banks, of short-term, liquid deposits into medium-term and long-term loans suitable for investment. The report he wrote at the end of his trip attracted the attention of his superiors and contributed to the advancement of his career. While Haberer's primary focus had been on banking, he had also collected many impressions on the securities market.

When Debré formed his staff in the Rue de Rivoli, Haberer's name was put forward by Maurice Pérouse, the directeur du Trésor, and he became one of the minister's conseillers techniques (technical advisers). His immediate superior, directeur de cabinet Antoine Dupont-Fauville, allowed him direct access to Debré.[42] His role was to come up with new ideas, to liaise with the powerful directeur du Trésor, and to act as Debré's enforcer. Haberer, who could rely on suggestions gathered from a network of young hauts fonctionnaires dedicated to the modernization of the French financial system, developed a productive working relationship with Debré: "This duo constituted by the politician and the expert was characterized by its persistence and determination, two qualities which allowed them to ignore administrative resistance and the risk of unpopularity. They shared the same proactive attitude, in which the willingness to take action was combined with a certain political courage, which does not mean that they were without personal ambitions or did not enjoy power."[43]

Profoundly impressed by the dynamism of American markets, Haberer had a hand in most of the financial reforms of the Debré era.

The 1966–1967 bank reforms were designed to "develop the practice of 'transformation' and make it the principal source of financing for the economy."[44] Several decrees eroded the distinction between deposit banks and investment banks (*banques d'affaires*), mergers were encouraged,[45] the opening of new branches by bank networks was facilitated, banks were given more flexibility to set their terms and conditions, and so forth. These reforms accelerated the bankarization process of French households.[46]

With the objective to create a liquid government debt market, Haberer focused on accelerating the transformation of the "Treasury circuit."[47] Devised and implemented in the immediate aftermath of the Second World War, the circuit was a complex set of administrative obligations that required "a vast number of institutions [. . .] to deposit a part of their resources with the treasury."[48] This architecture enabled the Trésor to finance the public deficit without borrowing from the central bank or issuing new bonds on the securities market. A decisive step in dismantling the circuit was the suppression of the requirement that banks retain a portion of their reserves in Treasury bonds.[49] Not surprisingly, Maurice Pérouse, the directeur du Trésor, was extremely reticent to endorse decisions that he believed would jeopardize the Trésor's access to its traditional funding resources and, possibly, the central position it occupied within the bureaucratic structure of the French state.[50]

Finally, a July 1966 report by René Larre, a director of the International Monetary Fund (IMF) who was soon to succeed Pérouse at the helm of the Trésor, diagnosed the weaknesses of the Bourse and advocated its liberalization.[51] Pursuant to the recommendations of the report, the Paris market was cautiously opened to foreign issuers. The degree of control exercised by the Trésor on the issuance of new stocks and bonds was progressively relaxed; securities placement procedures were modernized.

The creation of a securities regulator must not be viewed in isolation of the larger effort to enhance the role of the securities market in financing the French economy and make it more competitive internationally. French diplomatic outposts, which were best positioned to assess the strengths and weaknesses of foreign securities markets, were involved in the early stages of the process. According to Haberer, the French Embassy in Washington sent a detailed report on the role and responsibilities of the SEC; similar reports were requested from other embassies. Haberer did not remember that anything of interest had been identified, either in London or in continental Europe. Yet there did exist a securities regulator in one of the six nations that constituted the European Common Market: the Belgian Commission bancaire et financière, established in 1935.[52] The Belgian Stock Exchange, however, played a marginal role in the European economy—besides, seen from Paris, Brussels was an unlikely source of inspiration. As to the London Stock Exchange—which, in Haberer's own words, "was not a model of virtue"[53]—, its organization was perceived as the opposite of the Paris Bourse: "The regulatory history (*l'histoire réglementaire*) of the [London] Stock Exchange is that of a long duel between [market] professionals and the Civil Service. Professionals won and today the London market is independent from government. The fact that there is no official statute or office for intermediaries (*l'absence de charges officielles d'intermédiaires*) differentiates the London Stock Exchange from the Paris Stock Exchange."[54]

At that time, nobody seemed to be questioning the role played by the Compagnie nationale des agents de change; more importantly, French hauts fonctionnaires were not ready to follow the example of the British Civil Service and abandon all authority over the securities market—these were two good reasons the London Stock Exchange could not be seriously considered as a potential source of inspiration for reform. Later the SEC understood the benefits that could be derived from the existence of independent commissions regulating national markets abroad;[55] in the 1980s and 1990s, it actively encouraged the creation of such regulators. According to Haberer, however, American authorities were not consulted directly at any point in establishing the COB, and they did not try to influence French decision makers.[56] Historical records do not show any sign to the contrary: neither the archives of the Ministry for the Economy and Finance, the Banque de France, and the COB, nor the personal papers of Debré and Chatenet include any document emanating from an American institution or individual; the documents reviewed and analyzed for the purpose of this book never refer to a meeting or an informal discussion with American officials prior to Chatenet's appointment at the helm of the COB toward the end of 1967. The Casey papers do not allude to any attempt to "export" the SEC in France, and a targeted probing of available records from the State Department Central Files for the US embassy in Paris did not contradict Haberer's assertion.[57]

Although it has not been possible to find the report from the French Embassy in Washington in the archives of the Ministry for the Economy and Finance or of the Ministry of Foreign Affairs, there exists a very analytical three-column table comparing the composition and the powers of the French Comité des Bourses de Valeurs and the American SEC.[58] The first column, to the left of the table, is likely to have been copied, in whole or in part, from the report sent by the financial attaché at the embassy. It highlights what the drafters of the ordonnance believed were the most salient features of the SEC.

The table attempted to position the SEC within the organization of the US federal government:

Status

The SEC is an independent Federal agency. It has administrative and judicial authority. It is accountable to Congress exclusively. On an annual basis, it reports to Congress on its activity.

Composition

The five members are appointed by the President of the United States, with consent of the Senate, based on their professional skills (legal and financial education) and their political affiliation (no more than 3 commissioners might belong to the same party). The chairman is appointed by the White House.[59]

The independence of the SEC, along with the hybrid nature of its authority, both administrative and judicial, was to prove particularly problematic to transpose into French law. While the appointment powers of the president of the United States could easily be attributed to the French president or the French government, the dominance of the executive in the Fifth Republic precluded making the future commission accountable to the French Parliament.

The table added that the SEC was "a true administration, with permanent members, and not a *comité*"—so much for the colorless Comité des Bourses de Valeurs. The fact that all SEC members were appointed by the president of the United States to serve for a predetermined period of time, as opposed to being ex officio members, was viewed as a guarantee of their independence.

The powers of the SEC were presented with considerable detail:

Legislative and Regulatory Power (*Pouvoir législatif et réglementaire*)
Participation to the Lawmaking Process
a) When it deems it necessary, the SEC proposes to Congress amendments to the laws applicable to the securities market. It is consulted by Congress when laws covering the operations of the financial market or corporations are being discussed.
Regulatory Power (*Pouvoir réglementaire*)
b) The SEC is endowed with its own authority to issue regulations (*pouvoir réglementaire autonome*) with respect to the interpretation and application of laws pertaining to securities, intermediaries, the civil service, investment funds, etc.
Supervision of Intermediaries
a) Prior registration of Exchanges, the N.A.S.D.,[60] brokers, investment advisors, etc.
b) Audit and surveillance of activities
c) Disciplinary powers
Judicial Power
a) Inquiry powers. Whether or not cases fall under its jurisdiction, the SEC may investigate them. For this purpose, it may issue warrants, conduct inquiries, and collect testimonies.

b) The SEC must abide by its own "Rules of practice," oral, and written, which are designed to guarantee the rights of defendants. Its decisions are majority decisions and must be well-founded.

c) Cases are decided by a majority vote. These decisions must be motivated and might be appealed in federal court.

Proceedings

The SEC may be involved in civil or criminal proceedings:

• Civil proceedings: either as plaintiff, as assistant to the prosecutor, or as defendant when its own decisions are appealed in court;

• Criminal proceedings: the SEC forwards to the prosecutor cases which it investigated; it may assist the prosecutor.[61]

As indicated between parentheses in the translation above, the author of the table used the phrase *pouvoir réglementaire* on several occasions. The meaning of the French word *réglementation* is much narrower than the English word *regulation*. A réglementation, or a règlement, is an administrative rule, or set of rules, applying to a specific activity. The pouvoir réglementaire, therefore, is the power to enact such rules. The French word *régulation* does not appear in the table. At the time when the table was put together, it applied primarily to technical instruments, railway traffic, or the flow of a river but not to the operations of the securities market. It is only progressively that régulation acquired the broader meaning of *regulation*, that is, in the case of the securities market, a policy designed "to protect investors, maintain fair, orderly, and efficient markets, and facilitate capital formation."[62] While this translation has since been adopted by market professionals, lawyers, politicians, journalists, and so forth, French proponents of the "Regulation school" of economics (*Théorie de la régulation*) consider it misleading and argue that réglementation would be a more accurate translation.[63]

Under the caption "Missions of the SEC," a specific paragraph singled out the rules applicable to "insiders":

Rules applicable to insider trading (*Réglementation des transactions des "insiders"*)

Directors, senior management and shareholders owning, directly or indirectly, more than 10% of the capital of a company, must notify the SEC of the amount of shares they own. They must also report to the SEC all changes in the composition of their portfolio.

• Short-selling the company's securities, or borrowing money to buy them, is forbidden.

- Transactions performed by "insiders" are made public by the SEC
- Any profit resulting from illegal transactions must be disgorged.[64]

In this paragraph, the word *insider* was not translated into French and remained in English, between inverted commas. The French word *initié* was sometimes used in that context at the time—shortly after the merger between Ugine and Juhlmann, Mr. Delcassé, one of Ugine's disgruntled shareholders, had complained about the shenanigans of "*initiés* very close to the company."[65] An *initié* was an individual who had formally been accepted into a group after taking an initiation ceremony; more generally, the word designated an individual who had been informed of a secret. Prior to the December 23, 1970, act, trading on privileged information was not punishable by French law.

The content of the table was not limited to a presentation of the powers of the SEC. It also brought to the knowledge of the French hauts fonctionnaires a number of practical information. They learned that the SEC employed 1,400 individuals, including lawyers, certified public accountants, engineers, and financial analysts. Its 1965 budget amounted to USD 15.4 million (76.5 million French francs), of which USD 12.1 million came from the federal government and USD 3.3 million in transaction taxes collected by the SEC directly (0.1/1,000 on issuances, 0.02/1,000 on transactions). The contrast with the resources allocated to the comité was brutal: its expenses had not exceeded 195,000 French francs in 1965. Logically, the table concluded that the enlargement of the responsibilities of the Comité des Bourses de Valeurs would make it necessary to allocate supplemental personnel and increase its budget.

The table also included information on the fourteen American exchanges and on the National Association of Securities Dealers (NASD). The exchanges "set their own rules on all aspects of their operations, including the admission of members, the financial liability of members, the amount and conditions applicable to reserve funds, the fees, the listing requirements, the trading process." NASD was "made up of 3,900 broker-dealers (out of a total of 4,500) and was in charge of setting the rules applicable to the hiring of new members, of monitoring the professional activities of its members, and of taking first-level disciplinary action."

The middle column of the table recapitulated the organization and duties of the Comité des Bourses de Valeurs, as detailed in chapter 3. The third column, to the right of the table, was much less detailed. Under the title "Observations," it included a number of recommendations to improve the quality of investor information and upgrade the surveillance of transactions.[66] It suggested that the publication of consolidated financial statements be made mandatory and that offering memorandums be prepared prior to the issuance of stocks or bonds. The accuracy of such information would need to be verified systematically. The entity in charge of these verifications would also be responsible for the publication of the data in order to improve the quality of their dissemination and avoid overloading the *Bulletin des annonces légales et obligatoires* (*BALO*). This entity would be given authority to take sanctions (fines, suspensions, etc.), to make these sanctions public, and to refer civil or criminal cases to the relevant courts.

Creating such an entity was not an easy feat to accomplish: not only were legal concepts such as "regulation" or "insiders" problematic to transpose into French law, the promoters of the project were also to face skepticism, if not open hostility, from professional and administrative circles.

CHAPTER FIVE

Drafting the *Ordonnance*

On June 28, 1966, Michel Debré instructed the Direction du Trésor "to study the methods and the merits of the 'Securities and Exchange Commission' and to investigate whether adapting its most original features to France might improve the atmosphere of the stock market."[1] Obvious in the instructions he gave in the privacy of his Rue de Rivoli office, the minister's desire to take inspiration from America was also manifest in a speech he delivered at the beginning of July to an audience made up of market professionals. He elaborated on the stinging, yet very general, remarks of Pompidou about the moralization of the market:

> [. . .] it seems clear to me that an enhanced surveillance of the markets, particularly with respect to certain transactions, would allow an improvement in their operations, and would better convince public opinion that securities transactions, contrary to what people are inclined to think, are not necessarily, even if partially, mysterious and scandalous. Even if transposing national practices from one country to the other often clashes with markets' structural idiosyncrasies, I judged it necessary to order my Department to investigate whether certain practices of the New York market's *Securities and Exchange Commission* could be applied to the Paris market, particularly with respect to the information to be disclosed, at all times, by corporations; the procedure applicable to the listing of new securities; the surveillance of merger transactions, etc. [. . .] Ultimately, moralizing the Stock Exchange means giving maximum security and transparency to the transactions that are being conducted on it. It is on that second point [transparency] that an effort remains to be done. I am sure that the completion of this effort will contribute to bringing a larger number of customers to [the market for] securities transactions.[2]

By giving market professionals advance notice of the upcoming reform, Debré was trying to prevent predictable opposition. He assured the agents de change and the Comité des Bourses de Valeurs that they would be consulted and associated to the process. Diplomatically, he also encouraged agents de change to "educate the French investor"—an admission that progress on that front was sorely needed. Yet, in his use of the word "practices," he remained vague and abstained from disclosing his full intentions.

It took no less than six months for the report ordered by Debré at the end of June to be completed and delivered to his office—obviously, moralizing the market and, along the way, relinquishing a portion of its authority on it, were not priorities of the direction du Trésor's. The report could not be found in the archives, but its content can be surmised from a three-page memorandum, dated February 7, 1967, in which Haberer analyzed and criticized it at length.[3] The conseiller technique interpreted the delay in producing the report as a sign of hesitation. While he did not accuse his colleagues of voluntary pro-crastination, he observed that, with the upcoming March 1967 elections, it was too late for Debré to decide "on a problem the psychological importance of which cannot be underestimated"—the memory of the Ugine-Kuhlmann scandal remained very vivid.

Haberer's memorandum reiterated Debré's twofold objective: to attract to the Paris market new categories of investors, particularly executives aged between thirty and forty-five, even if this might "upset the Malthusian pro-fessionals who currently rule over the stock exchange";[4] to transform Paris into an international financial market, "moral" and well organized, capable of competing with other markets and of attracting foreign investors.

The Trésor's report claimed that significant progress had already been ac-complished on the path to moralization. But while the Chambre syndicale des agents de change and government services had indeed started to improve shareholder information and upgrade the IPO procedure, Haberer believed that it was pure rhetoric to pretend that these marginal reforms had been inspired by the SEC. Playing on Debré's impatience at administrative inertia, he added: "This is not what the Minister was expecting." Nothing short of a true "innovation" would satisfy Debré: "the foundation of a new ad-hoc entity, inspired by the Securities and Exchange Commission." The reader is given to understand that the Trésor had opined against Debré's desire to create a com-mission, or at least that the reservations expressed in the report were such that the creation of a commission would have been almost impossible.

More pointedly, Haberer took issue with a section of the Trésor's report which put undue emphasis on "the difficulties to transpose American law in France." The Trésor's main argument revolved around the legal status of the SEC, an agency independent from the federal government. Having dryly ob-jected that "it [was] pointless to take refuge behind legal categories in order to avoid a reform that is necessary," Haberer added that a precedent already existed: the Centre d'étude des revenus et des coûts (CERC), a public research center dedicated to the study of incomes and expenses, had been established in February 1966 as part of the "plan Debré." The chairman and board members of the CERC were appointed by the French government; they were chosen because of their reputation and their professional skills, either among government employees or businessmen. The CERC, Haberer argued, could serve as a model for the commission to be created. According to him, the powers of the new entity would not overlap with the regulatory powers (*attributions réglementaires*) of the Comité des Bourses de Valeurs or of the Chambre syndicale des agents de change. Haberer used the French word *réglementaire* to describe the powers exercised by the Comité des Bourses de Valeurs and the chambre syndicale over French agents de change. At that point in the process, *moralisation* and *réglementation* were being perceived as two very different things.

Haberer also stated that a crucial "test of the will to reform" would be the control of insider transactions: "One cannot pursue two contradictory objectives at the same time: on the one hand, to try to give access to the market to new categories of investors, the emergence of which results from the rise in living standards, and on the other hand to do nothing against demoralizing practices which, in France more than anywhere else, have transformed the market in a game where the same players always win (such is the belief which, even if not entirely true, determines people's behavior). This has been understood in the United States."[5] Apparently, the alliance of the Trésor and the "Malthusian professionals" denounced by Haberer had succeeded to halt the process initiated by Debré: for all practical purposes, the reform was on hold until the March elections—and who knew what their results would be?

The victory of procrastinators, though, turned out to be a pyrrhic one. As seen in chapter 1, Debré refused to view the disappointing outcome of the elections as an excuse for inaction. While the minister was working successfully to convince de Gaulle and Pompidou to activate article 38 of the Constitution, Haberer was putting together his ambitious reform agenda: "Thirty-three reform ideas applicable to saving, credit, and financial institutions."[6] Note number 32, dealing with the "moralization of the stock exchange," reiterated the two objectives outlined by Debré and, once again, refuted the arguments of the Trésor:

1. The creation of a new entity inspired by the Securities and Exchange Commission. Based on this model, the new entity could, without interfering with the regulatory (yet not moralizing) powers of the *Comité des Bourses* and the

Chambre Syndicale des agents de change, play a role which, today, is not performed by anyone: observations, investigations, recommendations, ample rights given to investors, governmental services, publicly traded companies and market professionals to bring a case to its attention. For that purpose, it would be advisable to appoint, in the Council of Ministers, members chosen for their great professional skills as well as for the authority that is theirs in government and business circles. If one wishes to complete this reform, one must not concern oneself with existing legal categories, but [one must] create something original.

2. The control of insider transactions, i.e., in concrete terms, transactions conducted by board members or senior managers of a given company in securities issued by this company. [. . .] On that specific point, the line of precedents of the Securities and Exchange Commission is very dynamic. Recently, the "insider" concept, which was initially limited to board members and senior managers, has been extended to geologists and even to a press attaché.[7]

After the vote of the Enabling Act on June 22, the road to reform was open again. While the lack of parliamentary debates on Debré's reform agenda upset lawmakers, it also sped up the drafting of the *ordonnances*. The constituting documents of the COB were discussed among a very small group of *hauts fonctionnaires*. The role of the French Parliament in 1967 cannot in any way be compared to that of the US Congress in 1934, when senators and representatives debated with great intensity the proposals put forward by the executive.[8]

Debré's staff, along with dedicated teams of the ministry, started to write the *ordonnances*. Haberer was instrumental in the choice of the word *commission* (as opposed to *comité* or *conseil*), an obvious reference to the SEC, to designate the new entity.[9] An undated preliminary draft, which would eventually bear little resemblance to the final *ordonnance*, contemplated the creation of a Commission de Normalisation des Opérations Boursières.[10] The resulting acronym, CNOB, was rather unfortunate, and did not survive the following iterations of the project.[11] The new entity was to be known as the COB, Commission des Opérations de Bourse, which was later to give rise to the expression *se faire cober* (to be caught by the COB), popular among market professionals.[12]

The Ministry for the Economy and Finance was determined to keep an eye on the deliberations of the future securities regulator. The first version of the draft *ordonnance* provided for the existence of a government commissioner—such was the case with the Comité des Bourses de Valeurs, where a government commissioner had the power to veto decisions going against "the general interest." During the summer of 1967, as a result of ongoing discussions between the *cabinets* of the prime minister and of the minister for the economy and finances, the original draft underwent several amendments; one of them resulted in the elimination of the government commissioner. In a letter to Debré dated August 4, René Larre, the new directeur du Trésor, agreed on all the amendments, with the exception of the suppression of the government commissioner. According to him, this was a matter of national interest: he had no objection to letting the COB include or exclude French companies from the official list of publicly traded companies, "but there would be a real risk to leave it up to [the COB] to define the policy to be implemented with respect to the listing of foreign companies."[13] Playing to Debré's jealous sense of power, he described a scenario whereby the COB might contradict one of his ministerial decisions and agree to list a company which had been deemed inappropriate by the services of his Ministry. The minister let himself be convinced by Larre's arguments. With the benefit of hindsight, Haberer later commented: "With Debré, Government was always there: this was not the Thatcherian or Reaganesque era, which came later, and when Government [became] the enemy, so there [was] a government commissioner."[14]

In the name of French national interest, therefore, the paragraph providing for the presence of a government commissioner was reinstated in the draft of the constituting documents.

The French presidency was regularly updated about the drafting of the ordonnances by the related ministerial departments. De Gaulle himself, who was busy attending to grander business, was not personally involved in the process—it is during the summer of 1967 that the president, while visiting the city of Montreal, issued a dramatic challenge to "Anglo-Saxon imperialism" in North America and uttered one of his most controversial lines: *Vive le Québec libre!* (Long live free Quebec!).[15] In a memorandum dated July 27, Jacques Chabrun, a member of the Élysée staff, informed Bernard Tricot, the general secretary, of the upcoming creation of the COB. He put it in the perspective of the much-needed revival of the Bourse:

> One of the most serious obstacles which hinder the smooth running of the financial market resides in the secrecy in which securities transactions are too often shrouded. In takeover-bids, for example, "insiders" can pocket significant gains, while small shareholders, with little information and left to their own devices, are at a disadvantage.

The revival of the *Bourse*, therefore, depends upon the improvement of investor information, so that investors, better apprised of the operations of [publicly traded] companies, be incited to buy shares and bonds again.[16]

Chabrun's memorandum was neutral. The following day, however, another memorandum to Tricot—unsigned, this time—expressed some reservations about the project:

> The preamble of this *ordonnance* reiterates the objective of [French] public authorities to develop long-term savings and facilitate access to the financial market for new categories of investors.
>
> It is doubtful that the [proposed] means will reach that objective if one considers that the *ordonnance* in question is based, principally, on the creation of a new investigative and inquiry body, on new legislation designed to punish speculative transactions by managers on securities issued by their own companies, and on the adoption of new criminal penalties.
>
> It might be appropriate to ensure a certain moralization of securities transactions, but in the present state of the financial market, it is more important to create new incentives for the general public to purchase securities.[17]

The anonymous staffer of the Élysée went on to recommend tax incentives in favor of security holders: according to him, they would be much more efficient to revive the Bourse.

At the end of August, Jean Dromer, a member of the Élysée *secrétariat général* in charge of economic and financial affairs, updated de Gaulle on "the *ordonnances* dealing with financial issues." The second section of Dromer's memorandum, which was devoted entirely to the creation of the COB, seemed to indicate that the text of the ordonnance had been modified at the request of the Élysée:

> A first draft had been presented and rejected by this *Secrétariat Général* because it looked unclear and essentially repressive.
>
> In its present format, it institutes, in a somewhat solemn manner, a control of securities transactions, with a "big commission" intended to avoid existing [deceitful] maneuvers which result in spoiling small investors to the exclusive benefit of bankers and managers of corporations.
>
> If the text is presented well, and if a big public relations campaign in favor of the *Bourse* comes along, it might be useful. Everything will depend upon the individuals who will be chosen, first and foremost the chairman, who will have to exercise his duties with authority and some solemnity.

It must also be noted that article 18 (repression) has been contracted and that it has been toned down. By now, it is less provocative.[18]

The final version of the ordonnance was significantly different from the drafts kept in the archives of Haberer and of the Ministry for the Economy and Finance. The differences, however, are more formal than substantial—the number and sequence of the articles, in particular, are not the same. Unfortunately, archival records do not include all the correspondence and related documents between the Élysée Palace, the Hôtel de Matignon, and the Rue de Rivoli during the summer of 1967.

In any event, Debré did not wait for all the stars to be aligned to make the future commission official. He presented it formally to de Gaulle and Pompidou during a meeting of the French government. Kept as part of the Haberer collection in the archives of the French Ministry for the Economy and Finance, a four-page note bears the title: "Presentation to the July 31, 1967 Council of Ministers."[19] It emanated from Debré's cabinet and, while unsigned, had probably been written by Haberer. It summarized the arguments in favor of the creation of the COB and was meant to be used as a support document for the presentation to be made by Debré to the French government. The note began with a reiteration of the ordonnance's three objectives:

At a time when international competition makes it a priority to develop the national industry, it is essential that corporations, particularly corporations from the private sector, have a large and rapid access to the capital market.

The progressive rise in the standards of living, the fast increasing number of middle and senior executives in modern society, make it possible for new strata of investors to access the market for securities, i.e. the kind of long-term investments which the French government wants to develop, consistent with the recommendations of the Fifth National Plan.

The freedom of foreign exchange transactions and the increasing solidarity among European countries give to the Paris financial market a serious opportunity to develop and diversify its international role, attracting foreign as well as domestic investors.[20]

The note reflected the evolution of official thinking about market surveillance; it also indicated a shift in the vocabulary used by French officials:

At the crossroads of these three preoccupations appears the necessity to transform the Stock Exchange into a veritable market, without mysteries or deceitful maneuvers, and where each and every investor might be comfortable that he might be informed loyally and that he might be able to appeal to an independent authority. [. . .] It is not so much a matter of "moralization", although the use of that word (contrasted against its opposite, "demoralization") was not illegitimate at the time of the incidents which occurred along the Ugine-Kuhlmann merger. It is a matter, rather, of normalization, i.e. the definition, through norms and technical dispositions, of the relationship between companies and the general public.[21]

Speaking in the presence of Pompidou, the man who had caused such a stir by his comments about the Ugine-Kuhlmann scandal, Debré duly referred to the "moralization" of the market. He also added, however, that the concept of normalization (*normalisation*, in French) was more appropriate. While drafting the ordonnance, Haberer and others had attempted to define "norms" and "technical dispositions" rather than "moral values."

Debré's statement explicitly mentioned the SEC. Assuming that he did indeed have the opportunity to read it in its entirety during the meeting of the Council of Ministers, it is tempting—and vain, unfortunately, in the absence of written records—to try to imagine de Gaulle's reaction about Debré's implicit celebration of the American model:

> In some foreign countries, everybody agrees that the regularity of stock market transactions and their attraction for individual investors are due to the success of a Commission endowed with adequate powers and in charge of enforcing the sincerity of the market. Such is the experience of, among others, the Securities and Exchange Commission in the United States.
>
> Prior to any initial public offering or any new issue of shares, companies will have to put together a document which will be submitted to and registered with the Commission, and will be made available to the general public. [. . .] This mechanism, designed to control information, already exists in the United States, where it applies to prospectuses designed according to regulation.[22]

A few days after the meeting of the French government, on August 9, *Le Monde* journalist André Vene informed his readers of the upcoming ordonnance. He put it in the perspective of recent market scandals:

> Three recent cases have convinced public authorities of the importance of filling the gaps in existing legislation. Two large corporations, one of which in 1967, suddenly disclosed important losses after publishing a series of encouraging information on their situation. The unexpected announcement of the terms of the merger between two other companies caused a sudden fall in the price of a

major stock, [a fall] which made a bad impression on the investing public and the *Bourse*.

In order to avoid such behaviors, a surveillance commission will likely be instituted, following the example of what exists in the United States and in Belgium.[23]

The Ugine-Kuhlmann scandal, obviously, was still fresh in memories. One of the two other incidents mentioned by Vene was even more recent: on April 24, 1967, two months after announcing a significant rise in its 1966 sales, Thomson-Houston disclosed a 5.3 million French francs loss. Between the February and the April announcements, for no apparent reason, the price of the Thomson-Houston shares mysteriously eroded from 100 to 70 French francs. Many observers suspected that senior management had benefited from insider information.[24]

American correspondents in Paris did not fail to notice the reference to the American model. In the *New York Times* dated August 31, 1967, journalist John L. Hess detailed the package of "wide-ranging economic reforms" introduced by Debré: "A new agency is to be set up to supervise the Paris stock market and give greater confidence to investors. Discussion on this area of reform here has often cited the United States apparatus for policing the securities markets.

"Incidentally, the Paris *Bourse* rose smartly today prior to the Cabinet meeting, and market sources said leaks of the measures to be taken had been responsible."[25] As per the procedure outlined in Article 38 of the Constitution, draft ordonnances had to be submitted to the Conseil d'État for review, and promulgated by the president prior to the expiration of the authority granted by the Enabling Act on October 31. The most significant change requested by the Conseil d'État was to extend the term of the chairman of the COB from three to five years.[26] The text of the ordonnance was modified accordingly.

The complete title of the ordonnance was *Ordonnance n° 67-833 du 28 septembre 1967 instituant une commission des opérations de bourse et relative à l'information des porteurs de valeurs mobilières et à la publicité de certaines opérations de bourse* (ordonnance number 67-833, dated September 28, 1967, establishing a *commission des opérations de bourse* and dealing with security holder information as well as the publicity of certain stock market transactions).

The ordonnance included a preamble, under the form of a "report to the President of the Republic." This preamble outlined two objectives: first, to

encourage the investment of long-term savings in securities; second, to reinforce the international role of the Paris Stock Exchange. The first occurrence
of the commission's name was immediately followed by a telling apposition:
"a *commission des operations de bourse* modeled after (*à l'image de*) what exists
in some foreign countries." The writers of the ordonnance stuck to a cautious
plural and did not mention the United States explicitly. The ordonnance was
signed by President Charles de Gaulle, Prime Minister Georges Pompidou,
and several members of the French government: Michel Debré (Economy and
Finances), Pierre Billotte (Overseas Departments and Territories), Louis Joxe
(Justice), and Olivier Guichard (Industry).

The ordonnance was made up of fifteen articles. With no pretense of literary
style, it enunciated the role and responsibilities of the commission:

> Article 1: A *commission des operations de bourse* is hereby established. It will
> be in charge of controlling information [disclosed] to security holders and the
> general public about publicly traded companies and the securities issued by
> them, and of watching over the proper functioning of the stock exchanges.

Article 1 added that the operating expenses of the COB were to be covered by
government. Article 2 outlined the composition of the COB. It would comprise
five members. The chair would be appointed by government decree for a five-
year term. Four other members would be designated by the minister for the
economy and finances for three-year terms. As was already indicated in the
preamble, "the number of members chosen for their experience in a profession
consisting in performing banking or securities transactions shall be equal to
two." All members of the commission would be subject to a two-term limit.
In addition to the chair and the four commissioners, the minister for the
economy and finances would appoint a *commissaire du gouvernement* (government commissioner) to represent the French government. The commissaire
du gouvernement would be given the right to request, within four days after
a decision had been rendered by the COB, a second discussion of the subject
under review.

The composition of the COB deviated from the typical postwar French
committee which aimed to include a representative of every "body" of the
nation.[27] In article 2, the American inspiration was obvious: similar to the
SEC's, the COB's board would comprise five commissioners. Yet differences
were no less striking. With the exception of the chair, they were appointed for
a shorter period (three years vs. five years). Besides, only the chair sat on the

board full time. The chair was appointed by government decree; no consent from the French Parliament (either the National Assembly or the Senate) was required. The procedure applicable to the designation of the four other commissioners was even less formal because they were designated by the minister for the economy and finances. The commissaire du gouvernement was in effect the sixth member of the board. The suspensive veto he could exercise over the board's decisions ensured that the interests of the French government would always be represented and defended.[28]

Article 3 endowed the COB with two essential missions:

To make sure that publicly traded companies fully discharge their legal and / or regulatory obligations with respect to the disclosure of information (*publications prévues par les dispositions legislatives ou réglementaires*).

To verify the information that publicly traded companies disclose to their shareholders or the general public.

Article 3 also gave the COB the authority (i) to order publicly traded companies to correct inaccuracies or omissions in documents they had disclosed, and (ii) to bring to the knowledge of the general public its observations about information released by publicly traded companies.

As per article 4, the COB would have the ability to receive complaints and petitions, and to act on them. It would have the right to propose changes to existing laws or regulations (*propositions de modifications des lois et règlements*). Each year, the COB would send a report to the president of the Republic; this report would be published in the *Journal Officiel.*

Article 5 empowered COB employees, albeit with some restrictions. They would have the right to access all the documents they deemed necessary to the fulfillment of their mission. Confidentiality duty could not be invoked to evade the obligation to give them access to the information they would request. They themselves would be bound by confidentiality duty.

Article 6 enshrined the principle of investor protection through the disclosure and dissemination of information. It did not apply to the COB but to publicly traded companies. To inform the general public, publicly traded companies (as well as companies in the process of going public) would have to print a document describing their organization, their financial situation, and the evolution of their activity.

As per article 7, the document mentioned in article 6 would have to be registered with the COB, which would stamp its seal of approval ("visa") and request, as the case may be, that changes be made or that additional information be inserted.

Article 8 was intended to complete the 1966 Company Law. Directors and senior managers of a publicly traded company holding shares of the company would have to hold them in registered form. The COB would have to be notified of the sale or acquisition of new shares. It stopped short, however, of offering a precise definition of "insiders" and "insider trading."

Articles 9 to 13 were meant to ensure consistency between the July 24, 1966, Company Act and the ordonnance. Article 14 added that it would apply to the French overseas departments and territories, and article 15 simply stated that its signatories were responsible for its execution.

Compared to the 1934 Securities Exchange Act, the 1967 ordonnance was much shorter: less than two pages in the *Journal Officiel*. It was also less ambitious: the independence of the COB was limited, and its powers were defined rather narrowly. While the words *réglementaire* and *règlements* appeared in the ordonnance, the word *régulation* was absent. Except for the responsibility "to watch over the proper functioning of the stock exchanges" enunciated in article 1, little was said about ongoing surveillance of trading transactions—in other words, the tasks that had so far been performed by the Comité des Bourses de Valeur. During its review of the draft ordonnance, the Conseil d'État had noted that the transfer of these responsibilities from the comité to the COB had to be treated separately: pursuant to Article 37 of the Constitution, the 1942 act, establishing the comité had to be amended by decree.[29]

On January 3, 1968, decree number 68-30 was published in the *Journal Officiel*.[30] Article 1 stated that the comité would be suppressed and that all its powers would be transferred to the COB. One exception was made, though: margin requirements applicable to forward transactions, which had so far been set by the comité, would from then on be set by the Banque de France, not the COB. During the review process, it had been noted that this was a central bank issue.[31] Because the governor of the Banque de France was not sitting on the board of the COB, as had been the case with the comité, the setting of margin requirements was transferred back to the central bank.[32]

On January 13, a press release issued by the Ministry for the Economy and Finance clarified that, while the powers of the defunct comité had been transferred to the COB, the recently established entity had also been endowed with a totally new responsibility: the information of investors and the general public.[33] The spirit of the press release was not unlike that of a letter sent by Debré to the chair of the comité at the end of December: "The broader mission, the status and the composition of the *Commission des Opérations de Bourse* make it an institution of a different nature than that of [the comité]."[34]

Debré's statement was correct, but, as indicated by Dromer in his August memorandum to de Gaulle, much would "depend upon the individuals who [would] be chosen" to fulfill the mission of the COB.

CHAPTER SIX

Takeoff

During his tenure in the Rue de Rivoli, Debré undertook a major overhaul of the top hierarchy of the Ministry for the Economy and Finances.[1] In July 1967, Directeur du Trésor Maurice Pérouse was appointed directeur général of the Caisse des Dépôts et Consignations, the ancient public institution viewed as the arm of the French government in a wide array of economic activities— financing of local development and of housing programs, management of solicitors' deposits and of "livret" savings accounts. In a 1965 memorandum to de Gaulle, his economic adviser Jean Dromer had offered the following description of the outgoing directeur du Trésor: "Mr. Pérouse is a civil servant of the highest intellectual and moral quality, but [he is also] traditional and conservative in his reactions."[2] Pérouse was succeeded by René Larre, the conseiller financier in the French embassy in Washington and a director of the International Monetary Fund (IMF), whose outlook was different from his predecessor's. In a 1990 interview with historian Sophie Coeuré, he was to declare that he "had been conquered by the American methods."[3] For all his appreciation and intimate knowledge of things American, however, he would not easily be lured into complacency toward the recently created, and still evanescent, COB. Challenged by the flurry of reforms initiated under Debré's authority, the new directeur could be counted on to defend the prerogatives of the Trésor.

On September 15, 1967, shortly after the French government approved the text of the draft ordonnance, Larre wrote to Debré to suggest the names of potential members of the Commission des Opérations de Bourse's *collège* (board).[4] He insisted on "the great autonomy [given to the COB] in the exercise of powers which, until then, had been the sole prerogative of government." He did not venture to recommend any name for the job of COB chairman, but he did have very clear views about what his credentials ought to be: "The considerations [developed in the first section of the letter] lead me to insist very strongly upon the appointment of a chairman who would be close to the services of the Ministry of Finances. According to me, this is why the chairman should be chosen among the highest ranking officials of the Department, with a wide breadth of experience in the fields of finance and the economy, as well a great deal of personal courage, social skills, and diplomacy."[5]

The chairman of the COB was to be appointed by government decree. In practice, it would be Debré's choice—unless of course de Gaulle or Pompidou had any objection. The minister was very much aware of the implications of his decision. The credibility of the Securities and Exchange Commission (SEC) had benefited from the qualities of its first chairmen. While Joseph P. Kennedy (1934–1935) had been a political appointee, his two immediate successors, James M. Landis (1935–1937) and William O. Douglas (1937–1939), counted among the most brilliant lawyers of the New Deal generation.

According to Haberer, Debré gave much thought to his decision and discussed it with him.[6] Both men agreed that the primary quality of the first chairman of the COB had to be his independence with respect to market professionals. Businessmen, stockbrokers, and bankers were therefore excluded. Haberer suggested that the chairman be chosen among existing or former members of the French government, in order to give him additional authority and prestige, particularly when time would come to wage political battles with the directeur du Trésor, the governor of the Banque de France, or other semigovernmental institutions. The name emerging from these discussions was Pierre Chatenet, who had held the position of minister of the interior in the Debré government from May 1959 to May 1961.

The son of a haut fonctionnaire of the French National Assembly, Chatenet, born in 1917, was five years younger than Debré. He received the same education (the Law Faculty, Sciences Po) and trained under his guidance for the difficult exam to become an auditor in the Conseil d'État, which he entered in 1941—in the colorful language of the ferociously competitive French higher education system, he called Debré his *maître d'écurie* (stable master).[7] The two men were former comrades in arms: during the war, Chatenet fought in the French Résistance alongside Alexandre Parodi, who played a decisive role in the liberation of Paris in August 1944. When Parodi was appointed minister of labor and social security in the provisional government headed by de Gaulle, he asked Chatenet to become his chief of staff. In 1945, Chatenet was one of the young officials selected by the French government to join the French delegation at the United Nations conference in San Francisco. In *Décolonisation*, a book he published in 1988 about his experience in the French colonies and in government, he reminisced about his discovery of the United States: "It was stunning to find oneself in the extraordinary setting of this magnificent city, amid an abundance of things which, after five debilitating years of shortages of all kinds, made Europeans dizzy. Had it not been for the wonderful kindness of the American environment, I would have felt, at times, somewhat uncomfortable, out-of-place, shy or clumsy. Americans were always willing to please people who, they realized, had been traumatized—not always understanding, in fact, what their sufferings had been. This was all the more generous of them."[8]

Chatenet spent about one year in New York as a member of the French diplomatic mission to the United Nations—Parodi, who had become his brother-in-law when Chatenet had married his sister Jacqueline, was the French ambassador. He enjoyed living in New York City and returned there several times over the following years.[9]

With hindsight, Chatenet later explained that his time at the United Nations had changed his perception of France and the rest of the world:

> Suddenly, one had to stop assessing problems within the very well defined framework of our nation's borders; [one had] to assess them in a much broader, and also much less focused, context. One realized, then, that it was not just in comparison with the war years that the situation had changed, but also in comparison with the pre-war years. Of course, at the time, men and ideas were already circulating very rapidly around the world, but I believe—at least as far as I am concerned—that I did not have the feeling, much less the certainty, of an imperious presence, of the influence of the outside, non-European world on the destiny of France and Europe.[10]

Chatenet then held several senior positions in the French administration, either abroad (chief of staff to the French resident general in Tunisia, member of the French permanent mission at NATO headquarters) or at home (*directeur de la fonction Publique*, a job that made him the equivalent of a director of human resources for the entire French Civil Service). He did not take a direct part, however, in the economic modernization of postwar France—he was never a member of the Commissarat général du plan, nor of the staff of the Ministry for the Economy and Finance.

In January 1959, Chatenet entered the French government as *secrétaire d'État auprès du premier ministre* (junior minister responsible to the prime minister): "I was very interested in what I was doing, and above all I loved being near Michel Debré, a friend who trusted me, and to whom, I felt, I could be useful."[11]

In May 1959, Chatenet was promoted to the strategic position of minister of the interior. In the context of the war in Algeria, his main responsibility was to maintain law and order—in January 1960, during the "week of barricades," a group of anti-independence activists attempted to seize control of Algiers. It is presumably under these tense circumstances that he earned de Gaulle's trust.

When illness forced him to leave the French government in May 1961, the president sent him a comforting note: "Of your presence at my side in the [French] government, I keep the fondest memory. In a very difficult task, during very tough times, you proved a very worthy Minister, and a big-hearted man."[12]

Chatenet's *Décolonisation* is suffused with the ethos of the French Civil Service (*l'esprit du service public*). Although the book is focused on the role played by Chatenet in the decolonization of French Northern Africa, it strikes a note similar to that of the memoirs written by many postwar hauts fonctionnaires involved in the modernization of the French economy.[13] In his 1982, seminal book on French executives, sociologist Luc Boltanski described the "reformist avant-garde," which played such a decisive role in the diffusion of American models in France: "This avant-garde cannot be identified with an association or a [political] party, it lacked a formal organization or representative bodies, it did not possess a flag [and was not defined by] clear borders; its members, however, were linked with each other through personal relationships in a network structure which continued, in peace and through elective affinities, the armed networks of the Résistance."[14]

In 1962, Chatenet was appointed chairman of the European Atomic Energy Commission in Brussels. His mission ended five years later, when the executive bodies of the three European executives were merged together. In 1967, therefore, Chatenet was out of a job and available.

Neither Debré in his memoirs nor Haberer in the recollections he shared mentioned that Chatenet, as a young man, had lived in the United States. Incidentally, we learn from the account of his time at the United Nations that, while he complied with the obligation to use the French language in official meetings, he did speak English with his foreign counterparts on more mundane occasions;[15] that skill, relatively uncommon for a Frenchman of his generation, proved particularly useful when he met with successive SEC chairmen.

Chatenet kept a relatively low profile in the media. In 1971, Georges Suffert, one of the most influential editorialists in Paris, painted a bittersweet portrait for the radio show *Le Club de la presse* on French radio Europe 1: "Mr. Chatenet, a friend of Mr. Michel Debré, was the Minister of the Interior until 1961. In this most difficult of jobs, he achieved the considerable feat of not being hated— let alone noticed. This is quite a success."[16] Suffert went on to tell his audience that Chatenet "belonged to the hard-line branch" of the Gaullist family. This was true enough, as long as one did not underestimate the complex and, at times, paradoxical nature of Gaullism.

An experienced negotiator, Chatenet was not afraid of making tough decisions. Nothing, however, had prepared him for the job of market regulator. During his varied administrative career, he had never worked in the Ministry for the Economy and Finance. Besides, he did not own an investment portfolio and had little interest in stocks and bonds.[17] Yet he was intellectually curious and liked the challenge of creating a new institution. During the time he spent in Brussels at the helm of the European Atomic Energy Commission, he had remained in touch with de Gaulle, who kept a close eye on atomic energy issues. The president appreciated his forthrightness, pragmatism, and integrity. When Debré suggested his name for the chairmanship of the COB, de Gaulle approved enthusiastically.[18]

On October 3, 1967, Debré formally proposed the appointment of Chatenet as chairman of the COB in a meeting of the Council of Ministers. Pursuant to the ordonnance, this appointment was made effective by a decree dated November 10, 1967. The decree was signed by de Gaulle, Pompidou, and Debré. On December 5, 1967, Dupont-Fauville, Debré's chief of staff, informed Haberer that Chatenet's salary would be a comfortable 12,000 French francs per month[19]—this was the minister's personal decision.[20]

"Personal courage, social skills, and diplomacy": such were the qualities outlined by Larre in his September 15 letter to Debré. Chatenet did not lack any of them, but he failed to pass what was probably the most important test in the eyes of the directeur du Trésor: he did not come from the ranks of the Ministry for the Economy and Finance and was not an inspecteur général des finances. Debré had deliberately chosen someone who would not be suspected of defending the interests of the department formerly in charge, if only partially, of market surveillance.[21]

In addition to Chatenet, the collège of the COB comprised four commissioners. The ordonnance stated that two of them had to be chosen "for their experience in a profession consisting in performing banking or securities transactions." In his letter, Larre was more specific about them than he had been about the chairman.[22]

Assuming that Debré had promised to pick one of them among the agents de change, he pointed out that the syndic was not a good choice: he was elected for a one-year term, and his authority could be diminished if, for some reason, he was not reelected. Larre, therefore, deemed it preferable to designate either another agent de change, or the general secretary of the chambre syndicale.

The directeur du Trésor also believed that the other commissioner chosen for his professional skills should be selected among the general managers of large French banks. Historically, however, bankers who had sat on the Comité des Bourses de Valeurs had been too busy to pay sufficient attention to their surveillance duties. He put forward the name of René de Lestrade, general manager of the Caisse nationale des marchés de l'État, a government entity in charge of facilitating the financing of corporations bidding for public contracts: not only did he enjoy considerable authority among his peers, he was also very imaginative—a "rare quality in administrative circles," according to Larre. As far as the two other commissioners were concerned, the directeur du Trésor abstained from recommending anyone in particular, noting briefly that a judge or a professor would bring additional authority and knowledge to the collège. Finally, he suggested the name of Marc Viénot, an inspecteur général des finances and an ÉNA graduate, to be the first government commissioner.

Larre's letter was not ignored by Debré's cabinet. The same day it was received, Haberer reacted to it in writing.[23] Contrary to the directeur du Trésor, the minister's adviser thought that the presence of the syndic des agents de change was essential. To mitigate the risk pointed out by Larre, he suggested that a letter be sent to the syndic, stating explicitly that his designation as collège member would be valid only for the period during which he would be heading the chambre syndicale. That solution was much better than the designation of an agent de change who would not have been elected by his peers, or of "the nice Mr. Petit," the general secretary, who was known to be close to the Trésor.[24]

Along with the governmental decree appointing Chatenet, the November 10 *Journal Officiel* included a more modest ministerial order (*arrêté*) announcing the nomination of the four other commissioners: Yves Meunier, the syndic; René de Lestrade, the general manager of the Caisse nationale des marchés de l'État; Arnaud de Vogüe, the chairman of Saint-Gobain, one of France's largest manufacturing corporations; and Albert Monguilan, a professional judge. Viénot, whose name had been put forward by Larre, was indeed the first government commissioner.

Being the shrewd administrator that he was, Larre did not ignore that collège members, with the exception of Chatenet, would have limited impact on the day-to-day operations of the COB. Much more essential to the success of the institution was the designation of a capable General Secretary. In his September 15 letter, the directeur du Trésor put forward the name of a Mr. X (his real name, which does not add much to this story, shall not be disclosed).[25] Judging from Haberer's reaction, Larre was being rather disingenuous: while both agreed that the general secretary had to be "active" and "efficient," "these two requirements [were] sufficient ground to dismiss Mr. X, whose subtlety is no sufficient substitute, sadly, for the two qualities that [were] absolutely necessary."[26] To this merciless assessment of Mr. X's character, Haberer added that, along with Lestrade and Viénot, he was too close to the Trésor.

For all his attachment to the principle of independence, Haberer had no objection to choose an inspecteur général des finances—after all, he was one of them: "The General Secretary will manage a team in charge of audits and investigations; these tasks will have to be performed with discretion, rapidity, and efficiency. Very few jobs would fit so well with the training and experience of an inspecteur des finances. Besides, the *inspection générale des finances* enjoys a well-deserved reputation of integrity, to which the Direction du Trésor cannot pretend." [27]

Haberer suggested that Dupont-Fauville, Debré's directeur de cabinet (chief of staff) and the nominal head of the Inspection, pick someone among his first-class inspecteurs. In the list of potential choices at the end of the memo, Debré underlined the name of Jean-Jacques Burgard. Haberer knew Burgard and had a lot of respect for his organizational skills, independence, and thoroughness. He later claimed that he had been responsible for selecting him, and it is not unlikely that he added a warm verbal recommendation to his more neutral memo.[28] Burgard himself gratefully acknowledged Haberer's role in his promotion.[29]

Burgard, born in 1926, belonged to the first generation of ÉNA students. After graduation, he joined the Inspection générale des Finances and held several postings overseas. In 1966, he became the deputy to the head of the Inspection.[30] As early as October 25, 1967, two weeks before he officially became chairman of the COB, Chatenet appointed him to the position of general secretary. This decision had been approved by Debré—decree number 68-23, issued on January 3, 1968, stipulated that the appointment of the general secretary by the chairman of the COB was "subject to the approval of the Minister of the Economy and Finances." The general secretary was to be an ex officio participant to the meetings of the collège.

At the helm of the COB, Chatenet and Burgard constituted a remarkably efficient duo. Chatenet was not afraid to delegate responsibility and supported his subordinates in difficult times. Years later, Burgard reminisced about "his high-mindedness, kindness, smiling authority."[31] The quality of their relationship was a great asset to their success: "We were very close. [Chatenet] had insisted on having a door opened in the wall between our two offices, allowing us to communicate without having to walk through the secretaries' office. He walked through it more often than I did, and gave me the benefit of his observations on all kinds of subjects, related not only to our mission, but also to the broader context."[32]

A deeper, if muted, connection existed between them: the memory of the war years.[33] In the 1940s, Jean-Jacques Burgard was too young to play a leading role in the Résistance, but his father was one of its heroes. A literature teacher at the Lycée Buffon in Paris, Raymond Burgard created the underground paper *Valmy* and was part of the leadership of Combat Zone Nord, one of the largest Resistance movements in the occupied zone. Arrested by the Nazis in 1942, he was beheaded in Cologne two years later.

When Burgard visited Chatenet for the first time, it was at his new superior's home:[34] the COB did not have its own premises yet—it did not even officially exist. Neither man was an expert of the stock market, but they were determined to seize the initiative and reach the objectives outlined by Debré and Haberer in the ordonnance. Even though he had not officially left the Inspection yet, Burgard started to work immediately. The priority was to build a team.

Chatenet was reluctant to inflate the size of his personnel. His intention was to combine the transfer to the COB of government employees with recruitments from the private sector. Some of the staff members would be working on the definition of rules and on the control of their application, while others would be conducting studies and analyses. Upon a recommendation from Debré's cabinet, an employee of the Minister of Finances was appointed administrative agent of the new institution.[35] His assigned priority was to draft employment contracts. During its first year of existence, the COB hired approximately forty individuals; they were seventy-five at the end of Chatenet's term. Chatenet never hid the fact that the COB was much smaller than the SEC. Explaining that the Washington staff of the American regulator amounted to 1,500 employees, he immediately added that it had never been the intention of the French government to build such a large institution. His objective, rather, was to operate "a small, but also a dynamic and responsive entity, able to fulfill the mission it [had] been entrusted with."[36]

On October 3—the day his nomination was discussed in a session of the Council of Ministers—Chatenet met with Haberer.[37] He asked many questions about the origins and the objectives of the institution he would soon officially launch and shared with him what he envisioned would be the timetable for takeoff:

- During the first month, building of the team
- For approximately four months, progressive start-up, "based on a temporary organization chart"
- Finally, cruising speed reached in the spring of 1968.[38]

Chatenet impressed Haberer, who sent Debré a summary of their conversation: "Overall, it seemed to me that Mr. Chatenet looked at things with the utmost realism. He will act with discretion, but also great efficiency, and he wishes to make the setting-up of the new entity a success."[39] In a handwritten comment on Haberer's memo, Debré set the date of January 1, 1968, for the official beginning of the COB's operations.

During the last months of 1967, Chatenet sent detailed reports to Debré to inform him about his activities and to enroll his support in the administrative skirmishes he had to fight with a number of adversaries. One of his first decisions was to issue a written set of rules applicable to the proceedings of the collège. He told Debré that his impression of the four designated commissioners was that they would be "very cooperative and very united." He was attached to collective decision making and wanted "all individuals sitting [on the collège] to feel personally committed to common action and to stand by the chairman"[40]—later, he was to take particular care of building consensus, in order to project an image of "respectability."[41]

Because the ordonnance stated that the operating expenses of the COB were to be covered by the government (*l'État*), an amendment to the nation's budget had to be prepared in order to include the 1968 preliminary budget of the new institution. Chatenet was cautious not to spend money unnecessarily—a particular concern of his were potential overlaps with existing government services—but he did not want to undermine the COB's credibility for lack of sufficient resources. In that difficult exercise, he told Debré, he had been able to rely on "the excellent cooperative spirit,"[42] which prevailed among his counterparts in the Direction du Budget—such was not the case in the Banque de France or the Direction du Trésor, as we shall see.

A decree implementing the ordonnance was discussed during a meeting that took place in October. Participants envisioned the allocation of specific revenues to the COB's budget: all or a portion of the taxes levied on trading transactions, a fee to be paid on new listings or on the registration of prospectuses or other documents, and so forth. This solution was finally excluded, and it was decided that 100 percent of the COB's operating expenses would be covered by the ministry.[43] The directeur du Trésor wrote to Debré that they could be expected to reach a minimum of 1.5 million French francs in 1968—a very modest amount compared to the budget of the SEC.[44]

Cases under investigation by the Comité des Bourses de Valeurs had to be transferred to the COB. Chatenet told Debré that the transfer of files was going smoothly, but he complained that the banque was not willing to let go any of its employees, except for secretarial staff. Analysts, lawyers, and press attachés would have to be hired from the private sector.

Nobody seemed to challenge the core missions of the COB: investor information and surveillance of the market. Unexpectedly, however, Chatenet's apparently innocuous initiative to create a research department within the COB ignited considerable passion. In a November 8 memorandum to Debré, the directeur du Trésor expressed strong reservations:[45] according to him, it would give rise to a regrettable overlap with the Trésor's Bureau du marché financier. This rather petty issue gave him an opportunity to develop his views on the independence of the COB:

> It seems to me that there is no legitimate legal foundation for giving these responsibilities to the department contemplated by Mr. Chatenet. Article 4, paragraph 2 of the *Ordonnance* establishing the COB defines, in a restrictive manner according to me, its power of initiative. The paragraph reads as follows: (the Commission) "may formulate proposals to modify laws and regulations (*propositions de modifications des lois et règlements*) applicable to the information of security holders and the general public, the stock exchanges, and the status of the *agents de change*." Under these conditions, I believe that it would be inappropriate to let the Commission engage, from the start, in tasks which are only remotely connected with its mission. Narrowly understood, this mission is actually extremely important. [. . .] The Commission should not [. . .] ignore the overall operations of the market, but I think that whatever observations or suggestions it might formulate on that subject must result from the exercise of its control powers and not from an ex-ante study of the various problems, well-known already, associated with the correct operations of the financial market.[46]

With ostentatious magnanimity, Larre recommended that the COB be invited to take part to several committees in charge of making proposals to reform the securities markets. He also conceded that the annual report to the president of the Republic might include proposals from the COB, to the extent that they derived "from the exercise of its control powers."

Debré rendered a Solomonic judgment. Through the intermediary of his cabinet, he let Larre know that he had approved the setting up of a "small" research department within the COB and that it would be up to him and Chatenet to agree on "the spirit of its mission."

Toward the end of the "start-up" phase, Chatenet sent a last interim report to Debré.[47] He did not elaborate on budgetary or other mundane issues, which were in the process of being resolved. His team had started to implement the registration procedure: a number of applications had been received and were being reviewed. Formal stamps of approval (visas) were to be issued on January 3, 1968, the inaugural trading session of the new year. To meet this extremely tight deadline, the COB had no other option but to rely on inspectors from the Banque de France: "To this end, the Minister [. . .]'s intercession with the Governor of the *Banque* appears to be essential."[48] Obviously, persuading Governor Brunet to be more helpful would require some coaxing.

Chatenet's second priority was to draft detailed guidelines for the transmission of accounting and legal information to the COB. He ordered an inventory of existing requirements, which showed that publicly traded companies were facing opaque and contradictory obligations. The COB also examined the questionnaire devised and implemented by the SEC: "As to the American questionnaire, it is extremely comprehensive, indiscreet even, and it is the product of the long line of precedents and of the authority of an institution which has been existing for thirty years; it suits an economy that is fundamentally dynamic and under no risk of being restrained, which might perhaps be the case here today."[49]

A draft questionnaire was sent to the Chambre syndicale des agents de change, to the Conseil National du Patronat Français (CNPF, National Council of the French Employers, the largest employer federation in France), as well as to a number of professional associations.

Chatenet informed Debré that the COB had already received several complaints from investors. Once again, he referred to the SEC: "For your information, it is interesting to note that 19,000 complaints of this type are brought before the American Commission each year. In his last hearing by the relevant Congressional Committee, [SEC] Chairman Cohen observed that a small number (less than 1,000) deserved to be investigated further, but that as a whole they were invaluable information for the Commission."[50]

By the end of 1967, the COB had a chairman, a board, a staff, and a budget. The decrees implementing the ordonnance were ready for publication in the *Journal Officiel*. Sitting en banc on January 3, 1968, commissioners issued their first visas. Debré was present on this solemn occasion. His speech received a large echo in the financial press.[51] He expressed his gratitude for the work that had already been accomplished by Chatenet and his team and reminded his audience of the missions of the new institution. First among them, "the noble task to inform" investors and the general public would differentiate the COB from its much less powerful predecessor entity. The minister was confident that Chatenet and the institution he presided over would make the demonstration of their independence—along the way, he pointed to the "precise," yet "limited" prerogatives of the government commissioner. True to his nature, Debré concluded on a political note:

> The Commission, therefore, will be able to contribute to the success of the economic policy conducted by the government. As we begin to implement a policy aiming at spreading more largely the benefits of saving and investment, in particular through the introduction of profit-sharing schemes, is it necessary to say how essential it is that this policy be implemented by an entity which is aware of the importance of its mission? At the same time, the development of share-ownership and of the bond market will allow companies to access the funds that are required for their development. The Commission will play its part through positive incentives, through improved operations, and also through the prevention, and possibly the punishment, of illegal or fraudulent acts. Thus the role of the Paris financial market will be able to expand at national, European, and international levels.[52]

The small investors of the emerging middle classes, so dear to Debré, could only rejoice at the news that a commission was created to protect them. Other segments of the French population, however, were indifferent—or even hostile—to "the benefits of saving and investment." Their voices were soon to be heard in the vicinity of the Palais Brongniart.

CHAPTER SEVEN

The Red Flag over the "Temple of Gold"

In the complex, yet largely unrehearsed, choreography of demonstrations and counterdemonstrations that graced the streets of Paris in May 1968, the night of May 24 stands apart. So far, the crisis had remained centered on the Sorbonne and its hilly surroundings, on the Left Bank of the River Seine. Since medieval times, students of the Montagne Sainte-Geneviève had looked down on the Right Bank, swarming as it was with craftsmen, shopkeepers, and money changers. That night, they crossed the Seine. The *New York Times* correspondent reported: "For the first time, the fighting overflowed to the Right Bank."

"One group of students penetrated as far as the *Bourse*, the Paris stock exchange, and set fires inside and in front of the building."[1]

The *Guardian*'s account of the incident was more picturesque: "The most dramatic moment in a night of unbelievable happenings was the invasion of the *Bourse* (Stock Exchange) by a mixture of Trotskyites, Anarchists, and revolutionary students who hoisted the Red Flag over the building of the 'Temple of Gold,' as it is called, built as it is in the Grecian style. After singing the 'Internationale,' the invaders set fire to the inside of the building, but it was extinguished soon afterwards."[2]

The damage was limited: only the flag of the Veterans' Association and the booths maintained by the banks within the building went into flames—the corbeille survived the attack. Someone wrote on the walls: "Moral values are not listed on the Stock Exchange"—a pun on the two meanings of the French word *valeur*, "value" and "security."[3]

The Palais Brongniart stood as a symbol of all that the May '68 students abhorred—money, capitalism, the traditions and privileges of the bourgeoisie. That after three weeks of unrest they finally attempted to ransack it and burn it down should not have come as a surprise—and maybe it did not: the *préfet de police* Maurice Grimaud, who was in charge of defending law and order in the French capital, had given instructions to let groups of demonstrators spread into wealthy neighborhoods—the much vilified high and middle classes, whose passivity had deprived the regime of its traditional support, would eventually be scared into action.[4] Reminiscent of the "Bloody Week" during the 1871 Paris Commune, the fire added dramatic color to the night. In the *Memoirs* of May 1968 he published nine years later, the otherwise cool-headed Maurice Grimaud painted an apocalyptic picture of the May 24 night: "The Parisians, on that side of the Seine, who so far had only heard muted echoes of the events on the other bank, [looked] with bewilderment at these galloping crowds of young devils, coming out of the night and disappearing again in darkness, while cars were ablaze in the sinister howls of fire trucks and the heartbreaking bursts of hand-grenades. Even movies had not prepared them for these emotions. Only men of sixty might remember stories they had collected from their grandparents about the 'Bloody Week.'"[5]

The nationwide student protests had originated in the campus of the Université Paris-Nanterre, West of Paris, in the early months of 1968. Much to the surprise of labor leaders, students had been joined by millions of workers coming out on strike—much less spectacular than the failed "attack" of May 24, a strike of agents de change employees had already paralyzed the Bourse in February.[6]

The French establishment was caught off guard by the revolt. De Gaulle himself, shaken by the apparently irrepressible turmoil, was desperately trying to regain the initiative. On May 24, he spoke to the nation on television. A defiant president announced a referendum on an ambitious social, economic, and institutional reform plan. Decree 68-468, dated May 27, set June 16 for the referendum. The question submitted to French voters was very general: "Do you approve the bill submitted to the French people by the President of the Republic for the renewal of higher education, social life, and the economy?"[7] In addition to the reform of national education, the proposed referendum was to remodel the economic and social structures of the nation along the following lines:

> The distribution of the benefits of expansion with a view toward continuing improvement of [standards of] living and of working conditions in [industrial] enterprises, agriculture and public services, principally in so far as the least favored [social] categories are concerned.
>
> The participation of the workers in professional responsibilities and at all levels of the economy.
>
> The drive toward full employment and professional training.
>
> The organization of economic activity within the regional framework with the increased participation of the locally elected bodies and the trade union and professional organizations and the decentralization and deconcentration of administrations.[8]

This translation, if a bit clumsy, was published in its entirety by the *New York Times*. Three days earlier, the newspaper had commented on de Gaulle's authoritarianism. Interestingly, the editorialist saw a direct connection between the ordonnance procedure and the recent unrest in Paris:

> The French President has had all the power needed for such reforms for a decade, but the current crisis testifies to the failure to employ that authority in any fundamental way. The far-ranging decree powers the French President obtained from the National Assembly just last year brought 35 "ordonnances"—an archaic term from monarchial days—in the social and economic field over a six-month period. Some of these decrees and, especially, the authoritarian way they were handed down, helped to provoke the current outbreak of strikes. There is little indication now of what new reforms the general has in mind apart from his old idea—unpopular with labor and business—of so-called worker "association" in management, a throwback to the corporate state of another era.[9]

Debré's combative astuteness when he had convinced de Gaulle and Pompidou to use Article 38 of the constitution after the March 1967 elections had come at a cost. The French people had grown tired of decrees, ordonnances, referendums, and the sidelining of Parliament—the "solitary exercise of power" criticized by former Minister Giscard d'Estaing in August 1967.[10] Events seemed to vindicate the prediction of a "shock wave in which everything can be washed away" made by resigning Minister Pisani one year earlier and reported by Mauriac in his *Bloc-Notes* column. It would be unfair, though, and grossly exaggerated, to blame Debré for an episode that mystified political analysts and still defies the sagacity of later historians and sociologists. Yet May 1968 also marked the outdated character of methods of government best represented by the minister for the economy and finances.

The old wizardry was missing in de Gaulle's May 24 televised address, which fell flat on the ears of his countrymen and did not reverse the growing flow of strikes and demonstrations. With the exhausted and depressed general seemingly unable to catch up with events, the Fifth Republic owed its survival to Pompidou, who never lost his composure amid the chaos. Shrewdly, the prime minister fragmented the united front of students and workers by negotiating the Grenelle Agreements with union leaders and representatives of French employers. He persuaded de Gaulle to dissolve the National Assembly and call for new legislative elections.

In his capacity as minister for the economy and finances, Debré should have been involved in the Grenelle negotiations, but Pompidou, with de Gaulle's assent, excluded him from the talks: known for his intransigence, his participation was deemed too risky.[11] Saddened and powerless, the former prime minister was reduced to marching on the front line of the big Gaullist rally on May 30: photographers immortalized an ecstatic Debré singing *La Marseillaise* in the crowd of demonstrators. Meanwhile, Pompidou was mulling over the events in the sanctity of his Matignon office.

Years later, Debré's bitterness had not disappeared. In his *Memoirs*, he penned an awkward lamentation on "the dramatic economic consequences" of the Grenelle Agreements:

> Sometimes, I hear people say that economic and financial losses do not matter. All revolutions have a dark side! What really matters is to be found elsewhere, first and foremost in the spirit of liberty which, once again, sprang from the paved streets of Paris. It is against this legend that I rise up! Where was liberty, in its highest meaning, that is to say tolerance and democracy? Definitely—and nobody ever doubted this seriously—on the side of the existing government. Facing it, that is to say on the side of rioters, there was the willpower of a tyrannical dictatorship on the breeding ground of anarchy. There is therefore no excuse to the ruin of the efforts undertaken to assert national power in the middle of the great competition that rules the world.[12]

The legislative elections were held on June 23 and 30. The Gaullist Union des Démocrates pour la République (UDR) party, allied to the Républicains Indépendants, won in a landslide, with a majority of 358 seats out of a total of 487. The disappointing outcome of the March 1967 elections was reversed.

In a cabinet reshuffle on May 31, Debré had left the Rue de Rivoli for the Quai d'Orsay, the seat of the French Foreign Affairs Ministry; Haberer followed him to the quai, where he became his directeur de cabinet.[13] They remained there when Maurice Couve de Curville succeeded Pompidou in the premiership on July 10. De Gaulle's choice of the rather bland former head of the French diplomacy was interpreted as a snub to Pompidou: "All the important Ministers of the outgoing Pompidou Cabinet were reappointed to similar or better posts in the new Government.

"This seemed to enhance the widely held impression that President de Gaulle, in announcing Wednesday that he had accepted Mr. Pompidou's resignation, was dismissing him rather than preparing him for a role as heir apparent."[14]

Pompidou's withdrawal, however, was temporary; Debré, his potential rival to de Gaulle's succession, did not benefit from it. In the ongoing administrative tug of war between the COB, the Trésor and the Banque de France, Chatenet had lost the support of his most powerful friend. Who knew whether the new resident of the Rue de Rivoli—Couve de Murville for a few weeks, then François-Xavier Ortoli from July 1968 to June 1969—would want to keep the COB alive? There had been precedents when a reform cherished by a minister had been silently smothered to oblivion by his successor.[15]

Meanwhile, the date of the referendum announced by de Gaulle had been postponed. La Participation, however, remained the order of the day. It had long been a cornerstone of Gaullist ideology: beginning with his speeches of the immediate postwar years, the general had constantly advocated the "association of labor and capital." The exact content of this "association," however, was lacking in specifics.

As a young man, de Gaulle had been exposed to Catholic social teaching. Along with other members of his generation, he had read Lyautey's opus "On the Social Duty of the Officer" and believed that businessmen, too, were endowed with social duties and responsibilities.[16] During his time at the helm of the Provisional Government (1944–1946), he presided over the great social reforms of the Libération. After he left government in January 1946, his main preoccupation was the threat of communism. In a speech delivered in Strasbourg in April 1947, he advocated a third way between capitalism and collectivism. He remained attached to the virtues of free enterprise and to individual property rights; yet, during the 1950s, he was also frequently critical of the power of money. The "association of labor and capital" would serve two purposes: (1) it would stimulate economic growth and increase productivity, and (2) through the eradication of social warfare, it would also steal the fire of communism.

While there is no reason to doubt his sincerity, de Gaulle's desire to reform the capitalist system came second after his ambition to restore the sovereignty of the French nation and provide for the long-term stability of its institutions. Back in power in 1958, his economic priorities were to fight inflation, restore the French franc, stimulate growth, and modernize the economy; social change would have to wait. Besides, his declarations on the "association of labor and capital" were not devoid of a touch of paternalism. As pointed out by the *New York Times* editorial, they were reminiscent of "the corporate state of another era," namely, the Vichy regime.

Profit-sharing programs were authorized by a 1959 ordonnance.[17] However, they remained optional and subject to an agreement between organized labor and business. The 1965 law on the taxation of corporate profits and capital income granted tax benefits to corporations distributing shares to their employees. Its final version included an amendment written by *député* Louis Vallon: Article 33 stated that the French government would send to Parliament, prior to May 1, 1966, a bill outlining "the right of workers to benefit from the increase in a company's assets resulting from self-financing."[18] In practice, "the amendment called for the preparation of a law that would make corporations give workers part of their profits in the form of stocks, while reinvesting the funds."[19]

The flamboyant Vallon belonged to the left wing of the Gaullist party (the Gaullistes de gauche). His amendment owed much to the thought of Marcel Loichot, an economist and a consultant, who had just published a little book on "the pancapitalist reform"[20]—the book had duly been sent to de Gaulle's attention at the Élysée. In a bombastic style, Loichot repudiated both Marxism and capitalism—incidentally, he devoted an entire chapter of his book to the nightmarish description of a capitalist dystopia in the United States. The prophet of "pancapitalism" advocated a society where all workers would become capitalists by receiving shares of the companies that employed them—the Vallon amendment was an attempt to reach that objective. The Gaullistes de gauche were a minority within the UDR party; many of their initiatives exasperated Pompidou and Debré, not to mention the more economically conservative Républicains Indépendants. Yet they always enjoyed the affectionate consideration of the president.

Reluctantly, the Pompidou government accepted the Vallon amendment. In a memorandum dated October 6, 1966, Henri Deniau, *chargé de mission* at the Élysée, put forward the following arguments: "The Fifth National Plan recommends an increase in corporate self-financing (*autofinancement*); this is possible only if sacrifices are demanded from shareholders, workers and consumers. Yet only shareholders benefit from such an increase.

"Another objective is to encourage the spreading of the ownership of securities. On that topic, several western nations, the United States and Germany in particular, are ahead of France."[21]

The second argument was not new. In another note to de Gaulle, Deniau had referred to the American model of "popular capitalism": "The development of savings and the creation of popular capitalism, as it exists in the United States, are obviously desirable, but they can develop only if wages increase substantially and exceed the ever-growing consumer needs."[22]

French business had been considerably irritated by the Vallon amendment, which they blamed for the persistent weakness of the Paris stock market in the

1960s.[23] Organized labor, on the other hand, was very reluctant to engage in profit-sharing negotiations with employers. Shortly after his arrival in the Rue de Rivoli, Debré had formed a committee, the Commission Mathey, to make proposals along the lines of the amendment. These proposals were extremely modest—for a time, it was believed that the Commission Mathey had quietly buried the Vallon amendment. De Gaulle himself, however, was intent to keep it alive. During a talk at a state savings bank in October, his comments favoring a sharing of ownership caused a drop in stock prices. *New York Times* journalist John L. Hess explained that the president's endorsement of "a reform of companies on the basis of an association" had revived the Vallon amendment:

> The project ran into practically unanimous opposition, both from labor, which is Marxist-oriented and whose members primarily want more take-home pay, and from business, which saw it as a capital levy and another attack on private ownership.
>
> Also opposed were Premier Georges Pompidou and Finance Minister Michel Debré. When a study commission this summer issued a report highly critical of the Vallon plan, the proposal was considered dead.
>
> The plan, however, had one important friend, the President, who has long believed in an "association" of interests that would soften traditional class hostilities in France. Mr. de Gaulle is said to have promised Mr. Vallon and his friends in writing that he would not let them down.[24]

La Participation figured prominently in the 1967 reform agenda. Ordonnance 67-693, dated August 17, 1967, made profit-sharing programs mandatory for corporations with more than 100 employees.[25] Its preamble outlined grandiose ambitions:

> The efforts made more than twenty years ago at the Liberation of France have permitted a considerable improvement in the living conditions of workers: the establishment of Social Security and of the child-benefit system, the steady increase in wages, laws in favor of employment have enabled them to access higher standards of living and to benefit from greater security.
>
> However, it appears now that a new step must be taken: workers must participate in the growth of corporations and they must be directly involved in the sharing of their profits; this is all the more important that the Fifth National Plan made economic growth subject to an increase in investments resulting from corporate self-financing. Under these conditions, progress, to which all

contribute, must be for all a source of enrichment, which means that all must share in the resulting increase in capital.[26]

There was a degree of paradox in the highly technocratic wording of a text meant to encourage workers' participation. The preamble ended with a paragraph designed to assuage the concerns of French business:

> The new right that is hereby extended to employees, far from jeopardizing economic progress, will allow the development of personal savings along with that of corporate investments: to this effect, it is provided that (i) the sums distributed to employees will not, except under exceptional circumstances, be made available to them prior to the expiration of a 5-year period, (ii) they will have to be allocated to the development of investments within the companies or at national level, and (iii) companies themselves will benefit from important tax measures designed to increase their capacity to develop.[27]

According to the testimony of Bernard Ducamin, a technical adviser who was working at the Élysée at the time, it had been de Gaulle's personal decision to include an ordonnance on la Participation in the reform plan made possible by the Enabling Act of June 22, 1967.[28] Debré had signed it in his capacity as minister for the economy and finances, but he and Pompidou were highly skeptical about its benefits. According to Haberer, la Participation had nothing to do with the establishment of the COB.[29] However, it was likely to result in a significant increase in the number of small shareholders; lacking in experience, this new breed of investors would be in need of protection. In the fluctuating political environment of 1968–1969, Chatenet and Burgard saw in it an opportunity to advance the interests of the COB and, possibly, to protect it against more powerful institutions.

The Chatenet papers at Sciences Po include a three-page memorandum on la Participation.[30] It is dated June 1968. A copy of this memorandum can be found in the Burgard papers, with an attached cover note stating: "Delivered to Mr. Tricot on June 27, 1968."[31] At the time, Tricot was the general secretary of the Élysée, a position he held since 1967. The memorandum had been written either by Chatenet alone or by Chatenet and Burgard together. It is impossible to assert with certainty whether they had been responding to a request from the presidency or whether they had volunteered their contribution to the Participation reform. Whatever the scenario might have been, the memorandum outlined the role that the COB might play in the reform.

According to the author(s) of the memorandum, informing employees about the operations of the company they worked with would not modify the chain of command, nor would it endanger its organization. While employees and their union representatives were reluctant to share management responsibilities with their employer, they were also frustrated by their insufficient knowledge of the overall situation of the company. The general increase in the standards of living had made it possible to satisfy the material needs of workers, but "a desire for dignity leads [them] to expand their demands beyond the satisfaction of strictly financial or material needs." For them, it was indeed a matter of dignity "to know what [they were] doing, to understand why [they were] doing it, and to better realize the extent to which [their] work was part and parcel of the overall operations of the company." The 1945 ordonnance establishing *comités d'entreprise* (works councils) had not improved this situation, partially because council members were not sharing information with the rest of the employees.

The memorandum proposed to institute "an obligation to disclose clear, understandable and controllable information to employees." Implementing this obligation should not be controversial and would change nothing to "the legal framework of the company." Chatenet went on to remind his reader that the ordonnance establishing the COB had opportunely instructed publicly traded companies to disclose information to their shareholders. He suggested to extend the right to be informed to all employees: "As far as information is concerned, shareholders and workers would be treated equally." While the scope of the 1967 ordonnance was limited to publicly traded companies, they were the largest and employed "a considerable quantity of workers." The memorandum ended with an offer in due form: "The COB, which would have completed the definition of norms applicable to large corporations, would undoubtedly cooperate usefully to the definition, by the relevant authorities, of minimal, yet particularly meaningful information requirements about the situation and the management of other corporations."[32]

The Burgard papers include another, shorter memorandum dated "July 1968." The cover note indicates that it was delivered to Tricot on July 5. It reiterated the argument that there existed a strong desire for information among workers, specifically about "structural projects," which might translate into mergers or targeted productivity measures.[33] The July memorandum also suggested to "objectify" the participation mechanism: to distribute macroeconomic profits more equally among the largest possible number of workers, collective investment funds should be developed.

Whatever ambitions Chatenet and Burgard might have harbored during the summer of 1968, they were soon to be disappointed. The reforms outlined by de Gaulle in his May 24 televised address involved the decentralization of France's highly centralized political institutions along with the reform of higher education and the participation of workers in profit sharing and in corporate decision making. The government headed by Couve de Murville was responsible for implementing the plan. Rescheduled several times, the referendum finally took place on April 27, 1969. It bore little resemblance to the original project—along the way, the reform of French universities had been taken care of by the November 1968 *loi Faure*, named after Education Minister Edgar Faure, and the texts institutionalizing la Participation had been postponed.[34] The scope of the referendum was narrowly institutional; the question submitted to French voters did not even mention higher education or the economy: "Do you approve the bill submitted to the French people by the President of the Republic regarding the creation of regions and the renovation of the Senate?"[35]

Opposition parties from the left campaigned for the no, while former Gaullist ally Giscard d'Estaing indicated that he would not vote yes. De Gaulle let it be known that he would resign if he did not receive sufficient popular support. In January, while visiting Rome, Pompidou had declared that he would be available for the presidency. This announcement, uncoordinated with the *Élysée*, had contributed to a further deterioration of his relationship with de Gaulle, but it had also reassured the UDR base, always fearful of a power vacuum. Eventually, de Gaulle's proposed reform was rejected by a majority of the French people. The following day, he announced his resignation: "I cease to exercise my functions as president of the Republic. This decision will take effect today at noon." The general retired in Colombey-les-Deux-Églises, where he died in November 1970.

In June 1969, Pompidou easily won the presidential election. The *New York Times* pondered the new orientation he might give to French foreign policy: "[Pompidou] has pledged, more significantly, to give priority treatment to housekeeping problems—such as the defense of the value of the franc—over prestige and grandeur. Gaullism without de Gaulle, after all, may be different."[36]

Jacques Chaban-Delmas, the former president of the National Assembly and the unofficial leader of the left wing of the Gaullist party, became prime minister. In the new cabinet, Debré was appointed minister of defense, a job he was to keep until April 1973 and which was to be his last governmental posting. A triumphant Giscard d'Estaing replaced the more technocratic Ortoli in the Rue de Rivoli. While Chaban-Delmas was trying to promote his progressive "new society" agenda, Giscard d'Estaing's main task was to revitalize the ailing French economy, badly shaken by the May 68 events. With support from Pompidou, he implemented another stabilization program and devaluated the French franc—a decision that de Gaulle, during his last months at the Élysée, had adamantly opposed. Débré's reforms of 1966–1967, however, were not called into question.

In July 1972, Chaban-Delmas was dismissed by Pompidou, who had grown increasingly uneasy with his "new society" initiatives—it probably did not help that the prime minister's image as a dynamic social reformer had been damaged by a series of financial scandals involving members of his entourage. Pompidou's selection of Pierre Messmer, the seasoned minister of Overseas Departments and Territories and a diehard Gaullist, to replace him in the Hôtel de Matignon was evidence of the increasingly conservative orientation of his presidency.

In later years, other laws amplified the ordonnances of 1959 and 1967; la Participation, however, never became the instrument envisioned by de Gaulle to democratize the capitalist system. In an article published in 1987, Tricot, whose role had been central during the last years of de Gaulle's presidency, regretted that the president's grand idea had produced so few results. Yet the man who chaired the COB at the beginning of the 1980s noted with some satisfaction:

> Regarding participation to administrative action, which is so necessary to inspire the consent of the various segments of the population affected by decisions made and implemented by the [French] government and its services, I do not see anything significant, with the exception of what applied to universities. Almost nothing. Nevertheless it is in 1967 that was established the first among these autonomous administrative bodies which, breaking with our Napoleonic traditions and inspired by American agencies, do not only have their own powers and a more or less complete freedom of action, but also gather, in their steering board, representatives of the professions involved, along with magistrates, high-ranking civil servants and, sometimes, lawmakers.[37]

Here and there in the documents published by the COB references to la Participation continued to appear, but Chatenet used other means to build the credibility of the institution he was in charge of developing (see chapter 8). Yet he never lost sight of the political dimension of the COB's role. The Chatenet papers at Sciences Po include a four-page article, dated January 1970, on "the securities market as an instrument of the evolution of capitalism."[38] In it and in other documents of a similar nature, the chairman of the COB developed his vision of the future of capitalism in France. Interestingly, the document abounds with references to the American securities market—a perspective very different from that of Loichot in his book on the pancapitalist reform.

In the United States, Chatenet observed, the number of shareholders had been multiplied by four over the preceding fifteen years.[39] The new shareholders came from middle-class wage earners. While a similar trend could be observed in Japan and, to a lesser extent, in Great Britain and Germany, it was just starting in France. Chatenet blamed the attachment to secrecy, the taste for bearer securities, the ignorance of corporate leaders, and the indifference of bankers. He believed, however, that the number of French shareholders should increase significantly, for economic and political reasons: "The economic necessity to remedy that situation, particularly with respect to private investments, has been emphasized so frequently that it is not necessary to insist upon it. But the political necessity, less frequently noted and understood, is of utmost importance."[40]

Chatenet thought that the two ideologies inherited from the nineteenth century, capitalism and socialism, were both being challenged by new economic and technological realities. Even "in the East," he observed, economists Evsei Liberman and Ota Sik were experimenting in the fields of market flexibility and profitability. The capitalist system was weakened by the widespread belief that it was less fair than the socialist system. Chatenet ventured that this might actually be an advantage: "Today, in this traumatic confrontation [between the two systems], the first advantage of the grandsons of Rockefeller over the grandsons of Karl Marx is that they are less stuck in dogma."[41]

Chatenet noted that Marx's prediction about the inevitable concentration of economic power in the hands of a few capitalists had been contradicted by the scattering of capital among the crowd of small investors. This resulted in an ever-stronger interdependence between the industry of the nation and an increasing portion of its population. Chatenet's idea of society associated stock ownership with economic growth, political freedom and regulation; it echoed the ideals of shareholder democracy enshrined and protected by the New Deal in the Securities and Exchange Act of 1934.[42]

Americans had long understood that investors had to be aggressively sought after. They used all the tools of marketing to sell securities. Chatenet had been impressed by the efficiency of the sales networks of brokers and mutual funds:

> The building of the Stock Exchange is here to keep a record of all these trading transactions, but it is not the place where the all-important task of spreading

security ownership among ordinary people is actually being conducted. Yet, from this standpoint, the French situation is very similar. Obviously, it is not in the *Rue du Quatre-Septembre* that equity ownership will become more popular. All over France, people must be sought after in their homes, and this can only be done by sales networks which would be specialized, and yet at the same time would take inspiration from standard marketing and advertising techniques.[43]

Chatenet believed that banks were the only players in a position to fulfill that role; they had to be persuaded to do it. This marketing effort had to be supported by a public relations campaign designed to improve investor education:

> A true psychological strategy is implemented so that, in the minds of investors, the idea of their solidarity with the company of which they are shareholders might take hold. Some of the actions [conducted in the United States] seem to us to be almost childish, but we are wrong, because they have produced astonishing results, particularly as concerns new shareholders belonging to the humblest classes of the population. In France, everything, or almost everything, remains to be done in that area. But what is absolutely certain is that, if one wishes to speak to the new shareholders, one cannot count on mysterious and distinguished boards of directors, or on ministerial officers who have a nineteenth century outlook on newly acquired wealth.[44]

Failing to seize the historical opportunity to spread equity ownership among the French population would be, according to Chatenet, a terrible political mistake.

CHAPTER EIGHT

In Search of Legitimacy

The district surrounding the stock exchange was known in Paris as the *quartier de la Bourse*, or *quartier Vivienne*, after the name of the street leading from the gardens of the Palais Royal to the Palais Brongniart, along the Bibliothèque nationale. Agents de change, *coulissiers*, and intermediaries of all kinds packed restaurants and haunted the picturesque shopping arcades, giving the quartier its distinct animation. In neighboring first arrondissement, the Banque de France was headquartered in the elegant Hôtel de Toulouse, once the Parisian home of a legitimated son of Louis XIV; it also occupied a number of other, less haughty, buildings, all located within walking distance of the Palais Brongniart.

One of Chatenet's priorities was to find adequate premises for the Commission des Opérations de Bourse (COB). This was to prove more difficult than he had originally anticipated. The Banque de France let it be known that the newly created commission would not be welcome in any of the many buildings it possessed in the quartier de la Bourse. In a letter dated November 19, 1967, Chatenet tersely informed Debré of this apparent lack of goodwill.[1] He also told him that he would reject the offer extended by the Chambre syndicale des agents de change to house the collège and its services—for obvious reasons, being the tenant of professionals he was supposed to supervise would not bode well for the COB's future reputation of independence.

Chatenet told Haberer at a very early date: "I am not going to settle down in the *quartier de la Bourse*, because then beggars and plaintiffs will crowd the hallways [of the COB] from day one. This is why I want to be situated in another Paris district, in order to show very clearly that I am a surveillance authority, and that I am not 'within the market.'"[2]

Whether Chatenet contemplated this symbolic move from the start or fell back on it for lack of better options, he made the decision to distance the COB from the Rue Vivienne.[3] He chose La Défense, the business district still under construction on the outskirts of Paris. In agreement with the Direction du Budget, he reviewed several acquisition and lease options. Finally, the COB settled down in the just-completed Tour Nobel; it later moved to the Tour Mirabeau. The opening of the COB's offices in La Défense paralleled the American situation where the Securities and Exchange Commission (SEC) had its headquarters in Washington, DC, and not in the immediate vicinity of Wall Street.[4] La Défense also had another advantage: it was a few kilometers away from the Rue de Rivoli—another sign of the COB's independence.

With its large central plaza, high-rise glass façades, and daring aesthetics, La Défense projected an image of transparency and modernity; its skyline bore a greater resemblance to that of Midtown Manhattan than to the refined and slightly haphazard urbanism of the old quartier de la Bourse. Ten years later, the *New York Times* marveled at "this Manhattanized section of Paris":

> Although there are other high-rise clusters in other outlying areas, a visit to La Défense reveals more than the famous disruption of a sacred skyline; this is a concentration of skyscrapers that dwarfs comparable new construction in American cities. Think of Pittsburgh's entire downtown, the rebuilt Golden Triangle, for comparable size. The difference here is that what would be the central business district anywhere else is pushed beyond the city's historic heart. [. . .]
>
> This is the outrageous and provocative creation in Paris of a new style of urban environment that has only been suggested, or threatened, elsewhere. La Défense is the Houston of Paris.[5]

The COB's installation in La Défense materialized, symbolically, the American inspiration that had presided over its creation. At a respectable distance from the historical nexus of power and money, the commission would also enjoy greater breathing space. Independence was indeed Chatenet's obsession during the start-up phase. In his November 19 letter to Debré, he made it the principal objective of the COB:

> [. . .] after two months spent assessing the task at hand, it seems obvious to me that the Commission will have a really meaningful role only if, beyond the implementation of legal and regulatory rules (*dispositions législatives et réglementaires*), *it acquires a true independence* [. . .]. Obviously, this independence will depend first and foremost upon what [the COB] will accomplish, but also upon the role the COB will be given and the respect it will command, as well as the development of a worthy and trusting relationship between its own leadership and those individuals, businessmen or government officials, who are in charge of our Economy.[6]

The "respect" that Chatenet deemed so important for his commission started with the consideration he enjoyed in government and business circles. In a country where former members of the government are addressed as *Monsieur le Ministre*—and this was the case in the letters sent to Chatenet when he was chairing the COB—it did not hurt that the chairman could claim this most exalted rank.

As per article 2 of the ordonnance, the commission comprised the chairman and the other members of the collège. The collège met forty-four times in 1968 and in 1969. The pace of the meetings slowed down in later years: forty in 1970, twenty-seven in 1971, and twenty-five in 1972. Subsequent articles dealing with the COB's powers and responsibilities referred to "members and agents of the Commission" or simply "the Commission." From inception, the name "Commission" applied to the collège and the services under its authority. When Chatenet met Haberer for the first time on October 3, 1967, he immediately raised the question of the legal status of the COB. A seasoned lawyer from the Conseil d'État, Chatenet envisioned two options. He recommended that they be followed sequentially. The first option was to set up an *établissement public* (public institution), governed by the rules of the French Civil Service (*statut de la fonction publique*), and under strict budgetary control from the Direction du Budget. In the long run, however, Chatenet preferred that the COB benefit from "the flexible status of an independent entity, with its own resources, which could be a dedicated portion of existing tax revenues (the tax on trading operations, for example)."[7] He believed that this would allow him more flexibility in the hiring of skilled financial analysts—what was apparently left unsaid during the conversation was the fact that the SEC did indeed collect taxes on transactions.

What Chatenet had in mind when he spoke to Haberer of "the flexible status of an independent entity" is not entirely clear. Because he had not taken part in the drafting of the ordonnance, he did not have the opportunity to insert language to that effect in the document. In his conversation with Haberer, he did explicitly advocate the allocation of specific tax revenues to the COB, but this was not necessarily incompatible with the rules applicable to *établissements publics*. While the COB later became a full-fledged autorité administrative indépendante (independent administrative authority), such a legal entity did not exist then. Only in 1978 was the Commission Nationale de l'Informatique et des Libertés (CNIL, National Commission on Information Technology and Liberty) explicitly referred to as an autorité administrative indépendante in the law that created it.[8] Chatenet might have been inspired by his recent experience as chairman of the European Atomic Energy Commission (EAEC) in Brussels, but the international organization in charge of nuclear development at a European level operated in a totally different environment—besides, because its members were representatives of their respective national governments, the EAEC could not be considered "independent." A sentence from a eulogy written by Burgard after Chatenet's death sheds an indirect light, if not on the intentions, at least on the context of Chatenet's musings: "This was a time when Government relied on the so-called *administrations de mission* [ad hoc, mission-specific administrative entities] to revitalize its policies."[9] Such administrations de mission had been responsible for some of the most successful achievements of the postwar decades in France: urban planning, developing seaside tourist areas, building transportation infrastructures, and so on. In a 1956 article in the prestigious *Revue française de science politique*, administrator and future member of the French government Edgard Pisani theorized the distinction between administrations de mission and administrations de gestion (management administrative entities)—interestingly, the article mentioned the Tennessee Valley Authority as an example to be followed.[10] While administrations de mission were designed to escape the debilitating routine of day-to-day management, they were a tool of government and were not supposed to be independent from it. Moreover, they remained in existence only for the time needed to complete their mission, whereas the COB was meant to be permanent.

Chatenet's attempt at administrative creativity was soon to be disappointed. The day following his meeting with him, Haberer met with Larre, other representatives of the Ministry for the Economy and Finance, and representatives of the Banque de France.[11] The participants to the meeting expressed their concern that the COB might be sued for negligence. They recommended that the decree implementing the ordonnance provide for integral payment, by the French government, of all expenses, irrespective of their nature, incurred by the COB—this arrangement gave additional legitimacy to Larre's repeated insistence on the presence of a government commissioner on the collège: since the French government might be deemed liable for decisions made by the COB, it made sense to keep a watchful eye on them.

Chatenet was determined to have the independence of the COB recognized in the decree. Debré, of course, was duly informed of his efforts. The chairman was not entirely successful: the "flexible status" he had envisioned in his conversation with Haberer was dismissed in favor of a more traditional one—in a memorandum to Debré, Chatenet blamed the "power of habit" prevailing in the French Civil Service.[12] Article 1 of decree 68-23, dated January 3, 1968, stated that the COB would be a "specialized institution of public character, the operating expenses of which are covered by the French government."[13] The decree added that the COB would have to abide by the accounting procedures applicable to French établissements publics; it did not mention any specific revenues that might be allocated to the COB—it would take years for the COB to be granted its own resources.[14]

Chatenet's fight for independence was an uphill battle: neither Larre, the directeur du Trésor, nor Brunet, the governor of the Banque de France, were warm supporters of the COB. The Banque de France, while "perfectly courteous" according to Chatenet, remained noncommittal. Brunet might have felt dispossessed of a portion of his authority. In a formal letter dated December 28, 1967, Debré thanked the governor for opening the archives of the Comité des Bourses de Valeurs and for having "contemplated sending some of his employees on temporary assignment to the COB."[15] Referring to article 5 of the ordonnance about professional secrecy, he also asked him to instruct his staff to cooperate with COB employees. One month later, Chatenet followed up in a letter to Brunet requesting that Burgard's access to Banque de France records be made easier.[16] Brunet annotated Chatenet's letter: "These projects must be brought down to their proper size . . . We can answer questions and follow up on requests for information. But it is out of the question to put our teams and our documentation at the disposal of Burgard & C°." Nevertheless, the General Secretary of the Banque de France eventually issued a memorandum outlining the procedure applicable to the treatment of requests for information emanating from COB employees[17]—in the end, Debré's diplomatic pressure worked wonders!

Even stronger hostility was to be expected from the agents de change. After it was announced that a commission would be established to supervise the Bourse, they expressed their displeasure: according to them, the reform would have a negative impact on trading volumes and revenues. While they were not ignorant of the need to improve their image in the eyes of public opinion, they intended to do it on their own terms. As far back as 1962, the chambre syndicale had felt compelled to launch a public relations program that included the participation of radio and television shows, the opening of a visitors' gallery in the Palais Brongniart, the publication of a dedicated magazine (*L'Année boursière*), and the periodic release of market statistics. The chambre's general secretary admitted that "the program was designed in order to convince the Comité des Bourses of the compagnie's willingness to innovate, at a time when the comité was getting ready to interfere in an area that was not normally falling under its authority."[18] Interfering with the chambre's prerogatives was precisely what the COB would be doing in the near future.

The syndic of the Compagnie nationale des agents de change was the of-ficial spokesman of the profession. At his request, he met with Debré to voice his colleagues' concerns. Later, Haberer fondly remembered the minister's colorful account of their conversation. The reform, the syndic had said, would undermine the foundations of the market and would inevitably lead to a resounding crash. Having listened patiently, Debré lavished appeasing words on his visitor and escorted him politely out of his office.[19] It probably did not hurt that Yves Meunier, the newly elected syndic, was de Gaulle's guest for lunch at the Élysée Palace in October 1967: the president, who could be charming if he wanted to, expressed his interest in the development of the stock market.[20]

For most of his tenure, Meunier's predecessor, the rather shallow Bottmer, had been eclipsed by the much more forceful Daniel Petit, general secretary of the Compagnie nationale des agents de change since 1960. Petit was the driving force of the compagnie—he had played a decisive role in the merger of the provincial and Parisian organizations.[21] Fortunately, he enjoyed a pleas-ant working relationship with Haberer, who had prepared for the ÉNA under his guidance at Sciences Po—besides, both men were of Alsatian descent.[22] Being the employee of the agents de change, Petit was careful to remain in the background, but informal, ongoing discussions were taking place between Haberer and his former professor.[23]

The agents de change, however, were not the only stakeholders of the re-form. After the decree appointing him to the chairmanship of the COB was published in the *Journal Officiel*, Chatenet met with bankers and corporate leaders. From his time at the helm of the EAEC, he knew many of them, which permitted, in his own words, "a rather great freedom of speech and, carefully avoiding the risk of being too naïve, an enlightening frankness."[24] As befitted fellow members of the French elite, their conversations were very civilized:

> The reactions to the initiative taken by the French government in the *Ordonan-nce* dated September 28, 1967, can be considered generally favorable, sincerely by some, at least verbally by others. Frontal hostility is very rare, which means, at the very least, that it is felt that this attitude would not be approved of. Con-versely, unconditional support, equally rare, only comes from circles which do not have much to do with the [market]. Reactions from the largest group of individuals affected [by the ordonnance] range from a majority expressing their sympathy, with a touch of skepticism in some cases, to a minority showing their concern, with a touch of interest in many cases.[25]

Leaders of large corporations were the most openly favorable, even though they would ultimately have to comply with additional information requirements. They knew that they would benefit from the modernization of the Paris market, as it would facilitate access to domestic and foreign capital. Yet they were also very realistic: the failure of the COB, while regrettable, would not really harm them. Theirs was a wait-and-see attitude. Nationalized and privately owned banks offered to help. They had an increasingly dominant role in the securities market, and they probably felt less threatened by the introduction of a securities regulator than did the increasingly challenged agents de change.[26]

All proclaimed their agreement with the COB's mission to improve investor information. Some hinted that it might be preferable if the new institution concentrated on writing a set of ethics rules, rather than on the actual performance of "routine" controls. Finally, the desire to eradicate insider trading attracted widespread skepticism, "amused at times," from the chairman's interlocutors.

Chatenet was under no illusions. He knew that the COB would have to prove itself: "The consensus is that the *Ordonnance* might very well turn into something real—or into nothing at all. Nothing if it results into [the creation of] one more bureaucratic department, another source of red tape and procedures. But there might be a chance that the *Ordonnance* will give birth to something real: if a body of decisions rendered by the Commission takes shape, and progressively wins the acceptance—respectful, disciplined, or simply resigned—of those who are concerned."[27]

Aside from the turmoil of the May events, 1968 turned out to be a difficult year. The COB was immersed in a flow of mundane tasks: visas were submitted to the collège by inexperienced employees who had to work under very tight deadlines.[28] Issuing visas constituted the bulk of the new institution's activity, but other tasks had to be performed as well, such as the review and approval of new listings, and the drafting of guidelines designed to improve the presentation of financial statements. A man of duty, the chairman himself endeavored to read all the annual reports published by the approximately 880 companies listed on the Paris Bourse.[29]

On December 31, 1968, a stinging article by René Tendron, entitled "Commission des Opérations de Bourse: A Heavy and Constraining Formalism," made the headlines of *Les Échos*, which could reliably be counted on to give voice to the concerns of French corporate leaders:[30] "Since its creation one year ago, the COB has attracted criticism, particularly from corporate leaders, who find its interventions too heavy and too constraining. Besides, to be really efficient, the COB should be able to escape the excessively narrow legal framework within which it is tightly bound. The COB, therefore, must be reformed."[31]

In October 1968, the COB presented a template for the prospectus to be issued as part of a capital increase in cash. According to Tendron, the instructions were twenty-five pages long; complying with them would be expensive and would add to unnecessary administrative hassle. He also warned that several weeks would be needed to complete the documents; the number of copies to be printed would represent "tons of paper." To make things worse, the COB demanded that confidential information be disclosed: "information about the suppliers and the customers of the company, as well as the organization of its commercial network, its research and development policy, and its projected investments."

The decree dated October 3, 1968, was meant to implement article 8 of the ordonnance, pursuant to which senior managers of a publicly traded company holding shares of the company would have to hold them in registered form.[32] The decree stated that they would have to notify the COB, within six days, of transactions on those shares. Tendron assured his readers that several managers had already sold their shares. Neither the ordonnance nor the decree gave a precise definition of who the "insiders" were: "The chairman of the board, of course [. . .], but also his driver, his friend, his banker, his broker, the usher, the chief accountant, the chief engineer, etc.—aren't they all insiders?" According to the journalist, Chatenet's intention was to delegate to CEOs the responsibility to establish a list of insiders within and outside their corporations. "If managers submitted to such procedures, it would be very close to informing on their employees. It is perfectly understandable that they should be reluctant to do that." Judging from Tendron's article, the French business community was loath to discard its traditions of secrecy.

The journalist's conclusion was more balanced than his merciless indictment of the COB. He acknowledged that the newly created commission did not have adequate resources: "The Stock Exchange and its participants cannot be recorded in a catalogue. It is not unlike the traffic code: it is possible to establish an ex-ante list of all possible violations, not of all violators. The COB must be able to conduct ex-post interventions. Just like the American Securities and Exchange Commission, it should have the power to investigate and punish [. . .], instead of being compelled to step in only as a preventive measure."[33]

Chatenet, who was sensitive to the reactions of public opinion, did not spare his efforts to improve the image of the commission.[34] In February 1969, the COB opened an Information and Documentation Center. Accessible to the general public on weekdays in the afternoon, it received many visits and phone calls. The annual report was circulated largely among French and foreign corporations, the press, and individual investors who requested it. An *Information Bulletin* was also issued on an almost monthly basis—in 1969, 3,000 copies were printed and circulated. The *Bulletin* included information on COB decisions regarding specific securities, along with paragraphs dealing with more general issues.[35]

While remaining faithful to his personal ethos of discretion and self-restraint, Chatenet had frequent meetings with French and foreign journalists. The media often referred to the COB as *le gendarme de la Bourse* (the Exchange cop).[36] On numerous occasions, a slightly exasperated Chatenet said that he disliked the phrase.[37] During a public lecture at the end of 1969, he explained at length the role of the COB and compared it instead to that of a *régisseur* (stage manager) in a theater—the theater, in this particular instance, being the Bourse.[38] He would also occasionally regret that the official name given to the COB did not reflect its actual activities. Because the COB's primary mission was to develop the securities market, he would have preferred a different name: Commission des valeurs mobilières, which he believed to be a more accurate translation of "Securities and Exchange Commission" into French.[39]

Always eager to compare the COB with the SEC, Chatenet was also careful to point to a major difference between the two institutions. In the same lecture, he emphasized that the COB had not been given judicial authority over market professionals and proclaimed that his main preoccupation was to stimulate the growth of the market, not to control its operations or punish crimes and offenses. In the first annual report of the COB, dated April 7, 1969, he articulated his philosophy:

> A rapid enumeration of the COB's powers reveals its original character. Indeed, it is in charge of supervising the behaviors [of market participants], while at the same time making general or specific decisions, and proposing [new] laws or regulations that would be more appropriate. In order to successfully fulfill these missions, it must rely on the support of [market] professionals. From the standpoint of the commission, it is less about punishing and governing than orienting attitudes, since it is well-known that new ways of doing things cannot be generalized without the active consent of a majority of those involved.[40]

Chatenet also had misgivings about the concept of "moralization," a word that rarely appears in his correspondence or in official documents published during his chairmanship. On February 21, 1969, he was the guest of journalist Georges Leroy on his radio show *Europe Soir* on Europe 1. Asked by Leroy to present the COB, he once again commented on the name of the institution: "The principal purpose of this institution is to develop and improve the securities market, and that is the reason why its name is slightly misleading: *Commission des opérations de bourse*. It might have been preferable to give it a name similar to that of the American entity which looks very much like it and which is, in many ways, its equivalent: Securities and Exchange Commission. Indeed, the objective is to improve investor information in order to attract the maximum number of people, and on that front, there is a lot to do."[41]

This opening was followed by a dialogue reminiscent of Pompidou's remarks after the Ugine-Kuhlmann scandal:

> Leroy—There is a phrase that you have not used and which is sometimes heard about your commission, and that is "the moralization of the *Bourse.*" It is often said that the COB is here, somehow, to moralize the *Bourse*. First of all, do you endorse that word, and then, do you think that the *Bourse* needs to be moralized?
>
> Chatenet—I do not particularly endorse that word because, undoubtedly, this institution was created in order to develop the market. It is with this objective in mind that it will be seen whether what we are doing is useful or not. What is at stake is an effort to build a French securities market on the same scale as our economy, which is not the case now. [. . .] To develop the market, it is certain that it must operate in a certain way, an honest way. As a consequence, insofar as there might be objectionable, criminal acts, they must be punished. If this is what you mean by moralizing, I agree but I find the word a bit naïve, and this is definitely not the reason why the Commission was created.[42]

Chatenet was not one to be content with a vague, symbolic mission. Not only was he determined to make full use of all the powers enunciated in the ordonnance, he wanted to clarify their definition and, if possible, extend them. At the beginning of his chairmanship, however, the French government seemed reluctant to follow up on his requests. In a June 1970 letter to journalist Michel Drancourt, then the editor-in-chief of *Entreprise*, he complained about the French government's apparent neglect of the COB:

> When creating a new institution, it is perfectly normal, for the government and for lawmakers, to be rather unsure about the resources this institution should

be given in order to accomplish its mission. Yet it is less logical to appear to lose any interest in it afterwards, and, having asked its founders, its chairman in particular, to conduct an initial experimentation, to fail to draw conclusions from this experimentation. If we set aside a number of very specific issues (certified public accountants, profit-sharing programs for example), the Commission has two major missions: shareholder information and market surveillance. Unfortunately, the name of my Commission, which I have not chosen, refers exclusively to the second mission, which is very misleading [. . .].[43]

While Chatenet congratulated himself on the significant improvement already achieved in the area of investor information, he resented the fact that this was not the case of the surveillance of trading transactions. Referring to the ordonnance, he pointed to the very specific wording of articles 3 to 7, all dealing with investor information, which contrasted with the very vague, cursory mention of the mission "to watch over the proper functioning of the stock exchanges."

Chatenet refreshed Drancourt's memory about the long history of the Paris market. Since Napoléon, market surveillance had been entrusted to a body of "ministerial officers," the agents de change, under the tutelage of the Ministry of Finances. What had been the intentions of the writers of the ordonnance, Chatenet asked, when they established an institution independent from the ministry and endowed it with the mission "to watch over the proper functioning of the stock exchanges"? This, according to him, was the "biggest ambiguity of [the COBs] constituting document"—he added that he had mentioned it in his annual report to the president of the Republic. The situation was all the more problematic as many had come to believe that the COB had the authority and corresponding powers to "prevent what is contrary to the proper functioning and the good reputation of the Stock Exchange from happening, and to punish it." Compared with the Commission de contrôle des Banques, the resources of the COB were dismal. The Ministry of Finances had agreed in principle to remedy that situation, but Chatenet remained skeptical. Confidentially, he told Drancourt that he would soon alert the French government.[44]

To assert the independence of the COB, Chatenet made use of all the tools at his disposal. One of them derived from article 4 of the ordonnance, which stated that each year, the COB would send a report to the president of the Republic and that this report would be published in the *Journal Officiel*.

The annual report of the COB, usually presented by the chairman in a press conference, proved a particularly efficient communication tool. Signed by Chatenet and the other four members of the collège, it bore the mark of both Chatenet and Burgard. Adorned with an increasing variety of charts and statistics, it grew in length over time: twenty-three pages for the 1968 report (published in March 1969), forty-six pages for the 1969 report, seventy pages for the 1970 report, eighty-eight pages for the 1971 report, and ninety-four pages for the 1972 report. Not surprisingly, it started with an executive summary (a mere introduction in 1968, a *sommaire* from 1969 to 1971). The report comprised an analysis of the international and domestic stock markets during the year under consideration and an overview of the activities of the COB: information on investors, accounting rules, surveillance of the Parisian and provincial bourses, and public relations. Along the way, some paragraphs dealt with specific technical issues. Beginning with the 1970 report, a nominative organization chart was included as part of the appendixes.

Written in a matter-of-fact style, without unnecessary flourishes, the reports reflected the increasing confidence of their authors, who did not hesitate to point at specific cases. They were peppered with references to the New York stock market, the SEC, and American securities regulation.

Each year, Chatenet and Burgard used the report to the president as an instrument to advocate an extension of the powers of the COB The last sentence of the first report set the tone: "The Commission believes, therefore, that with a modest improvement in the means at its disposal, legal powers in particular, it will be in a position, during the second year of its existence, to take significant steps in the fulfillment of the mission with which it has been endowed."[45]

The following year, the section on the surveillance of market operations indicated that "the Commission is still lacking the legal powers which would allow it to draw all the conclusions from the observations it has been able to make."[46] More specifically, it regretted that a number of market practices, while generally considered unsavory, were not punishable by law. This, the report indicated, was not the case in the United States, where the 1933 and 1934 acts, along with subsequent rule-making decisions rendered by the SEC, had clearly defined what was or was not legal.

Each year during his chairmanship, Chatenet did seek an audience with the president in order to formally present the commission's annual report. In 1969, de Gaulle did not pay much attention to its content and was more interested in discussing the overall political situation with a man whose opinion he held in high esteem.

From 1970 on, things were different: Pompidou's interest in financial and business matters was genuine and he read a synopsis of the report before the audience. In 1971, the meeting between Chatenet and Pompidou took place on March 26. The nine-page synopsis had been prepared by Jean Daney de Marcillac, an Élysée staff member in charge of economic and financial affairs. In the introduction, Marcillac was very appreciative of the report:

> I have only been able to take a cursory glance at the 250 pages of the several chapters and appendixes. I would simply like to express the very favorable impression it made on me: this report is very clear, and very well written, in a concise language, free of any kind of technical jargon. When necessary, the COB does not hesitate to call a spade a spade, and to say what it thinks of certain events which marked the stock market last year (for example, chapter VI, page 8 to 15: the SOCANTAR and BON MARCHÉ cases).[47]

The paragraph of the synopsis on employee participation in the benefits of company growth attracted the attention of the president, who gave the instruction, in a handwritten annotation, to "make a public relations effort about it."

In 1972, Marcillac renewed his praise of the report, "as well written, and as interesting, if much longer, than the previous one."[48] The presidential audience, which took place on March 23 at the Élysée, illustrated the interaction between Pompidou and Chatenet. In a confidential letter to Lestrade, a member of the collège of the COB, Chatenet gave a detailed account of their conversation.[49] Pompidou agreed with the arguments developed by Chatenet in the first chapter of the report—arguments that had "caused some difficulties with our government commissioner."[50] The president insisted on the necessity to prepare the Paris Bourse for competition from the City of London. He entered into the details of the British rules applicable to takeover bid transactions, which testified to his knowledge of technical intricacies. Finally, he congratulated the COB "for the place which it now holds in government, which certainly creates obligations for the members of its *collège*, but also for the French government."

Pompidou's concern about the city can be easily understood in the context of the upcoming accession of the United Kingdom to the Common Market. The time was gone when he and Debré were eagerly preparing the nation for the final opening of the European borders as a result of the Treaty of Rome. The preoccupation with British competition appeared repeatedly in the early 1970s. In the preface he wrote for Françoise Marnata's 1973 study of the Bourse, Chatenet noted a paradox: "Over the last few years, in countries which were both close geographically and of a similar industrial development, one could observe simultaneously, on one side of the Channel, a brilliant and attractive stock market [combined with] a badly hit economy, and on the French side, a gloomy and disconcerting Bourse [combined with] a nicely expanding and largely healthy economy."[51]

In February 1972, former Minister of Finances Wilfrid Baumgartner presented the conclusions of the committee he had chaired, upon the request of the Prime Minister, on "the financial market and shareholder information."[52] He insisted upon the necessity to draw inspiration from the London market: "Generally speaking, the Paris market should catch up, operationally, on large foreign markets, or at least should try to get closer, taking inspiration from the widely acknowledged qualities of the City of London, which will soon be part of the European Community."[53]

The text of his presentation was forwarded to Pompidou. In a two-page letter, the president told Baumgartner that he agreed with him, adding that the British entry into the European Community was "an opportunity to seize." Baumgartner had mentioned the creation of the COB, "taking inspiration from the methods of the American Securities and Exchanges [sic] Commission," and had reiterated the need to improve investor information and education. Pompidou, a late learner himself, concurred: "The mechanics of the financial market are no more complicated than many others, but an effort must be made to explain them. One can neither hope to increase the number of investors, nor to consolidate their investments, without having first made it clear to the general public, as well as to the students, what shares and bonds are, and how their holders contribute to the development of the nation."[54]

CHAPTER NINE

Mr. Chatenet Goes to Washington

The thirty-fifth annual report of the Securities and Exchange Commission (SEC) for fiscal year ending June 30, 1969, mentioned the existence of the Commission des operations de Bourse (COB) for the first time—albeit indirectly: "For the past 3 years the Commission had held one or two-week nationwide enforcement training sessions at its headquarters office in Washington, D.C. to which it has invited members of State and foreign securities commissions. The 1969 session was attended by government officials from France, Canada, Brazil, Puerto Rico and practically every State, as well as by staff members from each of the Commission's offices throughout the country."[1]

The report did not identify the French "government officials" who joined the training session in Washington, DC—they were likely to have been selected among the most promising employees of the newly created COB. Their attendance at this and later sessions was one of the results of Chatenet's meetings with his counterparts at the SEC: Manuel F. Cohen (1964–1969), Hamer H. Budge (1969–1971), and William J. Casey (1971–1973). In his administrative correspondence, Chatenet wrote that his relationship with Budge and Cohen had been "excellent";[2] the memorandums he circulated to members of the collège after his meeting with Casey do not indicate that it had been any different with their successor at the helm of the SEC. The Frenchman's command of the English language probably contributed to the quality of their exchanges.

At the end of 1967, as soon as his appointment was made official, Chatenet planned trips to Belgium and the United States "in order to study local experiments on site."[3] Archival records do not include any reports of visits to the United States for the last months of 1967 or 1968.[4] In a 1990 interview with historian Laure Quenouëlle-Corre, Chatenet mentioned a colorful meeting with Cohen in La Défense—apparently, Cohen had proudly declared that "he had sent to jail thirteen of them."[5]

At the end of 1969, Chatenet traveled to the United States. In Washington, DC, he and the French ambassador met with SEC chairman Budge, who told them that he spent a great deal of his time talking to Congress. Budge emphasized the necessity to cooperate with the judicial branch of government; he also told Chatenet that COB employees would be welcome at the SEC.

The chairman of the COB met with bankers, stockbrokers, managers of industrial corporations, journalists, and representatives of the New York Stock Exchange. The detailed visit report he wrote after he had come back was very informative;[6] it reflected his analytical approach of the securities market in the United States.

Chatenet was impressed by "the remarkable development (a four-fold increase at least) of the securities market, [caused] in particular by the incoming of shareholders from the lowest levels of the population." Over the preceding decades, wages had increased significantly, allowing "technicians and middle executives" to build their own investment portfolio. Chatenet the amateur sociologist acknowledged the role of mass advertising in this development—his attention had been attracted by the Merrill Lynch booth in the main concourse of Grand Central Station in Manhattan (the Merrill Lynch Investment Information Center).

Chatenet also commented on the press's role in the education of American investors. He had become acquainted with the American media during his time in New York in the late 1940s. In the many positions he had held during his varied career, he had continued to read British and American newspapers[7]—Burgard later confirmed that the chairman of the COB followed the London and New York markets in "the Anglo-Saxon press."[8] In his visit report, he quoted the *Wall Street Journal*, "the second largest daily, in terms of format and circulation, in the United States." The school system, too, was mobilized in this effort: "Economic education starts at school. All students from the schools in the New York area have been taken to the Stock Exchange at least once."

According to Chatenet, mutual funds had contributed to popularizing investment products. He thought the methods of American salesmen "very peculiar"—in other words, very different from the methods prevailing on the French market. He also noted that their compensation could exceed ten thousand dollars per month—a "considerable" amount of money for a Frenchman. Macroeconomic factors also played their part: the inflationary environment was less favorable to bonds; speculation in gold or real estate was inexistent. Finally, the stock market benefited from "a climate of trust created by the SEC, the interventions of which the general public is very much aware of." Understandably, the chairman of the COB made much of the beneficial effects of regulation. He went on to describe a kind of market utopia—very different from the French reality. Organized labor was not opposed, "as [was] often the case in France," to the development of share ownership; unions were "not insensitive to the notion of profit" and did not spread the idea that managers were "hiding profits" in order to avoid paying taxes. Bankers, corporate managers, journalists, regulators, all took part to "a large policy of disclosure": "the result of this is an environment in which the average American is really interested in his nation's industry." Interestingly, Chatenet used the English word *disclosure* in the French original (*large politique de disclosure*); he did not use the French word *transparence*, which would not have applied to accounting information then.

Chatenet was keen on sharing the information he gathered during his trips to America. Some of his observations, which would make their way into subsequent documents, such as the COB's annual reports, were not exempt from stereotypes or platitudes, as when he contrasted French and American attitudes with respect to taxes: "In the United States, when someone makes money, he hurries to let it be known, and everything is passed on to the newspapers because it shows that he is a clever man and, since he lives in an Anglo-Saxon country [*sic*], [it shows] that he is loved by God. In France, when someone makes money, he has only one thing in mind and that is to hide it—hide it from his wife, his employees, his tax collector."[9]

In addition to meeting with journalists from the financial press, Chatenet gave a number of high-profile lectures to selected audiences. One lecture attracted the attention of market professionals and the media. On December 10, 1970, the chairman of the COB was the guest of the Institut d'études bancaires et financières in Paris.[10] His lecture was entitled: "Dynamism and Control of the Securities Market in the United States, Great Britain and France." To an audience of bankers, journalists, and agents de change, he introduced himself as an outsider "looking at the French securities market with curiosity, interest, amusement sometimes, shock at other times—rarely I am bound to say—annoyance frequently, great alarm very often, an ever increasing alarm I must say."[11] This was the reason why he had felt compelled "to look at the outside," namely, at the American and British securities markets. While his presentation included a number of remarks about the British market, the gist of his argumentation relied on the observations collected during his trip to the United States. According to Chatenet, Americans considered that shares were commodities to be bought or sold on the marketplace; the creation of the SEC in 1934 had not changed the predominantly commercial nature of the securities market, where stockbrokers were free to compete. In France, the situation was different—Chatenet gently made fun of the innocent American stockbroker abroad, who would rely on his English-French dictionary to introduce himself as an agent de change. In the eyes of the French, who were excessively legally minded, shares were above all certificates of ownership of a portion of the equity of a company; agents de change were appointed officers endowed with public authority—a legacy of the Old Regime, along with other regulated professions. In exchange for its monopoly on all securities transactions, the Compagnie nationale des agents de change was subject to the authority of the Ministry of Finance. This authority had not been transferred to the COB, which was, therefore, much less powerful than the SEC.

Chatenet was never oblivious to the differences in the respective sizes of the French and the American markets. He had calculated that the total amount of securities outstanding in America was 6,000 billion French francs (85% shares, 15% bonds), whereas in France it did not exceed 110 billion French francs (45% shares, 55% bonds).

The much wider American securities market was also more "democratic": the number of shareholders had increased from 6 million in 1952 to 32 million in 1970, a pace that far exceeded population growth. Chatenet often confessed that, at the time he had been appointed chairman of the COB, nobody had been able to give him a precise estimate of the total number of French security holders. He thought that they were approximately 1.5 million. Chatenet believed that computers would soon revolutionize the organization of the securities market: "On that point, we are witnessing a very significant progress: the implementation of a new system which will be operational at the end of this year, and which may anticipate the securities market of the electronic age, a securities market without a trading floor."[12]

Chatenet was referring to the Nasdaq, of which he gave a detailed and rather accurate description for the benefit of his audience. Finally, he noticed that, even though the American market was freer and more modern, it had also been characterized, over the preceding thirty years, by resolute government intervention. The SEC, armed with a considerable budget, concentrated on its mission to protect investors—in the context of the "democratization" of the securities market, Chatenet emphasized the political nature of this mission.

The chairman of the COB asserted that no European market was immune to the long-term trends he described extensively. Compared to Wall Street, all of them were at an obvious disadvantage, but he feared that Paris would be much less reactive than London. According to him, the French were indifferent, hostile even, to the securities market; market professionals were too much attached to their centuries-old, and rather opaque, traditions. The very survival of the capitalist system, however, was at stake:

> In my conclusion, I would like to tell you, personally, as someone who is engaged in an effort that is, to some extent, political in its nature, that I see in this a double challenge: one for capitalism and one for France.
>
> A challenge for capitalism, as I have mentioned earlier. Being faced with the opposite system [socialism], what is at stake here is to win victory in the field of flexibility, of adaptability and, for lack of a better word [. . .], of democratization.
>
> For our country, and more specifically for the financial market of which the securities market is an important component, it seems to me that the challenge is to know how our organization, our system, our policy in this field, will survive the encounter with the double opening, social and European, offered to us, or imposed on us, by circumstances.[13]

Chatenet's lecture did not go unnoticed. A few days later, *Les Échos* reported that the chairman of the COB had criticized the traditional status of the agents de changes: "Mr. Chatenet has shown that the preoccupations of the *Commission des Opérations de Bourse* encompassed a much wider field than many had been led to believe after its two years of existence."[14]

In the summer of 1971, Chatenet decided that he would visit the United States one last time before the end of his chairmanship. He wrote to Marc Viénot, who had been the first government commissioner to sit on the collège of the COB and had recently been appointed conseiller financier at the French Embassy in Washington, DC. He wanted to gather further information about the beginnings of Nasdaq, to meet with William J. Casey, the new chairman of the SEC, and "to see the extent to which [he would] be able to institute, with the SEC, a system of reciprocity similar to that which already [existed] and [worked] very well between the COB and the Belgian Commission"[15]—the French-Belgian reciprocity agreement provided that a visa issued in either country would be valid in the other.[16] Such an agreement between the COB and the SEC would facilitate access of French companies to the American capital market. To illustrate his point, Chatenet mentioned a corporation that would remain linked with the COB for most of its history: "Undoubtedly, the Paris market is too narrow for French companies above a certain size; this problem will be raised in an obvious manner in the case of, for example, the merger between Pechiney and Ugine-Kuhlmann."[17] Initially scheduled in August, the trip finally took place in October. Chatenet prepared it carefully. In another letter to Viénot, he made a list of the individuals he wanted to meet in Washington, DC, and in New York, and shared with him, confidentially, what he called the "philosophy" of his trip:

> On the one hand, in the last report I will send to the President of the Republic, just before I leave office, I would like to insert a number of general observations about institutions, [observations] which echo personal opinions of mine, and of which I need to verify whether they are well- or ill-founded. [. . .] On the other hand, and on a more personal note, I have the intention to revisit and clarify the statements I made in a lecture I gave to the *Association Professionnelle des Banques* on December 10, 1970. At the time, this lecture had caused a stir; I let things calm down for a while, but I am determined to come back to my point.[18]

Chatenet spent eight days in New York (October 20–25 and 28–30) and two days in Washington, DC (October 26 and 27). In addition to Viénot and French ambassador Charles Lucet, he met an impressive list of people:

William J. Casey, chairman of the SEC;
William L. Cary, professor at Columbia University, former chairman of the SEC "during the Kennedy era";
William Mac Chesney Martin, former chairman of the N.Y.S.E., former chairman of the Board of Governors of the Federal Reserve, and author of a report on the securities market (August of 1971);
Gordon S. Macklin, chairman of the N.A.S.D.;
Mr. Cates, in charge of European affairs at the Treasury Department;
Mr. Turner, a senior executive "in charge of the N.A.S.D.A.Q. network";
Ralph Saul, former chairman of the American Stock Exchange, then chairman of First Boston Company, "an underwriter";
Felix Rohatyn, a member of the Big Board of the N.Y.S.E. and a managing partner of Lazard Brothers in New York.

Back in Paris, Chatenet sent a five-page confidential memorandum to the members of the collège of the COB, and to Haberer, who had succeeded Viénot as government commissioner.[19] At great length, he analyzed the crisis that had just struck the American securities industry. According to him, the number of security holders had remained stable over the preceding couple of years, and nobody seemed to be able to forecast how long the stagnation would continue. During the period 1950–1968, the steady increase in the number of investors "had given the impression that a market with limitless possibilities was emerging." A lot of new brokerage houses had been created, some of them undercapitalized and understaffed; among the older brokers, some had spent too much money on "very expensive, oversized telecommunication networks." After the crisis had started, 200 brokers had filed for bankruptcy; some of them had been taken over by their more robust competitors. The difficulties had been made worse by simmering conflicts between the National Association of Securities Dealers, the New York Stock Exchange, institutional investors, and the American Stock Exchange. Many of Chatenet's interlocutors told him that the market "had come very close to disaster, which would assuredly have dealt a serious blow to the enduring attachment of Americans to capitalism."

According to Chatenet, American federal authorities kept a watchful eye on the operations of the stock market. While the Treasury Department—in other words, the executive—was remarkably absent, the relevant committees of the House and the Senate followed Wall Street very closely—to the attention of his colleagues, presumably less versed in the subtleties of constitutional law, the former conseiller d'État added that "this [was] a consequence of the Constitution and of the way political life is organized in the United States." He ventured to predict that the SEC would emerge stronger from the crisis—an opinion shared by the individuals he met with. Some of them criticized the SEC for its passivity over the preceding three years, and for its narrow interpretation of "the powers, rather considerable in their vague formulation, which it received from Congress." Casey, though, was more nuanced: "His past and his political opinions do not make of him, a priori, an interventionist as Manuel F. Cohen, his predecessor, had been."

Chatenet, who considered Casey a politician and believed he owed his appointment to his friendship with Richard Nixon, also acknowledged his political skills in a delicate situation: "He understands perfectly well that the overall trend of the market, along with its increasingly centralized organization, leads inevitably to the development of the entity over which he presides, [a development] which probably exceeds what he personally wishes." The content of the report remained strictly professional; it did not allude to the one personal thing that the two men had in common, the memory of the Second World War: when Casey visited Paris in May 1972, he wrote that this was an opportunity to spend the weekend "at a reunion of his old Resistance friends in Paris"[20]—the chairman of the COB, however, was not one of them.

As indicated by Chatenet in the letter he had sent to Viénot in September, the 1971 annual report of the COB, published in March 1972, included some of the observations he had gathered in the United States, along with "personal opinions" he had already put forward in his lecture of December 1970. The section on "reform projects," in particular, drew extensively on foreign experiments, first and foremost American ones. The chairman also reiterated his criticism of the archaism of French securities distribution channels.[21]

Chatenet's attempts at developing a working relationship with American and other foreign regulators foreshadowed the rise of financial regulators as international actors—the "new diplomats," whose increasing role and visibility have not escaped notice by political scientists and legal scholars.[22] His visit reports read like diplomatic dispatches. Looking at them begs the question of how his American counterparts reacted to their meetings. The Casey papers at the Hoover Institution include a remarkably complete collection of documents pertaining to his chairmanship of the SEC. The examination of several boxes showed that the early 1970s were a time when American regulators were also taking an increasing interest in the international securities market.

Casey was the recipient of a number of memorandums from Allan S. Mostoff, associate director of the SEC's Division of Corporate Regulation. Mostoff proved a persistent advocate of international cooperation. On June 3, 1971, he updated the recently appointed chairman on the state of the relations between the SEC and foreign regulators: "The Commission has over the years provided a great deal of assistance to foreign regulatory authorities but always on an informal and very sporadic basis. Commission staff members have travelled to Germany, Korea, Japan and Brazil, Israel, Belgium and England, to provide limited assistance when requested. [. . .] In addition to such efforts, the Commission has many times played host to visiting officials of foreign regulatory agencies to explain to them the structure of our regulation and how the Commission functions."[23]

Interestingly, Mostoff did not mention France in the list of the countries visited by SEC staff, nor did he single out Chatenet among the "visiting officials." Meanwhile, a representative of the SEC had been participating to an Organisation for Economic Co-operation and Development expert group working on unregulated offshore funds. Mostoff pleaded for better coordination of these initiatives: "This would result in more effective employment of our limited resources and also more effective liaison with foreign regulatory bodies, an important by-product of which can be, I believe, cooperative enforcement work."[24]

Mostoff also regretted that the SEC had only limited knowledge of securities legislation passed in several foreign countries. He recommended that the SEC undertake a systematic evaluation of its international efforts in order to develop "sound and coordinated over-all programs."

Mostoff himself took an active part in several international meetings. In October 1971, he spoke at a seminar on offshore funds in Frankfurt, Germany. He confirmed that the United States would draft and sign treaties with a number of foreign governments to establish reciprocity in enforcement actions involving securities—he mentioned specifically "such improper practices as the use of foreign nominees for trading and selling of securities, or hiding the illegal gains of organized crime." The SEC representative assured his audience that this kind of inter-governmental enforcement cooperation would become increasingly necessary: "I think all of you have a vested interest in encouraging it to the extent that you can. It can only redound to your benefit: to establish the kind of sound regulatory atmosphere that I'm talking about will lead to investor confidence and investor expectations which will, in turn, stimulate the growth of your industry enormously. This has been demonstrated time and time again in the United States, where the rapid growth of the industry has followed the adoption of the regulatory statutes."[25]

Mostoff continued to lobby Casey on the topic of international cooperation. In another memorandum to his superior dated January 30, 1973, he offered a dim assessment of the SEC's approach of international matters—apparently, no significant progress had been made since he had first sounded the alarm almost two years earlier: "As you know, I have long felt that the Commission has not adequately considered the ramifications of the internationalization of (1) the securities markets, (2) investor preferences, (3) capital raising mechanisms and (4) the activity of the professionals and others regulated under our securities laws."[26]

To address "a number of very important policy questions [which] have arisen as a result of the foreign activities of US firms and the US activity of foreign firms," Mostoff recommended to the chairman that a staff task force be created. Among the matters with international ramifications, he mentioned "your own speech in Milan and your subsequent visits to the EEC and OECD, you informal contacts with foreign regulators." Casey had indeed taken part to two major international conferences (March and May 1972) in Europe.

In March, the first international meeting of stock exchanges took place in Milan, Italy. Casey delivered an address on the internationalization of the capital markets. He began his speech by observing that capital markets were becoming international and that domestic trading markets were "increasingly important to countries other than those in which they operate." Casey further noted the emergence of "an international public interest" in the international securities market—the meeting in Milan was indeed a manifestation of this interest. The internationalization process had had "its failures and its false starts"—Casey later referred to "the financial vicissitudes of certain well-publicized investment companies which had previously thrived in a regulatory vacuum." While the risk of losing money was inherent in any investment decision, it was irresponsible for regulatory authorities "to stand by and expect that the public will continue to commit their savings to markets which do not exhibit the kind of responsibility or adhere to the kind of public trust to which public savings are entitled."[27]

In an environment where capital flows were no longer restricted, a sound regulatory system constituted a decisive competitive advantage:

> I think it is clear that nations which provide these pre-conditions of investor confidence will succeed in attracting capital to their securities markets while those which do not will fail. Throughout the history of the US foreigners have consistently been investors in our economy. Recently, however, the interest in common stock has hightened [*sic*].
>
> Why? No doubt because foreigners—both individuals and institutions—have become more aware of the investment opportunities in the US securities market and the general long-term growth of our economy. But this development, which coincided with modifications in the US tax laws eliminating tax impediments to foreign investment, was no doubt considerably fostered by the sharp contrast between the extensive scheme of investor protections provided in the American securities markets and the absence of comparable protections in a number of foreign securities markets.[28]

Regulation, according to Casey, facilitated rather than impeded the development of the international securities market. American corporations and investors, which were responsible for a large portion of international capital flows, would benefit from the development of improved "schemes of investor protection" in foreign securities markets: "Americans today have a very substantial stake in other countries—both through direct corporate investment in foreign affiliates of US corporations and through indirect investment in the securities of foreign corporations—and, with improved regulatory techniques and tools to eliminate existing disparities in regulation, the flow of capital across national boundaries should accelerate in both directions."[29]

True to his reputation as a friend of Nixon, Casey quoted the president's report on US foreign policy for the 1970s. He emphasized the interrelation of

American domestic and international objectives: "I believe it is an important US national policy to assist and encourage the development of foreign local capital markets. The rationale is relatively simple: to the extent such markets prosper, we would expect better international relations. Furthermore, as I have noted, healthy and vigorous capital markets provide a source of capital to United States corporations to finance their operations outside of the United States."[30]

The development of a viable, efficient international securities market required some harmony among local regulators. Casey was confident that a number of reciprocity agreements between the SEC and non-American regulators would be signed in the near future. While the chairman of the SEC did not envision a unified, worldwide regulatory system, he did identify a number of areas where coordination was necessary: "Our securities markets and financial communities are diverse and unevenly regulated; while uniformity is not likely nor, perhaps, desirable, greater international cooperation, coordination and control will be needed. Stock exchange and market practices should be integrated, and corporate structures, financial analysis and disclosure practices, accounting and legal procedures, and disparate tax and fiscal policies require greater balance from country to country within our rapidly expanding international capital markets."[31]

The Milan meeting was followed by a conference on financial reporting held at the COB on May 19, 1972, in Paris. On the day of the conference, Casey was to have lunch with Chatenet, European Commissioner Raymond Barre, and other European officials. Mostoff put together a memorandum highlighting matters for possible discussion with his counterparts. Among them:

> d. The EEC has been attempting for some time to develop some sort of a minimum securities regulation code for its member countries. This development was one of the themes in your Milan speech. The desirability of moving ahead in this area and their progress could be a subject of discussion with Mr. Barre.
> e. Communication between the regulatory bodies represented at your luncheon and the SEC is inadequate. A subject of general concern would be techniques for improving communication.[32]

In his presentation at the conference, Casey advocated "some degree of commonality in [international] accounting standards," while admitting that it would take a long time to achieve that objective: "The history of improving accounting standards and practices in my own country shows that, although it took us almost 40 years to get as far as we have and there is still much to be done, each step along the way contributed to public confidence in the financial reporting disclosures as the basis on which investment are [*sic*] made. What is necessary is that we show a will to move together and the ability to make progress towards commonly accepted international standards."[33]

Casey identified several areas that might need standardization: security valuation based on earning power as opposed to dividends, the recognition of fair value as the best appreciation of economic reality, a more homogeneous presentation of profit-and-loss statements, and a move from historical to current values: "[. . .] what is the purpose of accounting and who is it for? In some countries, accounting is deemed being primarily for the purpose of guiding management and letting owners know where they stand. Increasingly, a country which has or hopes to have broad public participation in investing in its economic activity will have to accept that one of the primary purposes of accounting is to inform the investor and the potential investor."[34]

Judging from such public utterances, Casey and Chatenet agreed on the basic principles of what the Frenchman called a consistent *politique de l'information* (information policy). Casey's papers, unfortunately, do not include any documents mirroring the reports written by Chatenet after his visits to the United States—such memorandums would have offered a glimpse into Casey's and other American officials' visions of the COB at the time when it had just been established. As indicated in the introduction to this book, the quest for COB-related SEC administrative records proved eventually fruitless. For lack of better sources, though, a couple of press articles reflect the evolution of foreign perceptions of the COB between the beginning and the end of Chatenet's chairmanship.

An avid reader of the "Anglo-Saxon" press, Chatenet did not fail to notice the scathing article written by journalist Paul Lewis in the *Financial Times* on December 5, 1968—a copy can be found in his personal papers at Sciences Po. Adorned with a rather unflattering picture of the chairman, the article was entitled: "The Paris *Bourse* Watchdog: Kiss of Life Still Needed"[35]—the watchdog metaphor was no significant improvement on the gendarme one. A few months after the May 1968 events, Lewis noted that the Paris market remained extremely weak: in spite of de Gaulle's efforts to defend the French currency, stock prices were vulnerable to any bad news that might suddenly make the headlines, such as the recent threat of a strike of Renault workers. Trust had not returned, and the number of shareholders was going down—a very different trend from that of other European markets. Chatenet, whom Lewis had met in his La Défense office, observed that this number had been higher at

the end of the nineteenth century and that large stock portfolios were con-
tracting. The COB's chairman was doing his best to reverse this trend: "For,
although the COB is often compared with the US Securities and Exchange
Commission, its main duty is not so much the disciplining of an ebullient
market place as trying to put a little sparkle in France's lethargic exchanges."
To revive the market, Chatenet had two priorities: "better discipline and more
propaganda." As far as discipline was concerned, several new rules were soon
to be enacted: "In this way, the Commission hopes to deal a powerful blow to
the legend of the 'insider', which still figures prominently in the public attitude
towards the Bourse." Lewis praised the public relations effort of Chatenet, who
made several television appearances in order to convince his fellow Frenchmen
to invest in the stock market. His overall assessment, however, was far from
optimistic:

> But, even taken together, these measures represent no more than a start to the
> task of rehabilitating the *Bourse*, which Mr. Chatenet expects to take a long time
> and quite possibly not be fully accomplished, until the present generation of
> Frenchmen has been replaced by another and more progressive one. Moreover,
> the COB's own capacity for innovation is limited and even in such matters as
> improving company accounting procedure (for instance, by insisting on the
> publication of consolidated balance sheets which would at least make rational
> investments analysis possible) the Government has shown itself curiously slow
> to act.
>
> Some brokers report that the first signs of activity from the Tour Nobel have
> already had a favourable effect on sentiment in the Stock Exchange. However,
> declining company profits and monetary uncertainties still seem to be keeping
> the market as a while in its old groove and there is still little sign yet of that
> general rise in prices which would do more than any number of legal reforms
> to revive public interest in the Bourse.[36]

Two years after Lewis's article, however, the tone had changed radically. By the
end of 1971, the *New York Times* was full of praise for the COB: "French Version of SEC Unexpectedly Effective."[37] To illustrate the efficiency of the institution, the newspaper put forward three facts: (1) within the preceding month,
seventy-three companies had been delisted because they did not match the
new information requirements; (2) during the summer of 1971, the COB had
investigated a possible insider trading case when the price of the *rente Pinay*,
a very popular kind of government bond, had collapsed after inaccurate information had been disclosed; simultaneously, (3) Brasserie Bouchart, a large

brewing company, had been publicly reprimanded for having failed to disclose sufficient information in the context of a merger. "These three developments were evidence of the new broom that has been brought to the Paris Stock market by France's version of the Securities and Exchange Commission, a strapping institution, barely four years old, which takes very much after its prototype in Washington"—the broom, another uncomplimentary metaphor. The *Times* reminded its readers that the objective of the COB was twofold: to improve (1) investor confidence and (2) the international recognition of the Paris Stock Exchange. The record of the new institution was already impressive: the infamous Willot brothers, the masterminds of the Garantie Foncière real estate scandal. Burgard was quoted admitting that France was lagging behind the United States in terms of investor information, except on one point: "French companies are forced to disclose the sales of their subsidiaries." Overall, the success of the COB was good news for French investors: "Companies grumble about the new intrusion into their affairs. But France's 1.5 million stockholders have only dividends to gain."

The COB had exceeded the low expectations that the *New York Times*, along with other newspapers, had formed at the time of its creation.

CHAPTER TEN

Mission Accomplished?

The first annual report of the Commission des Opérations de Bourse, dated March 21, 1969, still bore the imprint of the May 1968 events. Its introduction regretted "the ever-increasing sentiment of pessimism" of the previous five years. The effects of the bear market of 1962–1967 had indeed been compounded by political instability:

> The situation could be considered all the more difficult that, as a result of unfortunate circumstances, uncertainty spread across public opinion about the economic, but also legal and even political future of French corporations.
>
> This uncertainty has been caused by that portion of public opinion which questions the organizational structure of corporations, which Parliament has just reasserted by voting the July 24, 1966 Company Act. For the financial market, it is a serious issue that the very status of corporations be questioned constantly, which jeopardizes the perception by the public of the safety of investing in securities.[1]

The report also criticized "the indecisiveness and the contradictions of our national will"—a veiled allusion to the Vallon amendment—and "the permanent questioning of too many texts." All this combined to create a very hostile environment: "Over the recent years, one could even wonder if developing the securities market was consistent with the needs of this nation and the interests of its investors. To this question, the preamble of the September 28, 1967 *Ordonnance* answers positively, and the *Commission des Opérations de Bourse* embraces this act of faith in the vitality of the market."[2]

The COB believed that "the development"—one had to understand "the survival"—of the securities market depended on its "transformation"—a process in which it volunteered to take a leading role. The COB focused on educating French investors: "The mentality of investors must continue to evolve so that the benefits of securities be well understood and [so that securities be appropriately] utilized. It would also be a good thing if the *Bourse* could lose, in the eyes of the general public, its reputation of being a place where profits can be made quickly, under conditions which are closer to gambling than to reasonable speculation." Unknowingly, the writers of the report echoed Roosevelt's 1934 fireside chat quoted in chapter 4, in which the president hoped that "as a result [of the *Securities Exchange Act*] people [would be] discouraged in unhappy efforts to get rich quick by speculating in securities."[3] Improved information on corporate activities would also contribute to changing the state of mind of French investors:

> One sometimes puts forward as an excuse the smaller size of French corporations, their insufficient desire to present their activities to the general public, and their neglect of profitability. This opinion is far from always being legitimate, as evidenced by the commercial and industrial achievements of some [French] corporations. Mergers and take-overs that are currently happening point to the growing awareness of a much-needed structural transformation in order to face competition. On the other hand, the improved disclosure of information is evidence of a change in attitude with respect to investors. In addition, it will have to be admitted that the legitimate goal of a corporation is to make profits. Selectivity, which has never been absent from the Bourse, can only increase in the future; corporations will be able to request from the financial market the capital they need only to the extent that they will compensate their shareholders adequately by allowing them to benefit from expected growth.[4]

While the report reasserted the legitimacy of corporate profit and the need to prepare for international competition, it also proclaimed the rights of investors, large and small, to be treated fairly, that is, to receive adequate dividends and to benefit from the increase in shareholder value—the memory of the Ugine-Kuhlmann scandal was still fresh. Pierre Chatenet's vision was based on a very basic sociological observation: assuming that investors would not be discouraged by corporate scandals and anticapitalist propaganda, their number was bound to rise in the years to come. On December 4, 1969, in the lecture he gave in Toulouse on "the information of shareholders," he mused on "the shareholder of tomorrow": "Who will be the shareholder of tomorrow? Either there won't be any, or he will belong to these new [social] classes who did not own shares, or whose parents did not own shares. The need for housing being met, living standards continuing to rise, immediate consumption needs brought by industrial civilization being progressively satisfied, at least partially, it is logical to think that potential shareholders should come back to the stock market."[5]

Chatenet's "shareholder of tomorrow" matched, more or less, the model new investor of the early 1970s: having earned, and not inherited, his wealth, he was much more demanding than the gullible investor of olden days; he wanted to know where his money was invested and what risks were being taken; he also had a very different relationship with his banker and his agent de change.

If one were to attract "the shareholder of tomorrow," it was necessary to revisit the question of investor information. In the successive annual reports of the COB, Chatenet articulated and defended a consistent politique de l'information (information policy)—what he had called "a policy of large disclosure" (large politique de disclosure) in the report written after his 1969 visit to the United States.

Persistently, the COB attempted to educate issuers of securities and market professionals. The argument was made that French corporations were competing for capital with foreign issuers: in order for their securities to be attractive, the quality of accounting information had to be upgraded to international standards. The 1970 annual report noted that while significant progress had been accomplished, it remained insufficient: "As early as its first report, the *Commission des Opérations de Bourse* highlighted the fact that French rules [applicable] to investor information were second only to American rules. But actual practices do not always confirm that hierarchy. In a study published in August 1970 by the European Federation of Financial Analyst Societies (EFFAS), which was based on financial statements published by a selection of large corporations from six European countries, France ranked after Great Britain and Germany, on par with Switzerland."[6]

The reports identified recurring shortcomings: lack of global perspective on company performance, nonconsolidation of key figures, publication of contradictory press releases, erroneous data given to the media, and inconsistencies in the series of statistics submitted to financial analysts. For the sake of investor protection, the COB recommended that all major French corporations devise and implement, at a consolidated level, a coordinated "information policy."

The COB supported the efforts of French accountants to modernize their profession. The 1968 report acknowledged that the presentation of financial statements had so far been designed to meet tax requirements, which made comparisons between corporations extremely difficult.[7] Traditionally, auditors had interpreted their responsibility very narrowly, much to the detriment of French investors:

> The experience of the main industrialized countries is entirely different. Certified public accountants in charge of auditing the financial statements of corporations most frequently belong to numerous and powerful partnerships. They perform

an ongoing audit mission, based on detailed examinations of, in particular, inventories and accounts payables. Their compensation varies according to the service provided. The contrast with the French approach is so marked that subsidiaries of foreign corporations located in France usually turn to auditors from their own countries and hire a French auditor for the sole purpose of complying with their legal obligations.[8]

The writers of the report went on to observe that the number of qualified accountants in France was dramatically insufficient: 2,400 *experts comptables* (chartered accountants was the translation proposed by the report) and 7,000 *comptables agréés* (certified public accountants) against a total of 40,000 in Great Britain. While the COB saluted the improvement resulting from the July 24, 1966, Company Act and the August 12, 1969, decree establishing a nationwide professional organization of auditors, it also admitted that upgrading the profession to international standards would take a very long time: too many French managers were indifferent to the very notion of external control, and too many accountants were attached to the status quo.[9]

The reports also reflected Chatenet's preoccupation with the quality of French financial journalism:

> In that area, as in others, significant progress has been observed over the last few years. Two examples can be given: on the one hand, generalist newspapers published in Paris have markedly increased the size and the quality of their financial sections, which magnifies the impact of that kind of information on the public at large; on the other hand, many newspapers, specialized or not, have gotten into the habit, which must be warmly encouraged, to clearly distinguish, in different sections, news and communiqués emanating from companies from information coming from the editorial staff.[10]

The point made in this excerpt from the 1970 report was reiterated in the following years, sometimes in blunter language, as in the 1971 report:

> The role of the press is important in all major capitalist countries, and particularly in France, where corporations have a very imperfect knowledge of who their investors are, as a result of the traditional popularity of bearer securities among intermediaries and the investing public.
>
> Yet, for a long time, the way this channel of information used to operate left much to desire because of an interdependence [between business and the media] that was harmful to sincerity. The provisions of article 14 of the August 26, 1944

ordonnance on the organization of the French press, which forbade editorial advertising, were ignored.[11]

If investor information figured prominently in the annual reports, surveillance of the securities markets was not absent. For all Chatenet's qualms about the COB being called "the cop of the *Bourse*," this was indeed how the commission came across: during his chairmanship, several high-profile cases contributed to building its reputation as a stern enforcer of the law. At the beginning of 1969, glass manufacturer BSN (Boussois-Souchon-Neuvesel) launched a hostile takeover bid on the much larger Saint-Gobain—a corporation established during the reign of Louis XIV. The takeover bid process, recently imported from the United States, was still relatively new in France; the conflict between BSN's Antoine Riboud, a maverick businessman, and Saint-Gobain's aristocratic chairman Arnaud de Vogüe, pit against each other two generations of French capitalists. The COB abstained from direct intervention and let the market react to the assault on Saint-Gobain, which eventually failed—Saint-Gobain was to merge with Pont-à-Mousson, giving birth to a multinational construction giant, while BSN was to concentrate on the food industry. Once criticized for its bureaucratic overreach, the COB was accused of inaction. The situation was complicated by the fact that Vogüe was one of its collège members—he left the collège for the duration of the takeover. Later, Chatenet claimed that it had been perfectly fair to "let the best man win," but the reality, according to Jean-Jacques Burgard, was that the COB had not been ready to arbitrate a conflict between two major French corporations.[12]

The COB, however, did soon have the opportunity to prove its usefulness. The ordonnance restricted the scope of its intervention to the securities market. It did not say anything about the real estate market, which was booming during the late 1960s and early 1970s. *Sociétés civiles de placement immobilier* (SCPIs, real estate investment trusts) were being marketed aggressively, and many an investor was lured by excessive return expectations. Aware that these products were competing with stocks and bonds, the COB alerted the Ministry for the Economy and Finance. It took the French government three years to react—meanwhile, massive frauds were occurring. A number of real estate scandals, involving members of the Gaullist establishment, made the headlines of the French and foreign press. The *New York Times* reported: "The real estate scandals, involving the company of Mr. Rives-Henry, La Garantie Foncière, and others, have become a cause célèbre here in part because of a vigilant Opposition intent on embarrassing the Government and its Gaullist-dominated majority. The debate has widened to include questions about the financial backing of political parties, the money candidates spend in elections and the independence of elected officials and of the civil service from financial and other pressure groups."[13]

During the first two years of its existence, the COB was powerless. The only way Chatenet could express his concern was through the issuance of a press release: "We are not in charge of real estate investment-trusts [September 23, 1969]."[14] Alerted by the COB, the French government was slow to take action. Finally, an act voted on December 31, 1970, extended the jurisdiction of the COB over SCPI.[15] Chatenet proceeded swiftly to clean up the market: twenty-seven companies were investigated immediately.[16] In these delicate circumstances, he supported his staff and defended them against pressures from the outside.[17] In the aftermath of the Garantie Foncière scandal, the French Parliament debated rules governing conflicts of interest between business and government. Not only did opposition politicians denounce cronyism, they also questioned the intrinsic morality of the capitalist system: "There was general agreement with the Government that in the final analysis it is the public servant's own conscience that provides 'the surest guarantee of a correct functioning of our democracy.' But Socialists and Communists also insisted that the profit system of capitalist society was a fundamental source of dishonesty."[18]

Three years after the failed attack on the Palais Brongniart, as the much-celebrated trente glorieuses were about to end, financial scandals were giving ammunition to those who still questioned the legitimacy of the capitalist system. In that context, Chatenet argued in favor of a reinforcement of the COB's powers. Insider trading was his priority.

Pursuant to the amendment incorporated in the 1966 Company Act as a result of the ordonnance, directors, senior managers, and key personnel of publicly traded companies having access to insider information had to hold their shares in registered form; these individuals also had to notify the COB of the sale or acquisition of new shares. It quickly became clear, however, that these provisions were inefficient: it was extremely difficult to list all individuals having access to material, nonpublic information; the obligation to notify the COB had given rise to an influx of documents that were difficult to use and were, for the most part, uninteresting. As early as April 1969, the 1968 annual report of the COB concluded that it was desirable "to change the system." The report included a discussion of insider trading legislation in the United States and in the United Kingdom—the paragraph on the United States did not fail to mention the 1934 act and the role of the SEC. Only the United States, though, was referred to as an example to follow: "Controls should not prevent corporate executives and other insiders to risk a portion of their savings by investing in the companies for which they are working. This is demonstrated by the example of the United States, where the severity of these controls does not in any way prevent corporate executives from personally benefiting, via stock options mechanism, from the increase in shareholder value."[19]

The 1968 report gave advanced notice of upcoming proposals by the COB but did not enter into details about them. They eventually resulted in the December 23, 1970, act, which reinforced its investigative powers and instituted new penalties to punish insider trading.[20] While the act did not include the phrase *délits d'initiés*, it did provide a definition of insider trading: trading on nonpublic information and disseminating inaccurate information to manipulate prices. The 1970 annual report of the COB, published on March 26, 1971, welcomed the vote of the new law, particularly the provisions granting the Commission the authority to summon individuals who might give them information on cases which had been referred to it: "The *Commission des Opérations de Bourse* now has at its disposal an investigation procedure comparable to the hearings of Anglo-Saxon commissions."[21]

The COB's increasing workload provided Chatenet with additional arguments in favor of an increased budget. On July 28, 1971, he answered a letter from René Pleven, the Minister of Justice:

> It is true that, since the beginning of 1971, the COB has found itself caught between a brutally increasing workload and the absolute inelasticity of its human resources, kept unchanged by the budgetary authority for the past two years. In light of the atmosphere resulting from the recent scandals, I have some hope that the situation will improve in 1972. [. . .]
>
> Aside from present circumstances, the fact remains that these difficulties also come from constraints that are specific to the COB's activity. To be worth it, accounting verifications must be very thorough, even though they must be performed on elements that have been complicated voluntarily, or even concealed on purpose by those concerned.[22]

These issues were discussed with the Ministry for the Economy and Finance, which retained control of the COB's operating expenses—for all Chatenet's persuasion, the COB continued to operate with a very tight budget and strictly limited human resources.

Another aspect of the COB's organization, however, attracted the attention of the highest level of the executive. President Pompidou kept a watchful eye

on the composition of the collège. While it was the prerogative of the Rue de
Rivoli to appoint the four nonchairing members of the COB's collège, the
president demanded that the list be submitted to him prior to publication. In
January 1971, his aide Marcillac reviewed and approved the minister's recommendations.[23] Two members left the collège: Vogüe was replaced by Maurice
Borgeaud, the chairman of Usinor, a large steel-making conglomerate, and
Monguilan was replaced by Gilbert Lancien, another professional judge from
the Cour de Cassation. Meunier, the syndic, and Lestrade, the representative
of the banking profession, retained their seats. Marcillac's memorandum indicated that Lancien's name had been put forward by the minister of Justice,
and that Chatenet would have preferred to replace Lestrade with Rémy Schlum-
berger, chairman of the Banque Neuflize-Schlumberger, "who was more distant
from the Minister of the Economy and Finances." Chatenet's recommendation
was not followed and the minister—who, at the time, was none other than
Valéry Giscard d'Estaing—prevailed.

The 1971 annual report, dated March 24, 1972, was the last to bear the
signature of Chatenet. The first paragraph quietly acknowledged the recent
extension of the powers of the COB:

> The year 1971 has been important for the Commission. Its action with respect
> to S.C.P.I.s, and the judicial repercussions of several of its interventions in other
> areas, have made those who already knew it more aware of its ability to take
> action, and have revealed its existence to a wide audience. What has sometimes
> appeared, from the outside, as a brutal change in its orientation was simply the
> effect of the enactment, in December of 1970, of two new pieces of legislation,
> which, as per the Commission's own recommendation, have granted it the
> additional legal powers which it had declared necessary as early as its first annual
> report.[24]

Chatenet sent a copy of the report to François Bloch-Lainé, former directeur
du Trésor and chairman of Crédit Lyonnais, with a short cover note: "In four
years, we did try to do something, finally. But entrenched positions are so
difficult to move!"[25]

On December 31, 1970, the term of the chairman of the COB had been
reduced from five to four years, while the terms of the other members of the
collège had been extended from three to four years.[26] The expiration date of
Chatenet's term, however, had been left unchanged.

By the end of 1972, as Chatenet's chairmanship was about to end, time had come for a first assessment of his action. On October 24, he wrote to Edgar Faure, the minister of Social Affairs in Pierre Messmer's government.[27] As far as la Participation was concerned, Chatenet said, progress had been real in spite of initial skepticism from employers and trade unions: 2.5 billion French francs had been invested in securities on behalf of employees; at least 2 million employees had become, directly or indirectly, security holders. These numbers had to be put in perspective with Chatenet's estimate of the number of shareholders in France at the beginning of his chairmanship, 1.5 million. "Until recently, shareholders in France were individuals whose parents already owned shares; today, the majority of shareholders are individuals whose parents did not own shares. After all, this also is a way to make a revolution happen, and in my opinion it is as good as any other."[28]

Tongue in cheek, Chatenet was comparing himself to the May 68 would-be revolutionaries—the ever ironic and witty Faure must have appreciated.

Pompidou took a personal interest in the choice of Chatenet's successor. In April, Jean-René Bernard, conseiller technique in charge of economic and financial affairs at the Élysée, put forward the name of Raymond Barre. Barre, a brilliant and independent-minded professor of economics at Sciences Po, would soon be back in Paris after a six-year stint as European commissioner for Economic and Financial Affairs in Brussels. The president annotated Bernard's memorandum with the following remark: "The succession of Mr. Chatenet is important. Names will have to be submitted to me. As far as Mr. Barre is concerned, it seems difficult to me, because of the timing and because he may see it as a being stuck in a siding."[29]

Pompidou proved remarkably prescient about the political stature of the professor: two years after his name had been discussed as a potential COB chairman, Barre was to join the French government in the capacity of *Ministre du Commerce extérieur* (minister in charge of Foreign Trade); in 1976, he was to become prime minister under President Giscard d'Estaing. Eventually, Chatenet was replaced by André Postel-Vinay. Postel-Vinay had been a major figure of the French Résistance; he was also an inspecteur général des finances. Postel-Vinay's tenure as chairman of the COB was short, as he became a member of Jacques Chirac's government in May 1974. His successor, Jean Donnedieu de Vabres, had a lot in common with Chatenet: born in 1918, the former student in political sciences, who had entered the Conseil d'État in 1941, had joined the French Résistance alongside Michel Debré and Alexandre Parodi; after World War II, he had made a distinguished administrative career, serving his country in the capacity of general secretary of the French government between 1964 and 1974. In 1980, Donnedieu de Vabres was to be succeeded by another conseiller d'État, Bernard Tricot.

For all the frustration expressed at times by Chatenet when he complained about the limitations to the COB's authority, his chairmanship was generally considered a success, particularly by those who had entrusted him with this mission. In January 1973, Debré, then the minister of Defense in Messmer's government, sent him a very warm farewell message:

> My dear Pierre,
>
> You are going to leave the chairmanship of this Commission, the creation of which had caused so much noise! I can testify to the kindness and courage which prevailed in your mind when you accepted my offer. I can also testify to the surprise of all those concerned when your nomination was made public. Well! Quietly, with no advertising, you have accomplished an enormously important work. Thanks to the talent you displayed, this COB is now an essential compo-nent of French finance—and I really mean essential. If, tomorrow, "economic agents," as they say, are willing to break into a gallop and give our nation a Stock Exchange corresponding to its new economic capacity, [then] a necessary mech-anism will be in place, with its traditions, its prestige, its audience. Of that, my dear Pierre, you are responsible. For that, I congratulate you—and I congratulate myself for having sought you![30]

Chatenet's departure from the COB at the beginning of 1973 did not mark the end of his career. In 1968, he had joined the Conseil Constitutionnel, where he sat for almost ten years—apparently, nobody found it inappropriate that a member of France's highest constitutional court would simultaneously head the securities market regulator. He also presided over the destinies of Créditel, a leasing company specializing in telecommunications, and Cofiroute, a mo-torway concessionary company. In 1986, Édouard Balladur, the minister for the economy and finances in another Chirac government, asked him to chair the commission in charge of advising the French government about the pri-vatization of a number of state-owned companies.

In 1974, Burgard moved from the general secretaryship of the COB to that of the SNCF (Société nationale des chemins de fer français), France's state-owned railway company. He sat on the board of a number of corporations, professional associations, and charities; for many years, he taught at Sciences Po and authored several books and articles. When Chatenet died in 1997,

Burgard paid an emotional tribute to the memory of the former chairman of the COB.

During the last decades of his life, the unanimously respected Chatenet rarely ventured into the political field. He made an exception, though, for the sake of old friendship: in December 1980, he joined a committee in support of Debré's candidacy to the presidential election to be held in May 1981.[31] With less than 2 percent of the vote, de Gaulle's former prime minister suffered a humiliating defeat. He died on August 2, 1996.

Debré's political fortunes had never recovered from the May 1968 events—in his memoirs, he referred to them as "an earthquake in French political history."[32] Pompidou, his great rival to de Gaulle's succession, did not live to complete the task for which he had been called by the French people in 1969. On April 2, 1974, death put a brutal end to the term of the second president of the Fifth Republic.

Giscard d'Estaing, Debré's immediate predecessor as minister for the economy and finances, had returned to his Rue de Rivoli office in June 1969. In 1974, he ran successfully for president and succeeded Pompidou. Yet the year 1981 saw his defeat to Socialist François Mitterrand, whose unexpectedly strong performance as candidate of the left had so annoyed de Gaulle in 1965. Ironically, while Mitterrand's election caused much anxiety among French and foreign investors, his fourteen-year presidency was to be marked by a series of landmark reforms of the financial markets[33]—by then, no one was thinking of setting the Bourse ablaze any more.

During the early 1970s, Haberer had remained a close adviser to Debré, managing his cabinet at the Ministry of Foreign Affairs and later the Ministry of Defense. At the time of Mitterrand's election in 1981, he had held the position of directeur du Trésor for four years, playing an active role in laying the foundations of the European Monetary System. In 1982, the loyalty he had transferred to the newly elected socialist president was rewarded by his appointment as chairman and CEO of French investment bank Paribas, which had just been nationalized, along with other banks and major industrial corporations. Summarily dismissed after the victory of a Gaullist-led conservative coalition at the 1986 parliamentary elections, he was promoted to head Crédit Lyonnais, one of the three largest state-owned banks, when Mitterrand was reelected in 1988. Haberer's five years at the helm of Crédit Lyonnais ended in a dramatic crisis combining a brutal downturn in the real estate market, a swindle of international proportions, and the unintended consequences of an ill-fated acquisition policy. The resulting bailout by the French government exposed the inadequacies of the state-ownership architecture so artfully designed by the post–World War II generation.

The so-called Crédit Lyonnais affair has obscured the memory of Haberer's role in the reforms of the late 1960s. Debré's voluminous memoirs, less notable for their literary grace than for the passionate sincerity of their author, provide a detailed account of his two-and-a-half-year stewardship of the French economy. True to his reputation as a considerate manager, he did not fail to acknowledge what he owed individual members of his staff—among them, Haberer was praised with particular warmth.

Debré also dedicated several pages of his memoirs to the creation of the COB. With the benefit of hindsight, he had come to regret the limitations of the 1967 ordonnance. According to him, the objective had been to proceed gradually: first, to build legitimacy for a newly created institution; second, within two to three years, to define and transfer to the COB "additional powers, inspired by those of the SEC, particularly with respect to 'insiders.' "[34] This cautious approach had had mixed results: "More than twenty years and the emergence of grave shortcomings in the action of the COB would be needed for Parliament to be asked to vote a new law, which, according to me, remains too moderate, considering the need for disciplinary measures, i.e. the penalties that are inevitably needed to guarantee to investors that transactions and the issuance of securities will be transparent."[35]

Debré, whose memoirs were published in 1993, was referring to the 1989 act "on the security and the transparency of the financial market":[36] in the aftermath of another insider trading scandal, involving this time Pechiney, French lawmakers deemed it necessary to reinforce the independence and enlarge the powers of the COB. The Pechiney-Triangle scandal had international ramifications. By then, American regulators no longer looked at France with indifference; the SEC, willing to exercise its power as the regulator of the dominant state, put pressure on the French government to bolster the repression of insider trading. Seven years later, in 1996, another major piece of legislation continued on the same trend.[37] The incremental remodeling of the collège of the COB took place in the context of ongoing administrative changes, liberalization pressure emanating from European institutions, and increased international competition.

Chatenet's austere demeanor did not match the stereotype of the disheveled prophet. As early as 1972, though, he had predicted the emergence of a European securities market and the connection of traders via an electronic network.[38] However, neither he nor Burgard had anticipated that the Compagnie nationale des agents de change would one day disappear and that the corbeille would survive only as a picturesque ornament in a deserted building. In January 1988, a radical overhaul of the professional organization put an end to the monopoly of the agents de change; the compagnie and the chambre syndicale were dissolved.[39] The powers formerly exercised by the compagnie were transferred, respectively, to two professional organizations, the Conseil des Bourses de Valeurs (CBV, Council of Stock Exchanges, established in 1988) and the Conseil du Marché à Terme (CMT, Council of Forward Markets, established in 1987). From then on, market professionals were affiliated with the Association française des sociétés de bourse, later called the Association française des marchés financiers. Most agents de change eventually merged with investment banks. A privately owned company, the Société des Bourses françaises (SBF), was incorporated in order to operate the Paris securities market and serve as a clearinghouse. Xavier Dupont, the last syndic, became chairman of the SBF and the CBV. His tenure, however, was short-lived, as he was forced to resign when it was discovered that the guarantee fund of the former chambre syndicale had lost millions on forward positions on the Marché à Terme International de France (MATIF, the Paris futures exchange).[40] Dupont was replaced by individuals put forward by the Direction du Trésor, which seized the opportunity to tighten the control it exercised on the Bourse.[41] In 1991, the six provincial exchanges closed and became representative offices of the SBF.[42]

After the end of the ancient organization of the Paris agents de change, the COB had to adapt to a new environment. Enhanced independence resulted from significant changes in the composition of the collège. The 1989 act amended several articles of the 1967 ordonnance. In organizational terms, the changes concerned primarily article 2. The term of the chairman was extended to six years and was made nonrenewable. While the chairman was still appointed by government decree, the other members of the board were no longer designated by the minister for the economy and finances. Three members were to come from high jurisdictions (Conseil d'État, Cour de Cassation, Cour des Comptes); two from the recently created professional organizations (Conseil des Bourses de Valeurs, Conseil du Marché à Terme); one from the Banque de France. Two additional members, chosen for their competence and experience, were to be co-opted by the above six and the chairman. The new collège comprised nine members (including the chairman).

Further revisions were made to article 2 of the ordonnance in the 1996 act. The number of board members was increased from nine to ten. Nothing changed with respect to the chairman and the four members coming from the

Conseil d'État, the Cour de Cassation, the Cour des Comptes, and the Banque de France. Because the Conseil des Bourses de Valeurs had merged with the Conseil du Marché à Terme, the resulting Conseil des Marchés Financiers (CMF, or Council of Financial Markets) was given the right to designate one single collège member. Another collège seat was allocated to the Conseil National de la Comptabilité, the organization in charge of setting accounting standards. Three additional members, chosen for their legal and financial expertise, would be designated by, respectively, the president of the Senate, the president of the National Assembly, and the president of the Conseil Économique et Social.

Gradually, budgetary control from the Ministry for the Economy and Finance was alleviated; in 1985, the COB was allocated its own, independent resources—fees collected on transactions and instruments subject to its oversight. Meanwhile, the powers of the COB were enlarged and aligned, at least partially, on those of the SEC. The December 14, 1985, act, which revised article 4 of the 1967 ordonnance, gave the COB the power to issue its own regulations (règlements)—these regulations, however, had to be made official by a ministerial order issued by the minister for the economy and finances.[43] The 1989 act inserted an article that did not exist in the 1967 ordonnance.[44] This new article 9 gave the COB the authority to impose fines or penalties for infringements of its own regulations.

As a result of the 1985 and 1989 acts, the COB was granted a portion of the legislative and judicial powers; this extension of its powers was subsequently deemed constitutional by the French Conseil Constitutionnel. By the end of the 1980s, therefore, the COB became a full-fledged "independent administrative authority" at the crossroads of the three branches of government: "as a lawmaker, it makes rules; as a policeman, it investigates violations of these rules; as a judge, it punishes these violations."[45] In 1996, an Act of the French Parliament explicitly referred to the COB as an autorité administrative indépendante.[46]

Many European nations followed France's path in adopting the US model of securities regulation. According to Haberer's testimony, Italian authorities requested documentation about the COB when they established the Commissione Nazionale per le Società e la Borsa (CONSOB) in 1974.[47]

When the COB was created, international governmental organizations (IGOs) were not playing the role that was to become theirs in later decades. While Debré spent a great deal of his time preparing for, and attending meetings at, the IMF in Washington, DC, the Basle-based Bank for International Settlements (BIS) was yet to transform into the main coordination venue for bank supervision, and the International Organization of Securities Commissions (IOSCO) was not even in existence.[48] "International meetings of securities regulators were virtually unprecedented until the 1970s, and significant efforts at cooperation began only in the 1980s."[49]

Once IOSCO had been instituted, in 1983, the COB proved a most convenient tool for the French government.[50] IOSCO was to turn into one of those international club-organizations of which the Basle Committee, an emanation of the BIS in charge of setting capital adequacy standards, offers the best example.[51] Few French citizens, however, are aware of its existence,[52] and its accomplishments remain modest—compared with the Basel Accord little progress has been made on the front of international securities regulatory standards.

The COB also entered into a number of international cooperation agreements with its foreign counterparts. On December 14, 1989, SEC chairman Richard C. Breeden and COB chairman Jean Saint-Geours jointly signed an administrative agreement.[53] The agreement itself was preceded by an "Understanding Regarding the Establishment of a Framework for Consultations," which emphasized the interdependence of the US and French securities market:

> The SEC and the COB share a common goal of developing and maintaining open, fair, efficient and secure markets. [. . .] The Agreement signed today provides a framework for the Authorities to exchange information necessary to maintain the integrity of the securities markets of the United States and France. This Understanding reflects the Authorities' additional agreement to engage in mutual consultations about subjects of common interest in order to coordinate market oversight, and to resolve differences that may exist between their respective regulatory systems. These consultations will assist in the development of mutually agreeable approaches for ensuring the continued strength and growth of the securities markets of the United States and France.[54]

The SBF merged with the MATIF in 1999; along with the Amsterdam and Brussels Stock Exchanges, the resulting Paris Bourse S.A. became part of the Euronext alliance in 2000. Euronext then acquired the London International Futures and Options Exchange (LIFFE) and the Lisbon Stock Exchange. Euronext merged with NYSE Group, owner of the New York Stock Exchange, in 2007. In 2014, shortly after Intercontinental Exchange (ICE) acquired NYSE Euronext, Euronext became public and split from ICE.

By the early 2000s, it had become clear that the French supervisory architecture was in dire need of rationalization: the COB and the CMF coexisted uneasily, with a risk of unnecessary duplications, contradictions in their respective bodies of rules and regulations, and potential loopholes. The August 1, 2003, Act on Financial Security established a new authority, the Autorité des Marchés Financiers (AMF), which absorbed the COB and the CMF.[55] The number of collège members was aligned on that of the CMF (sixteen), with a greater number of seats reserved for representatives of market professionals. To reflect that the CMF had been defined as a corporate body, which the COB was not, the AMF was defined as an *autorité publique indépendente dotée de la personnalité morale* (independent, incorporated public authority), a legal status slightly different from that of an independent administrative authority.

On September 26 and 27, 1997, *Les Échos* celebrated "the 30th birthday of the cop of the *Bourse*"[56]—Chatenet, who had passed away at the beginning of the month, would probably have noted with melancholy that the expression he had loathed so much was still commonplace among French journalists. The article, based on interviews with Michel Prada, then the chairman of the COB, and some of his predecessors, told the story of the progressive "legitimization" of the French securities regulator. The two journalists inserted a shorter piece on "the American model, child of the stock market crash of 1929"; incidentally, they also informed their readers that the COB was relocating from La Défense to the quartier de la Bourse, across the street from the Palais Brongniart.

Conclusion

Financial crises are often interpreted as a failure of regulation; conversely, new regulation is usually seen as the product of financial crises. In the wake of the 2008 Lehman Brothers trauma, former Fed chairman Paul Volcker famously noted: "There is a certain circularity in all this business [. . .]. You have a crisis, followed by some kind of reform, for better or worse, and things go well for a while, and then you have another crisis."[1]

Rarely does a nation undertake an overhaul of its financial regulations without being forced to do so by a stock market crash or the collapse of its banking system.[2] This, however, is what happened in France in 1967. Amid the protracted decline and stagnation of the Bourse, French policy makers seized the opportunity offered by a spectacular, if not isolated, insider trading case to establish an independent commission in charge of regulating the Paris securities market. Paradoxically, they used regulation as a tool to attract foreign investors and to revive the market, rather than as a limitation to its development— regulatory competition among nation-states, then, was not synonymous with the race to the bottom of regulatory standards, which is so frequently viewed as its necessary outcome.[3] Even more surprisingly, they drew their inspiration from an American model, the Securities and Exchange Commission—a powerful testimony to the innovative nature of the New Deal, so vividly captured by Roosevelt's call for "bold, persistent experimentation" in his 1932 speech at Oglethorpe University. The reformers of the late 1960s modeled the COB on an institution created after a stock market crash and in a "market-based" financial system, and they transferred it in the context of the French "overdraft economy." Along with the bank reforms of 1966–1967 and the attempt to create a liquid money market in the early 1970s, the creation of the COB makes sense in the long process of government intervention to develop the financial market. This challenges the view that such action started much later, in the 1980s, and primarily through waves of deregulation[4]—the adoption of the American model of securities regulation had very little to do with the subsequent ascent of neo-liberal ideology.[5]

While the examination of archival records confirms that the COB was indeed modeled after the SEC, it also shows that there were significant differences between the model and its imitation. The securities regulator established by the 1967 ordonnance was a hybrid creature sharing American and French characteristics; in this hybridization process, moral preoccupations and cultural factors were essential—as much, if not more than rational economic arguments.

In the analysis of the politics of financial reform, it is essential, yet problematic, to separate rhetoric from reality. The "moralization" of the Paris Bourse is a case in point. As indicated by his openness to Marcel Loichot's rather awkward economic theories and his persistent defense of la Participation, Charles de Gaulle was not enamored with the state of the capitalist system as he knew it. His economic vision owed much to the paternalistic teachings of nineteenth-century Social Catholicism; it took shape in the early years of the Cold War, at a time when he thought it necessary to find a third way between capitalism and communism. De Gaulle's rhetoric, however, evolved over time, along with the political situation and under the influence of his economic advisers. His vision was not always consistent, and Gaullists themselves were far from unanimous in their idea of society. For all their protestations of fidelity to the great man of the Fifth Republic, Georges Pompidou and Michel Debré shared a cautious skepticism toward la Participation. Their ambition was to modernize the French economy, not to move away from capitalism. They sincerely believed, however, that stock ownership had to be promoted and that large and small investors had to be protected. Their appeal to morality was more than a cynical attempt to cloak their technocratic objectives under the guise of de Gaulle's grandiose oratory.

The story of the COB began with Pompidou's ringing call to "moralize" the Paris Bourse. If the prime minister's words resonated so strongly, it is not so much that the Ugine-Kuhlmann scandal had generated a wave of outrage beyond the confines of the stock exchange floor but, rather, that a great number of French people were convinced that there was something intrinsically immoral in the mechanics of the securities market. Nongovernmental organizations— domestic groups promoting shareholder activism or transnational networks opposing the power of global finance—did not appear in this story; they did not exist then.[6] Policy makers, however, could not ignore the outrage of the small investors who felt robbed by the merger between Ugine and Kuhlmann; they were not oblivious to the fact that the perceptions and reactions of public opinion had to be factored into their decision process. Twice in two years, in May 1966 and in May 1968, the hall of the Palais Brongniart proved a spectacular stage and a powerful echo chamber for the grievances and protests of civil society. Aware that hostility to the capitalist system was one of many obstacles to the development of mass investment and, ultimately, to the competitiveness of the Paris market, French reformers set themselves to the task of reversing these negative perceptions. "Moralizing the market," therefore, became a key component of their strategy to revive a sluggish Bourse.

The uncompromising—and at times slightly priggish—Debré was not one to let himself be taught moral lessons by anyone, much less Pompidou, who had unheroically kept quiet during the German occupation. He seized the opportunity to add an emblematic reform to his economic program geared toward enhancing French power in Europe. In the postelectoral context of 1967, political expediency was crucial in setting the agenda; it also dictated a swift execution of decisions made at the highest level of the executive. As noted by Elliott Posner in his analysis of the 1983 reform instituting the Second Marché, financial decision making in France was "top-down, insular and incremental."[7] Debré, whose acquaintance with the United States was limited, could rely on Haberer's craftsmanship, persistence, and intimate knowledge of the American banking system and securities market. To a variable extent, large corporations, banks, and agents de change were involved in the process. Market professionals, however, were kept on a tight leash by the Ministry of Finance, and, in the context of a state-based economy, their nonstate status can be considered a matter of debate. The ordonnance procedure circumvented the French Parliament and avoided long and—in Debré's eyes—sterile debates. Imitating an existing institution—or pretending to do so—was more expedient than establishing an independent committee of experts, collecting the recommendations of lawyers, market professionals, and opinion leaders, debating competing options in Parliament—all that the reform process, in a modern democracy, normally entails.

In the troubled context of the last two years of de Gaulle's presidency, Pierre Chatenet's political shrewdness and direct access to the inner sanctum of Gaullist power protected the still fragile COB from administrative predators and market pitfalls. His undisputed honesty and unimpeachable background made him the ideal incarnation of morality—even though he was always cautious to avoid that word. The first chairman of the COB proved a zealous enforcer of the Brandeisian principle that small investors had to be protected through the disclosure of complete, accurate accounting information.

It is pointless to second guess Debré's assertion that he became aware of the existence of the US system of securities regulation when he read, inadvertently, a magazine: in the 1960s, the reputation of the SEC made it a perfectly legitimate source of inspiration—besides, no competing models were imme-diately available. That the model was American added piquancy to the process—unfortunately, no records have been found of the moment when de Gaulle was informed of the urgent need to imitate an American institution. The so-called Americanization of France generated a great deal of anxiety among the French population; yet, it does not seem that the modeling of the COB on the SEC attracted much popular attention at the time.

The creation of the COB does testify to the pressure of external economic competition, the importance of transnational networks of managerial elites, and the constraints of domestic politics, but it does not fit easily into the an-alytical frameworks developed by political scientists to account for the diffu-sion of regulatory policies on a global scale. The existence of an independent securities regulator and the resulting improvement of the quality of accounting information were indeed a prerequisite for France to take an active role in the debate about international regulatory standards, but fifteen years ahead of the creation of the International Organization of Securities Commissions, this was obviously not what Debré, Haberer, and Chatenet had in mind.[8] The creation of the COB did not result in a transfer of authority from the national to the supranational level of governance, be it European or global. Establishing a global regulator for the world securities markets was not discussed during the conferences held in Milan and Paris in 1972—almost half a century later, this scenario is not even remotely close.[9] In the late 1960s and early 1970s, regulatory convergence was yet to happen. American regulators, however, were soon to notice that their foreign counterparts could be valuable partners in defining international accounting standards and the enforcement of secu-rities regulations. The Americanization of accounting and regulation gained speed as globalization unfolded; for the most part, however, it was to take place after the end of Chatenet's chairmanship.

In the early decades of the COB's existence, the Ministry of Finance kept a close eye on its activities and continued to use it "as a means for controlling the brokers and modernizing the stock exchanges and the securities industry."[10] It took years for the securities regulator to conquer its independence and become a full-fledged independent administrative authority. Chatenet was not oblivious to the limitations to the COB's independence. The reports he wrote after his trips to the United States indicate that he viewed the American securities market as an ideal toward which it was his responsibility to progress. In his dealings with business leaders, market professionals, administrative rivals, and, more generally, public opinion, he was always sensitive to mischaracterizations about the COB's real powers. Yet he also made effective rhetorical use of the American model to promote his vision of a competitive marketplace and to advance the interests of the COB.

During the late 1960s and early 1970s, the old French word *régulation* acquired a new meaning. Applied to the securities market—which was a novelty— it became the French translation of the American word "regulation." In the financial media, the speeches of politicians and the lingo of bankers and agents de change, régulation quickly superseded *moralisation*. While the word *réglementation* did not disappear, its meaning became much narrower. A new concept came into being, along with that of *transparence, délit d'initié*, or autorité administrative indépendante; as time went by, laws, decrees, ordonnances and the action of market professionals gave flesh to these concepts.

All this did not take place in a secluded environment. Yet while implementing the Treaty of Rome was a political decision that, arguably, could have been reversed, this was not the case of technological innovation and the growth of international capital flows, which were happening with only marginal intervention of national governments. Pompidou and Debré did not attempt to resist them; foreshadowing the liberalization process of the 1980s and 1990s, the reforms of the late 1960s initiated the transformation of the French banking sector and capital markets. De Gaulle's presidency, remembered today as a moment of national assertion, also marked a decisive step toward France's integration to the European Common Market and, more largely, the global economy.

This combination of deliberate strategic choices and reactive adaptation to external changes was made possible by the political settlement of 1958. For most of the 1960s, de Gaulle's historic stature, Pompidou's command of governmental machinery, and Debré's zeal for legislative and economic reforms seemed to do wonders. Ten years after de Gaulle's return to power, the events of May 1968 dissipated the illusion that the French people had unanimously and forever aligned with their leaders. The Fifth Republic endured, though, in part as a result of Pompidou's tactical skillfulness. If Debré turned out to be—after de Gaulle—one of the main political casualties of May 1968, it is not only because he was outmaneuvered by a smarter Pompidou but also because his successful advocacy of the ordonnance procedure brought to light the painful shortcomings of a "government for the people, without the people"—or without its elected representatives. That he failed to comprehend the inherent contradiction between the methods he recommended and the transparency objective he pursued did not in any way diminish the historical importance of his reform of the Bourse.

Ironically, the 1967 accidental reform turned out to be a very consequential one. The SEC has been called "the most enduring legacy of the New Deal."[11] The COB—and the Autorité des Marchés Financiers, its successor entity— might also be regarded as "the most enduring economic legacy" of Gaullism. This assertion, obviously, is both simplistic and arbitrary; yet, the same cannot be said of the "new" French Franc, which had to suffer many devaluations before it was replaced by the euro, or of the much vaunted "restoration" of French public finances, which gave way to chronic deficits.[12] More pointedly, the COB encapsulates something of the composite nature of the Gaullist economic doctrine in its Fifth Republic incarnation. In the section of his memoirs quoted in chapter 1, Debré invoked the spirits of Colbert, the *dirigiste*, and Turgot, the *libéral*. The 1967 decision to create an *autorité administrative indépendante* was not a strategy to scale down the size of government or limit the scope of its interventions; rather, it was an attempt to reinvent government intervention and design new instruments of public policy—a transition from the traditional exercise of power to what Michel Foucault, ten years later, was to call a new form of "governmentality."[13]

While focused on the creation of an independent market regulator, this investigation also casts a revealing light on the paradoxical combination of cosmopolitanism and parochialism that was typical of the French elite. Chatenet and Haberer, along with lesser characters in this story, were durably impressed by their visits to the United States. At the same time, their careers illustrate the revolving door system favored by French civil servants and businessmen. There was more than unabashed cronyism in these quid pro quos, however. For the most part, these individuals were both talented and disinterested; the sense of solidarity was particularly strong among those who had come of age during World War II and had taken an active part in the French Resistance. Imbued with the ethos of the French Civil Service, hauts fonctionnaires of the postwar decades acted as the ultimate guarantors, if not of the democratic nature of the decision-making process, at least of its efficiency and conformity with the legal traditions of the French Republic.

Beginning with the election of Pompidou in 1969, Gaullist grandees had to make room for a younger, more heterogeneous generation. After his election to the presidency in 1974, Giscard d'Estaing, whose loyalty had seemed dubious enough to justify Debré's recommendation to use article 38 of the Constitution, did not reverse a reform he had not supported; what his successor François Mitterrand might have thought of the COB in 1967 is uncertain, but it is during his time in office that the powers of the COB were considerably enlarged—partially as a result of another Pechiney scandal, involving this time a close friend of the president.

Over the years, the fervent advocacy of la Participation has disappeared from political rhetoric; to an even greater extent than other shibboleths of Gaullist ideology—the celebration of France's *grandeur*, the quest for a third way in international politics, the "empty chair policy," and the rejection of all kind of supranational authority—it has been unceremoniously discarded by de Gaulle's successors and their speechwriters. French policy makers, however, never lost sight of their objective to promote equity ownership. Indeed, it was at the core of the 1978 "Monory laws," and of the reforms of the 1980s. La Participation somewhat anticipated on the "more extreme ideal" of a later era:[14] the "ownership society," so ardently promoted by British Prime Minister Margaret Thatcher and American President George W. Bush. Since 1967, the number of French investors has indeed increased significantly: by 2009, the number of individual, direct shareholders had reached 6.6 million, compared to an estimated 1.5 million at the time Chatenet became chairman of the COB.[15] In a society that remained suspicious of capitalism and its minions, the COB did not conjure these investors out of nothingness, but it can be credited for having created an environment that was more favorable to the spreading of security ownership—many a student who demonstrated against de Gaulle in May 1968 was to become the proud owner of a stock portfolio.

By the time Debré was writing his memoirs in the early 1990s, computer systems permitted twenty-four-hour trading, and money was flowing freely across borders. De Gaulle's former prime minister was not blind to these realities. Yet his defense of government's authority over the financial market remained as passionate as ever: "*To maintain the national character* of certain economic activities that are crucial to the security and the independence of the nation and to make sure that the key areas of our economy do not fall under foreign control; *to enforce the basic morality* which must inspire not only law, but also the way business is actually conducted. One must not give up on these two points."[16]

The Paris Bourse of the 1960s has been transformed by globalization, new technologies, and financial innovation. Along with some of its former competitors, it is now part of a multinational financial services network. Policy makers willing to regulate financial markets are facing increasingly complex dilemmas. The creation of the COB is a compelling story, but it would be hazardous to generalize the findings of a single case study. The modest objective of this book was to historicize its origins, not to build an analytical framework for explaining the emergence of independent market regulators, nor to draw conclusions for the present. The problems outlined by Debré in his memoirs, however, will likely continue to be debated—if at a different, much larger scale.

Introduction

1. Bernard Tricot, *Mémoires* (Paris: Quai Voltaire, 1994), 413. All English translations are the author's.

2. In chapter 6 of *The French Way*, Richard Kuisel explains how the Fifth Republic liberalized the French economy in the 1990s: "[. . .] none of this, or so it was claimed, was an imitation of the Americans. To paraphrase Philip Gordon and Sophie Meunier, who explained the process of 'globalization by stealth,' one might speak, in this case, of 'liberalization by stealth.'" Kuisel, *The French Way: How France Embraced and Rejected American Values and Power* (Princeton: Princeton University Press, 2012), 283. There was nothing stealthy, however, in the imitation of the SEC by Gaullist reformers of the late 1960s.

3. For a history of the Paris securities market, see Laure Quennouëlle-Corre, *La place financière de Paris au XXe siècle: Des ambitions contrariées* (Paris: Comité pour l'histoire économique et financière de la France, 2015); Paul Lagneau-Ymonet and Angelo Riva, *Histoire de la Bourse* (Paris: Éditions La Découverte, 2012). For a short monograph on the COB, see Marie-Claude Robert and Béatrice Labboz, *La Commission des Opérations de Bourse* (Paris: Presse Universitaires de France, 1991).

4. See in particular Pierre-Henri Conac, *La régulation des marchés boursiers par la Commission des Opérations de Bourse (COB) et la Securities and Exchange Commission (SEC)* (Paris: Librairie Générale de Droit et de Jurisprudence, 2002).

5. For a detailed analysis of the 1930s financial reforms in the United States, see Michael E. Parrish, *Securities Regulation and the New Deal* (New Haven: Yale University Press, 1970); Joel Seligman, *The Transformation of Wall Street: A History of the Securities and Exchange Commission and Modern Corporate Finance* (Boston: Houghton Mifflin, 1982); Michael Perino, *The Hellhound of Wall Street: How Ferdinand Pecora's Investigation of the Great Crash Forever Changed American Finance* (New York: Penguin, 2010).

6. Sabine Effosse, *Le crédit à la consommation en France, 1947–1965: De la stigmatisation à la réglementation* (Paris: Comité pour l'histoire économique et financière de la France—IGPDE, 2014), 100–104.

7. Bertrand Blancheton, Hubert Bonin, and David Le Bris, "The French Paradox: A Financial Crisis during the Golden Age of the 1960s," *Business History* 56, no. 3 (2014): 391–413.

8. Other aspects of transatlantic policy transfers, however, have been thoroughly investigated by historians. To name but one, Daniel T. Rodgers revealed the international roots of American social politics of the Progressive Era. Rodgers, *Atlantic Crossings: Social Politics in a Progressive Age* (Cambridge, MA: Belknap Press of Harvard University Press, 1998). The subject of the Americanization of France has also been much debated among historians and the general public. Richard Kuisel, among others, explored France's response to American influence during the second half of the twentieth century. Kuisel, *Seducing the French: The Dilemma of Americanization* (Berkeley: University of California Press, 1993) and *The French Way*.

9. The Palais was named after its architect, Alexandre-Théodore Brongniart (1739–1813), who died before completing the building he designed.

10. "Palais Brongniart–Paris," accessed October 2015, http://www.palaisbrongniart.com /?langue=en. The website describes a project to be completed by 2013.

11. Eric Helleiner and Stefano Pagliari, "The End of an Era in International Regulation? A Postcrisis Research Agenda," *International Organization* 65 (Winter 2011): 169–200.

12. Tony Porter, *Globalization and Finance* (Cambridge: Polity Press, 2005), vii.

13. Porter, *Globalization and Finance*, 67–84; David Andrew Singer, *Regulating Capital: Setting Standards for the International Financial System* (Ithaca: Cornell University Press, 2007), 67–95.

14. Ordonnance no. 67-833 du 28 septembre 1967 instituant une commission des opérations de bourse et relative à l'information des porteurs de valeurs mobilières et à la publicité de certaines opérations de bourse.

Chapter 1 · A Minister on a Mission

1. "Long a Loyal Gaullist," *New York Times*, January 10, 1966.

2. In an article he wrote about the beginnings of the European Union, Chatenet commented on de Gaulle's friendship with German chancellor Konrad Adenauer: "[The] complementarity [between de Gaulle and Adenauer was] very important for the General, who was still influenced by the strong Germanic culture of those who had studied before 1914, whereas he seemed, at times, intellectually and instinctively, more distant from the Anglo-Saxons." Pierre Chatenet, "Aux sources de la construction européenne: des crises et des hommes," *Commentaire* 65 (1994): 73–76.

3. As explained by Philippe Roger in his book on French anti-Americanism, de Gaulle's frequent opposition to US foreign policy did not make him a rabid anti-American. Roger, *L'ennemi américain: Généalogie de l'antiaméricanisme français* (Paris: Éditions du Seuil, 2002), 436–438.

4. Henry Tanner, "De Gaulle Starts 2d Term and New Cabinet Is Announced," *New York Times*, January 9, 1966.

5. The street itself was named after a 1797 victory of Bonaparte over the Austrians in Northern Italy.

6. "Long a Loyal Gaullist," *New York Times*, January 10, 1966.

7. "Long a Loyal Gaullist."

8. Jérôme Perrier, *Michel Debré* (Paris: Ellipses, 2010), 364.

9. Michel Debré, *Trois républiques pour une France: Mémoires—IV: Gouverner autrement (1962–1970)* (Paris: Albin Michel, 1993), 66.

10. Debré, *Mémoires—IV*, 88.

11. Debré, *Mémoires—IV*, 96.

12. On the many autobiographies, memoirs, and personal testimonies published by high-ranking French civil servants of the postwar era, see Brigitte Gaïti, "Les modernisateurs dans l'administration d'après-guerre: L'écriture d'une histoire héroïque," *Revue française d'administration publique* 2, no. 102 (2002): 295–306.

13. Debré, *Mémoires—IV*, 81–82.

14. From F. Caron, *Histoire économique de la France*, 158, quoted in Jean-Charles Asselain, *Histoire économique de la France du XVIIIe siècle à nos jours: 2—Depuis 1918* (Paris: Seuil, 1984, 2011), 105.

15. John Zysman, *Governments, Markets, and Growth: Financial Systems and the Politics of Industrial Change* (Oxford: Martin Robertson, 1983), 114.

16. Michael Loriaux, *France after Hegemony: International Change and Financial Reform* (Ithaca: Cornell University Press 1991), 149–153. See also Benjamin Lemoine, *L'ordre de la dette: Enquête sur les infortunes de l'État et la prospérité du marché* (Paris: Éditions de la découverte, 2016), 50–52.

17. Luc Boltanski, *Les Cadres: La formation d'un groupe social* (Paris: Les Éditions de Minuit, 1982), 177–178.

18. Peter Braestrup, "Despite de Gaulle's 'Serenity and Ardor,' a Slowdown," *New York Times,* January 21, 1966.

19. Tanner, "De Gaulle Starts 2d Term," *New York Times,* January 9, 1966.

20. Author's interview with Jean-Yves Haberer, April 12, 2014. Antoine Dupont-Fauville, "Michel Debré Ministre de l'Économie et des Finances," in *Michel Debré, un réformateur aux Finances 1966–1968,* ed. Eric Bussière et al. Histoire économique et financière de la France (Paris: Comité pour l'Histoire économique et financière, 2005), 5–11.

21. French historian Laurent Warlouzet calls for a reassessment of the role played by Debré— among others—in Gaullist France's rallying to the European project. Warlouzet, *Le choix de la CEE par la France: L'Europe économique en débat de Mendès France à de Gaulle (1955–1969)* (Paris: Comité pour l'histoire économique et financière de la France–IGPDE, 2011), 500–502.

22. *New York Times's* John L. Hess asked rhetorically, "Can the Communists under their General Secretary, Waldeck Rochet, and the moderate leftists in François Mitterrand's Federation of the Left go on to achieve a viable program for coalition government? That is still uncertain, but it is a great deal less unlikely today than it was a week ago." Hess, "Vote in France II: Communists Escape 'Ghetto,'" *New York Times,* March 19, 1967.

23. Georges Valence, *VGE: Une vie* (Paris: Flammarion, 2011), 200.

24. Debré, *Mémoires—IV,* 88.

25. Article 38 of the Constitution of the Fifth Republic. English translation as per the French Conseil Constitutionnel, accessed February 27, 2015, http://www.conseil-constitutionnel.fr /conseil-constitutionnel/english/constitution/constitution-of-4-october-1958.25742.html.

26. Alain Peyrefitte, *C'était de Gaulle,* vol. 3 (Paris: Éditions de Fallois, Fayard, 2000), 233.

27. Edgard Pisani, *Persiste et signe* (Paris: Éditions Odile Jacob, 1992), 165.

28. François Mauriac, *Bloc-notes* (column) dated May 11, 1967, in Mauriac, *Bloc-notes,* vol. 4, *1965–1967* (Paris: Éditions du Seuil, 1993), 450–451.

29. Charles de Gaulle, "Press Conference," May 16, 1967, accessed June 17, 2016, http:// fresques.ina.fr/de-gaulle/fiche-media/Gaulle00129/conference-de-presse-du-16-mai-1967.html.

30. André Ballet, "L'Assemblée nationale a entendu la déclaration du Premier ministre sur les pouvoirs spéciaux," *Le Monde,* May 20, 1967. Emphasis added.

31. "Minutes of parliamentary proceedings," May 19, 1967, *Journal Officiel de la République française,* May 20, 1967.

32. "Minutes of parliamentary proceedings," May 19, 1967, *Journal Officiel de la République française,* May 20, 1967.

33. Éric Roussel, *Pierre Mendès France* (Paris: Gallimard, 2007), 474–475.

34. Giscard d'Estaing, "Interview with *L'Express,*" May 8, 1967, quoted by Socialist *député* Gaston Deferre during the May 20 session of the French National Assembly, "Minutes of parliamentary proceedings," May 20, 1967, *Journal Officiel de la République française.*

35. Valence, *VGE,* 250–251.

36. "Minutes of parliamentary proceedings," May 20, 1967, *Journal Officiel de la République française.*

37. "Minutes of parliamentary proceedings," June 16, 1967, *Journal Officiel de la République française,* June 17, 1967.

38. "Minutes of parliamentary proceedings," June 16, 1967, *Journal Officiel de la République française,* June 17, 1967.

39. During the first decades of the Fifth Republic, however, formal ratification of ordonnances was often delayed or even nonexistent. Marc Guillaume, "Les ordonnances: Tuer ou sauver la loi?," *Pouvoirs,* no. 114 (3rd quarter 2005): 117–129.

40. Loi no. 67-482 du 22 juin 1967 autorisant le Gouvernement, par application de l'article 38 de la Constitution, à prendre des mesures d'ordre économique et social, *Journal Officiel de la*

République Française, accessed March 4, 2015, http://www.legifrance.gouv.fr/jopdf/common/jo
_pdf.jsp?numJO=0&dateJO=19670623&numTexte=&pageDebut=06211&pageFin.

41. Emphasis added. John L. Hess, "French Cabinet Approves Wide-Ranging Economic Reforms," *New York Times*, August 31, 1967.

42. Centre d'histoire de Sciences-Po, Fonds Michel Debré, Archives de Michel Debré, ministre de l'Économie et des Finances 1966–1968 4DE, Box 4DE35: dossier rigide "Marché Financier–Epargne," dossier souple "Idées de réforme dans le domaine de l'épargne, du crédit et des institutions financières," note no. 421/CAB8 dated April 1, 1967, signed by Jean-Yves Haberer.

43. "Ordonnances relatives au crédit, à l'épargne et au marché financier," Centre d'histoire de Sciences-Po, Fonds Michel Debré, Archives de Michel Debré, ministre de l'Économie et des Finances 1966–1968 4DE, Box 4DE29: dossier "Ordonnances financières," no date, no signature, no addressee.

Chapter 2 · "Thieves!"

1. Michel Debré, *Trois républiques pour une France: Mémoires–IV: Gouverner autrement (1962–1970)* (Paris: Albin Michel, 1993), 100.

2. Laurent Warlouzet, *Le choix de la CEE par la France: L'Europe économique en débat de Mendès France à de Gaulle (1955–1969)* (Paris: Comité pour l'histoire économique et financière de la France–IGPDE, 2011), 446.

3. Cinquième Plan de développement économique et social, vol. 1, 68–69.

4. Alphonse Thélier, "Le nouveau groupe Ugine-Kuhlmann sera d'après la capitalisation boursière le second de l'industrie française," *Le Monde*, May 27, 1966.

5. Michel Beaud, Pierre Danjou, and Jean David, *Une multinationale française: Pechiney Ugine Kuhlmann* (Paris: Éditions du Seuil, 1975), 43.

6. Philippe Thaure, *Pechiney? . . . vendu!* (Paris: Presses des Mines, 2007), 45.

7. Thélier, "Le nouveau groupe Ugine-Kuhlmann."

8. Memorandum dated July 6, 1966, from Maurice Pérouse to Michel Debré, "Fusion des Sociétés UGINE, KUHLMANN et PRODUITS AZOTÉS: Répercussion sur les cours de bourse des actions de ces sociétés," CAEF, Archives Jean-Yves Haberer, 5A0000350/1.

9. Author's interview with Jean-Yves Haberer, April 12, 2014; Jacques Seyler, "Des torts partagés," *Le Monde*, November 12, 1966.

10. "La Bourse croit à une fusion Ugine-Kuhlmann," *Les Échos*, May 25, 1966.

11. Alain Vernay, "Il est urgent de substituer des précisions aux rumeurs," *Les Échos*, May 25, 1966.

12. Jean Saint-Geours, *Pouvoir et Finance* (Paris: Fayard, 1979), 163–167.

13. Vernay, "Il est urgent de substituer des précisions aux rumeurs."

14. Vernay, "Il est urgent de substituer des précisions aux rumeurs."

15. Vernay, "Il est urgent de substituer des précisions aux rumeurs."

16. "La fusion Ugine-Kuhlmann provoque des remous sur les cours," *La Vie Française*, May 27, 1966.

17. Letter to Ugine shareholders, June 6, 1966, Rio Tinto France, Archives Pechiney–Collection historique, Secrétariat général: Box 072-2-24974, Société des Produits Azotés–Fusion Ugine Kuhlmann/SPA (1966).

18. Letter to Ugine shareholders, June 6, 1966.

19. "Un entretien avec M. André Lebreton, Directeur général d'UGINE," *La Vie française*, June 10, 1966; "Les assemblées dans la chimie . . . UGINE-KUHLMANN Les Présidents exposent les raisons du projet de fusion," *La Vie française*, June 24, 1996.

20. Memorandum dated July 6, 1966, from Maurice Pérouse to Michel Debré, "Fusion des Sociétés UGINE, KUHLMANN et PRODUITS AZOTÉS, Répercussion sur les cours de bourse des actions de ces sociétés," CAEF, Archives Jean-Yves Haberer, 5A0000350/1.

21. Memorandum dated July 6, 1966, from Maurice Pérouse to Michel Debré.

22. In the case of Kuhlmann, Pérouse's rough estimate was confirmed by the report presented by auditors to the extraordinary general meeting of Ugine shareholders on December 7, 1966.

Kuhlmann net asset value (NAV) calculated by auditors: FRF 685,215,072.35
Number of Kuhlman shares outstanding: 3,446,397
NAV / Number of shares: 198.82

In the case of Ugine, no such calculation was included in the report put together by auditors.

Rapport des Commissaires aux apports à l'Assemblée générale extraordinaire à forme constitutive du 7 décembre 1966, Rio Tinto France, Archives Pechiney—Collection historique, Secrétariat général: Box 072-2-24974, Société des Produits Azotés–Fusion Ugine Kuhlmann / SPA (1966).

23. Memorandum dated July 6, 1966, from Maurice Pérouse to Michel Debré.

24. Minutes of the December 29, 1966, extraordinary general meeting of Ugine shareholders, Rio Tinto France, Archives Pechiney–Collection historique, Secrétariat général: Box 072-2-24929 / 24913: SECEM et AEU (1965–1966).

25. Memorandum dated July 6, 1966, from Maurice Pérouse to Michel Debré.

26. The *Syndicat* was chaired by André Bassinet from *La Cote Desfossés*. The vice chairmen were René Sédillot (*La Vie Française*) and Roger Gicquel (*L'Opinion*). "M. Pompidou déclare," *La Vie Française*, June 10, 1966; "Le Premier Ministre et la Bourse," *Les Échos*, June 13, 1966.

27. Loi no. 65-566 du 12 juillet 1965 modifiant l'imposition des entreprises et des revenus de capitaux mobiliers. *Journal Officiel*, July 13, 1965, 6003–6008. The Vallon amendment echoed the famed Wallon amendment, named after French *député* Henri Wallon (1812–1904). In 1875, the vote of the Wallon amendment by the National Assembly formally established the republican nature of the political regime in France.

28. "M. Pompidou déclare," *La Vie Française*, June 10, 1966.

29. "Le Premier Ministre et la Bourse," *Les Échos*, June 13, 1966.

30. "Le Premier Ministre et la Bourse."

31. Note no. 409/CAB8 de Jean-Yves Haberer à Michel Debré, 7 février 1967: "Adaptation de certains dispositifs américains destinés à "améliorer" la Bourse," CAEF, Archives Jean-Yves Haberer, 5A0000362.

32. Pompidou used the word *cadavérique* (corpse-like) to characterize the state of the securities market. Televised interview of Georges Pompidou by journalist Roger Priouret, economic editorialist of French magazine *L'Express*, September 26, 1966. Transcript communicated by Emilia Robin, Institut Georges Pompidou, April 27, 2015.

33. Albin Krebs, "Pompidou Rose in Classic French Manner and Became de Gaulle's Successor," *New York Times*, April 3, 1974.

34. Éric Roussel, *Georges Pompidou, 1911–1974* (Paris: Jean-Claude Lattès, 1994), 89–110.

35. Krebs, "Pompidou Rose in Classic French Manner."

36. "Comment moraliser la Bourse," *La Vie Française*, June 17, 1966.

37. "Intervention de Michel Debré du 6 juillet 1966," CAEF, Trésor, Marchés financiers: Box B-0051929/2.

38. Interview of Bottmer by M. Monty, *Fortune française*, 1966, CAEF, Compagnie des Agents de change–Secrétariat général: Box B-0067977/1.

39. "Retour au calme sur Ugine et Kuhlmann," *La Vie Française*, June 3, 1966.

40. Seyler, "Des torts partagés."

41. Minutes of the June 22, 1966, ordinary general meeting of Ugine shareholders, Rio Tinto France, Archives Pechiney–Collection historique, Secrétariat général: Box 072-2-24929 / 24913: SECEM et AEU (1965–1966).

42. Minutes of the June 22, 1966, ordinary general meeting of Ugine shareholders.

43. Minutes of the June 22, 1966, ordinary general meeting of Ugine shareholders.

44. Minutes of the June 22, 1966, ordinary general meeting of Ugine shareholders.

45. Minutes of the June 22, 1966, ordinary general meeting of Ugine shareholders.

46. Seyler, "Des torts partagés."

47. Minutes of the November 14, 1966, extraordinary general meeting of Ugine shareholders, Rio Tinto France, Archives Pechiney–Collection historique, Secrétariat général: Box 072-2-24929 / 24913: SECEM et AEU (1965–1966).

48. Minutes of the November 14, 1966, extraordinary general meeting of Ugine shareholders.

49. Minutes of the November 14, 1966, extraordinary general meeting of Ugine shareholders.

50. Société d'Analyse Financière et Économique (Mme Vidart), Ugine Kuhlmann, Archives historiques BNP Paribas: Box IND/3316.

51. Thaure, Pechiney? . . . vendu!, 48–49.

52. Ugine-Kuhlmann internal memorandum, October 10, 1969, Archives historiques BNP Paribas: Box IND/3316.

53. Interestingly, the report put together by auditors prior to the merger between Ugine-Kuhlmann and Pechiney was much more detailed than the 1966 report on the merger between Ugine and Kuhlmann. Rio Tinto France, Archives Pechiney—Collection historique, Direction générale: Draft report on the merger between Pechiney and Ugine-Kuhlmann: Box 200-6-55024 / 55025, Fusion Pechiney–Ugine-Kuhlmann (1971).

54. Beaud et al., Une multinationale française.

55. "Communication faite au conseil d'administration de la B.N.P. du 3 août 1966 par M. Défossé," CAEF, Trésor–Marchés financiers: Box B-0051929/2.

Chapter 3 · The Paris Bourse in the 1960s

1. Jean Lacouture, De Gaulle: 1—Le rebelle, 1890–1944 (Paris: Éditions du Seuil, 1984), 187–188.

2. Commission des opérations de Bourse, "Rapport annuel 1969," Journal Officiel de la République française (March 11, 1970): 128.

3. Yves Meunier, "Où va la Bourse?," Conférences des Ambassadeurs, April 20, 1967, CAEF—Compagnie des Agents de change—Secrétariat général: Box B-0067977/1.

4. Guy Chaussinand-Nogaret, Gens de Finance au XVIIIe siècle (Paris: Éditions Complexe, 1972), 36–40.

5. Charles P. Kindleberger, A Financial History of Western Europe (New York: Oxford University Press, 1993), 99.

6. Charles P. Kindleberger and Robert Aliber, Manias, Panics, and Crises: A History of Financial Crises (Hoboken: Wiley, 1978), 128.

7. Kindleberger, A Financial History of Western Europe, 100.

8. Romuald Szramkiewicz and Olivier Descamps, Histoire du droit des affaires (Paris: Librairie Générale de Droit et de Jurisprudence, 2013), 137–138.

9. Paul Lagneau-Ymonet and Angelo Riva, Histoire de la Bourse (Paris: Éditions La Découverte, 2012), 19–20.

10. In a 1990 interview with historian Laure Quenouëlle-Corre, Chatenet himself quoted Les Boussardel, a fictional saga by twentieth-century novelist Philippe Hériat, to describe the Parisian milieu of agents de change dynasties. Archives orales Pierre Chatenet (September 27 and October 12, 1990, interviews conducted by Laure Quenouëlle-Corre). Interview 6, tape 8, September 27, 1990, Comité pour l'histoire économique et financière de la France / Institut de la gestion publique et du développement économique (IGPDE).

11. Stendhal, *Lucien Leuwen II* (1834; Paris: Pocket, 1999), 322.

12. Honoré de Balzac, *La Maison Nucingen* (1837; Paris: Gallimard, 1989), 180.

13. Bernard Colasse, *Les fondements de la comptabilité* (Paris: La Découverte, 2012), 90.

14. Szramkiewicz and Descamps, *Histoire du droit des affaires*, 409–411; Colasse, *Les fondements de la comptabilité*, 90.

15. Pierre-Henri Conac, *La régulation des marchés boursiers par la Commission des Opérations de Bourse (COB) et la Securities and Exchange Commission (SEC)* (Paris: Librairie Générale de Droit et de Jurisprudence, 2002), 8.

16. Alain Supiot, *La Gouvernance par les nombres: Cours au Collège de France (2012–2014)* (Paris: Fayard / Institut d'Études avancées de Nantes, 2015), 128.

17. Laure Quennouëlle-Corre, *La place financière de Paris au XXe siècle: Des ambitions contrariées* (Paris: Comité pour l'histoire économique et financière de la France, 2015), 49.

18. "[. . .] much against his will, Sacha Stavisky ignited an explosion that briefly engulfed the entire system of government. His affair had inverted Captain Dreyfus's, substituting a guilty man gone free for an innocent one sent to Devil's Island, civilian for military justice, and a defensive for a missionary Republic. But each expressed the conflict between ideals and realities that had plagued France since the Revolution, and that in this regime accounted for the frequency of scandal." Paul F. Jankowski, *Stavisky: A Confidence Man in the Republic of Virtue* (Ithaca: Cornell University Press, 2002), 264.

19. Conac, *La régulation des marchés boursiers*, 12.

20. Along with other organizations established by the Vichy government, the OECCA was "refounded" in 1945.

21. Yves Bouthillier, *Le drame de Vichy: II. Finances sous la contrainte* (Paris: Librairie Plon, 1951), 411.

22. Loi no. 290 du 14 février 1942 tendant à l'organisation et au fonctionnement des bourses de valeurs, *Journal Officiel de l'État français*, February 15, 1942, 662–665; "Tableau en trois colonnes: États-Unis, France et observations," CAEF, Trésor–Marchés financiers: Box B-0051929/2.

23. "Tableau en trois colonnes: États-Unis, France et observations," CAEF, Trésor–Marchés financiers: Box B-0051929/2.

24. Claire Andrieu, *La Banque sous l'occupation: Paradoxes de l'histoire d'une profession* (Paris: Presses de la Fondation nationale des sciences politiques, 1990), 207–208.

25. On the "overdraft economy," see Michael Loriaux, *France after Hegemony: International Change and Financial Reform* (Ithaca: Cornell University Press, 1991), 55–75, 168–178; Laure Quennouëlle-Corre, "Les réformes bancaires et financières de 1966–1967," in *Michel Debré, un réformateur aux Finances 1966–1968* (Paris: Ministère de l'Économie, des Finances et de l'Industrie, Comité pour l'Histoire économique et financière de la France, 2005), 104–117.

26. Loriaux, *France after Hegemony*, 56–57.

27. Loriaux, *France after Hegemony*, 111.

28. Raghuram G. Rajan and Luigi Zingales, "The Great Reversals: The Politics of Financial Development in the 20th Century," *Journal of Financial Economics* 69 (2003): 15. See also John Zysman, *Governments, Markets, and Growth: Financial Systems and the Politics of Industrial Change* (Oxford: Martin Robertson, 1983), 124.

29. Jean-Pierre Patat, *Monnaie, institutions financières et politique monétaire* (Paris: Economica, 1986), 248.

30. Olivier Feiertag, "The International Opening-Up of the Paris Bourse: Overdraft-Economy Curbs and Market Dynamics," in Youssef Cassis and Éric Bussière, eds., *London and Paris as International Financial Centres in the Twentieth Century* (Oxford: Oxford University Press, 2005), 229–246.

31. Georges Lutfalla, "Étude du marché financier," *Journal Officiel de la République française*, November 14, 1952, 409–468.

32. Lutfalla, "Étude du marché financier," 410.

33. Francis Auboyneau, "Paris Bourse Faces Hardships in Process of Developing Market," *The American Banker*, March 26, 1965. The article was written in French and translated into English by the newspaper. CAEF–Compagnie des Agents de change–Secrétariat général: Box B-0067977/1. Emphasis in original.

34. Auboyneau, "Paris Bourse Faces Hardships."

35. Jacques Seyler, "Des torts partagés," *Le Monde*, November 12, 1966.

36. Colasse, *Les fondements de la comptabilité*, 90.

37. Until 1994, auditors and certified accountants were affiliated to two different organizations, respectively, the Compagnie nationale des commissaires aux comptes and the Ordre des experts comptables et des comptables agréés. Colasse, *Les fondements de la comptabilité*, 25.

38. "Réunion du 15 juin sur les problèmes actuels de la Bourse," aide-mémoire daté du 27 juin 1967, CAEF, Trésor–Marchés financiers: Box B-0051929/2.

39. "Communication faite au conseil d'administration de la B.N.P. du 3 août 1966 par M. Défossé," CAEF, Trésor–Marchés financiers: Box B-0051929/2.

40. Lagneau-Ymonet and Riva, *Histoire de la Bourse*, 88.

41. Jeanne Lazarus, *L'épreuve de l'argent: Banques, banquiers, clients* (Paris: Calmann-Lévy, 2012), 24.

42. Quennouëlle-Corre, *La place financière de Paris au XXe siècle*, 227.

43. Paris, France: Archives historiques du Crédit Agricole, Box DAF 3343–2: Comité des Bourses de Valeurs, Dossier général: correspondance, décisions, procès-verbaux et ordres du jour.

44. Quennouëlle-Corre, *La place financière de Paris au XXe siècle*, 298.

45. Memorandum from Jean Dromer to Général de Gaulle, May 17, 1966, Archives nationales, Présidence de Charles de Gaulle, Dossiers AG/5(1)2318–2322.

46. "Communication faite au conseil d'administration de la BNP du 3 août 1966 par M. Défossé," CAEF, Trésor–Marchés financiers: Box B-0051929/2.

47. Françoise Marnata, *La Bourse et le financement des investissements* (Paris: Armand Colin, 1973), 34.

48. For a detailed analysis of the French stock market crisis of the 1960s, see Bertrand Blancheton, Hubert Bonin, and David Le Bris, "The French Paradox: A Financial Crisis during the Golden Age of the 1960s," *Business History* 56, no. 3 (2014): 391–413.

49. Marnata, *La Bourse*, 34–38.

50. Interview granted by Georges Pompidou to French newspaper *L'Aurore*, February 13 and 14, 1967, excerpt communicated by Emilia Robin, Institut Georges Pompidou, April 27, 2015.

51. "Réunion du 15 juin sur les problèmes actuels de la Bourse," memorandum dated June 27, 1967, CAEF, Trésor–Marchés financiers: Box B-0051929/2.

Chapter 4 · France Looks at America

1. Richard E. Mooney, "France Shifts View toward Welcoming Foreign Investment," *New York Times*, March 24, 1966.

2. Mooney, "France Shifts view Toward Welcoming Foreign Investment."

3. According to Richard Kuisel, "De Gaulle consented to the shift in policy rather than ordering it." Kuisel, *Seducing the French: The Dilemma of Americanization* (Berkeley: University of California Press, 1993), 176.

4. Michel Debré, *Trois républiques pour une France: Mémoires—I: Combattre* (Paris: Albin Michel, 1984), 98.

5. Debré, *Mémoires—I*, 103. Murphy, in his own book *Diplomat among Warriors*, mentioned Debré in a very different, if still African, context. In 1957, as the war in Algeria was raging, the French Air Force bombed the Tunisian village of Sidi Sakiet. Murphy and a British diplomat

were members of a "good offices" mission formed at the request of the French government. They were violently attacked by members of the Gaullist party, which was in the opposition at the time: "Perhaps the most prominent writer for De Gaulle at that time was Senator Michel Debré, who later became Prime Minister in the De Gaulle Government. Debré wrote several articles attacking the Good Offices mission and his thesis was, in effect, "Yankee Go Home!" Sidi Sakiet, he declared, was a French problem and France would settle it without American or British intervention." Murphy, *Diplomat among Warriors* (Garden City: Doubleday, 1964), 395–396.

6. Couve de Murville enjoyed the utmost trust of de Gaulle. According to French historian Laurent Warlouzet: "As [regarded] European matters, he was considered so close to General de Gaulle that he did not seem to have ideas of his own. Such was the criticism often directed at him by, among others, Michel Debré." Laurent Warlouzet, *Le choix de la CEE par la France: L'Europe économique en débat de Mendès France à de Gaulle (1955–1969)* (Paris: Comité pour l'histoire économique et financière de la France–IGPDE, 2011), 260.

7. Michel Debré, *Mémoires–IV,* 165.

8. Michel Debré, "Independence: Key to French Economic Aims," *American Banker*, April 20, 1966.

9. Debré, "Independence."

10. John L. Hess, "Paris Opens Doors to U.S. Investment," *New York Times*, January 16, 1967.

11. Kuisel, *Seducing the French*, 178. On *Le Défi américain*'s reception, see also Laurent Warlouzet, *Le choix de la CEE par la France. L'Europe économique en débat de Mendès France à de Gaulle (1955–1969)* (Paris: Comité pour l'histoire économique et financière de la France–IGPDE, 2011), 451–452.

12. Jean-Louis Servan-Schreiber, *Le défi américain* (Paris: Denoël, 1967), 115. Italics in original.

13. Servan-Schreiber, *Le défi américain*, 225. Servan-Schreiber mistakenly dated Roosevelt's famous phrase, which was included in his 1936 acceptance speech at the convention of the Democratic Party in Philadelphia, and not in his 1932 inaugural address.

14. Michael Perino, *The Hellhound of Wall Street: How Ferdinand Pecora's Investigation of the Great Crash Forever Changed American Finance* (New York: Penguin, 2010), 284.

15. Quoted in Louis D. Brandeis, *Other People's Money and How the Bankers Use It* (New York: Frederick A. Stockes Company, 1914), 10.

16. Brandeis, *Other People's Money,* 79.

17. "The epithet 'blue sky' was attached to the laws by one midwestern state legislator who [. . .] declared that, if securities legislation was not passed, financial pirates would sell citizens everything in his state *but* the blue sky." Michael E. Parrish, *Securities Regulation and the New Deal* (New Haven: Yale University Press, 1970), 5–6.

18. Julia C. Ott, *When Wall Street Met Main Street: The Quest for an Investors' Democracy* (Cambridge: Harvard University Press, 2011), 188.

19. Herbert Hoover, *The Memoirs of Herbert Hoover: The Great Depression, 1929–1941* (New York: Macmillan, 1952), 7.

20. Democratic Party Platforms: "Democratic Party Platform of 1932," June 27, 1932, online by Gerhard Peters and John T. Woolley, The American Presidency Project, http://www.presidency.ucsb.edu/ws/?pid=29595, accessed June 17, 2016.

21. Franklin D. Roosevelt, "Making Suckers of Americans," *Liberty* (August 20, 1932). Hoover also referred to "the Mississippi bubble of 1927–1929" in his memoirs. *The Memoirs of Herbert Hoover*, 11.

22. Franklin D. Roosevelt, "Inaugural Address," March 4, 1933, online by Gerhard Peters and John T. Woolley, The American Presidency Project, http://www.presidency.ucsb.edu/ws/?pid=14473, accessed June 17, 2016.

23. Raymond Moley, *After Seven Years* (New York: Harper & Brothers, 1939), 155.

24. William O. Douglas, "Protecting the Investor," *Yale Review* 20 (Spring 1934): 521–533. Reprinted in Howard Zinn, *New Deal Thought* (1996; Indianapolis: Hacket, 2003), 117.

25. Parrish, *Securities Regulation and the New Deal*, 142.

26. David Andrew Singer, *Regulating Capital: Setting Standards for the International Financial System* (Ithaca: Cornell University Press, 2007), 21.

27. Joel Seligman, *The Transformation of Wall Street: A History of the Securities and Exchange Commission and Modern Corporate Finance* (Boston: Houghton Mifflin, 1982), 100.

28. Franklin D. Roosevelt, "Government and Modern Capitalism," Fireside Chat, September 30, 1934, in Russel D. Buhite and David W. Levy, *FDR's Fireside Chats* (Norman: University of Oklahoma Press, 1992), 56.

29. Secretary of the Interior Harold L. Ickes famously noted in his diary: "At Cabinet meeting yesterday afternoon the President talked over the appointments he had in mind on the new commissions that have been created by act of Congress. I am afraid I do not agree with him as to the chairman he is going to name for the Securities Commission. He has named Joseph P. Kennedy for that place, a former stockmarket plunger. The President has great confidence in him because he has made his pile, has invested all his money in Government securities, and knows all the tricks of the trade." Harold L. Ickes, *The Secret Diary of Harold L. F*, vol. 1, *The First Thousand Days, 1933–1936* (New York: Simon & Schuster, 1953), 173.

30. Daniel Yergin and Joseph Stanislaw, *The Commanding Heights: The Battle between Government and the Marketplace That Is Remaking the Modern World* (New York: Simon & Schuster, 1998), 53–55.

31. Bernard Baruch, *The Public Years* (New York: Holt, Rinehart and Winston, 1960), 234.

32. Baruch, *Public Years*, 234–235.

33. Georges Lutfalla, "Étude du marché financier," *Journal Officiel de la République française*, November 14, 1952, 427. On the SEC's reputation as one of the New Deal's most successful agencies, see also Jessica Wang, "Imagining the Administrative State: Legal Pragmatism, Securities Regulation, and New Deal Liberalism," *Journal of Policy History* 17, no. 3 (2005): 257–293.

34. "Résumé d'un rapport sur le marché financier, son rôle économique, sa situation actuelle et les réformes que celle-ci appelle, présenté par Georges Lutfalla au nom du Conseil Économique les 12 et 13 novembre 1952," Banque de France, Direction Générale des Études et du Crédit, 27 mai 1959, Archives de la Banque de France, Box No. 77, 1370198301, "La banque, la bourse, l'assurance 1959–1972," dossier 260/03: Marchés Financiers, projets de réforme jusqu'en 1959.

35. Debré, *Mémoires–IV*, 108.

36. This was typical of the way Debré interacted with his subordinates, as indicated by a short note dated November 23, 1966. Dealing with a similar issue, the note was sent to his adviser Haberer: "I have read in *L'Information* that a bill regulating take-over bids had been introduced in the U.S. Congress. Try to find this document and tell me what you think." Note de Michel Debré à Jean-Yves Haberer, 23 novembre 1966, CAEF, Archives Jean-Yves Haberer, 5A0000350/1.

37. As early as November 1966, in an article that alluded to the Ugine-Kuhlmann scandal, *Le Monde* mentioned the creation of a commission—and dismissed it offhandedly: "In order to moralize the *Bourse* and avoid fiddling of data before the release of account statements, capital increases, take-over-bids or mergers, it has been envisioned to create a surveillance commission. [Such a commission] does not seem to be needed since there already exists a *Comité des Bourses* and a *Chambre syndicale des agents de change* to fulfill this mission. But it might be possible to get some inspiration from the American example. In the United States board members and managers must disclose trading transactions on the securities of their corporations. This rule also applies to shareholders who own 10% of the equity of a company, even if they are not board members or managers." Jacques Seyler, "Des torts partagés," *Le Monde*, November 12, 1966.

38. Debré, *Mémoires–IV*, 108.

39. The 1959 promotion Vauban was named after Louis XIV's famous military engineer, who

was a pioneer of economic thought. Future French president Jacques Chirac also graduated from the ÉNA in 1959.

40. Beginning in 1949, French trainees (primarily businessmen, engineers, and workers) were sent to the United States to study American prosperity. "By the end of the 1950s, more than 4,000 'missionaries' had visited the United States and written voluminous reports [. . .]." Richard Kuisel, "L'*American Way of Life* et les missions françaises de productivité," *Vingtième Siècle, revue d'histoire* 17, no. 1 (1988): 22. See also Luc Boltanski, *Les Cadres: La formation d'un groupe social* (Paris: Les Éditions de Minuit, 1982), 157–164.

41. Jeanne Lazarus, *L'épreuve de l'argent: Banques, banquiers, clients* (Paris: Calmann-Lévy, 2012), 26.

42. Laure Quennouëlle-Corre, "Les réformes bancaires et financières de 1966–1967," in Michel Debré, ed., *Un réformateur aux Finances 1966–1968* (Paris: Ministère de l'Économie, des Finances et de l'Industrie, Comité pour l'Histoire économique et financière de la France, 2005), 92.

43. Laure Quennouëlle-Corre, "Les réformes bancaires et financières de 1966–1967," 92.

44. Michael Loriaux, *France after Hegemony: International Change and Financial Reform.* 174. See also Pierre-Henri Cassou, "La réglementation bancaire, entre intérêt général et intérêts particuliers," in Hubert Bonin and Jean-Marc Figuet, eds., *Crise et régulation bancaires. Les cheminements de l'instabilité et de la stabilité bancaires.* Genève: Droz, 2016, 243–269.

45. In 1966, the Comptoir National d'Escompte de Paris (CNEP) and the Banque Nationale pour le Commerce et l'Industrie (BNCI) merged to create the Banque Nationale de Paris (BNP).

46. Jeanne Lazarus, *L'épreuve de l'argent: Banques, banquiers, clients* (Paris: Calmann-Lévy, 2012), 28–32.

47. Benjamin Lemoine, *L'ordre de la dette: Enquête sur les infortunes de l'État et la prospérité du marché* (Paris: Éditions de la découverte, 2016), 73–79.

48. Loriaux, *France after Hegemony*, 149–150.

49. In his analysis of the attempt by the Banque de France to create a liquid money market in the early 1970s, Eric Monnet also highlights the reforms of the late 1960s as part of the strategy to develop the role of French banks in the financing of the economy. See Éric Monnet, "La politique de la France au sortir des Trente Glorieuses: Un tournant monétariste?," *Revue d'histoire moderne et contemporaine* 1, no. 62-1 (2015): 147–174.

50. Lemoine, *L'ordre de la dette*, 75.

51. Laure Quennouëlle-Corre, *La place financière de Paris au XXe siècle: Des ambitions contrariées* (Paris: Institut de la gestion publique et du développement économique, 2015), 306–307.

52. The Belgian Commission bancaire et financière was created in 1935 in the context of a severe banking crisis (*Arrêté royal sur le contrôle des banques et le régime des émissions de titres et valeurs*, July 9, 1935). While the primary mission of the commission was the supervision of the Belgian banking system, it was also charged with the responsibility to review and opine on the issuance of new securities. Its powers and resources were much more limited than those of the SEC. Jacques H. Verteneuil, "La Commission bancaire a vingt-cinq ans," *La Revue de la banque*, nos. 9–10 (1960): 607–618.

53. Author's interview with Jean-Yves Haberer, April 12, 2014.

54. "Résumé d'un rapport sur le marché financier, son rôle économique, sa situation actuelle et les réformes que celle-ci appelle, présenté par Georges Lutfalla au nom du Conseil Économique les 12 et 13 novembre 1952," Banque de France, Direction Générale des Études et du Crédit, 27 mai 1959. Archives de la Banque de France, Box No. 77, 1370198301, "La banque, la bourse, l'assurance 1959–1972," dossier 260/03: Marchés Financiers, projets de réforme jusqu'en 1959.

55. Nicole de Montricher, "Norme légale et internationalisation des marchés boursiers: la délinquance financière en liberté surveillée," *Droit et société* 1, no. 71 (2009): 133–160.

56. Haberer was adamant on this point. Author's interview with Jean-Yves Haberer, April 12, 2014.

57. National Archives and Records Administration: RG59, Subject-Numerical File, 1964–1966, Boxes 711–712 [subject France E(conomics), 857–860 subject France Fin(ance)], RG59, Subject-Numerical File, 1967–1969, Boxes 614–615 (France E), 750–754 (France Fin).

58. "Tableau en trois colonnes: États-Unis, France et observations," CAEF, Trésor–Marchés financiers: Box B-0051929/2.

59. "Tableau en trois colonnes: États-Unis, France et observations."

60. National Association of Securities Dealers.

61. "Tableau en trois colonnes: États-Unis, France et observations," CAEF, Trésor–Marchés financiers: Box B-0051929/2.

62. From the mission statement of the SEC on its website at: http://www.sec.gov/about /whatwedo.shtml (Accessed June 17, 2016).

63. Conversely, "regulation" would not be the correct English translation of *régulation*, which designates, according to these economists, a new paradigm in the understanding of the economic system. Robert Boyer, *Économie politique des capitalismes: Théorie de la régulation et des crises* (Paris: La Découverte, 2015), 9.

64. "Tableau en trois colonnes: États-Unis, France et observations," CAEF, Trésor–Marchés financiers: Box B-0051929/2.

65. Minutes of the June 22, 1966, ordinary general meeting of Ugine shareholders. Rio Tinto France, Archives Pechiney–Collection historique, Secrétariat général: Box 072-2-24929 / 24913: SECEM et AEU (1965–1966).

66. "Tableau en trois colonnes: États-Unis, France et observations," CAEF, Trésor–Marchés financiers: Box B-0051929/2.

Chapter 5 · *Drafting the* Ordonnance

1. Note No. 409/CAB8 de Jean-Yves Haberer à Michel Debré, 7 février 1967: "Adaptation de certains dispositifs américains destinés à 'améliorer' la Bourse," CAEF, Archives Jean-Yves Haberer, 5A0000362.

2. "Intervention de Michel Debré du 6 juillet 1966," CAEF, Trésor–Marchés financiers: Box B-0051929/2.

3. Note No. 409/CAB8 de Jean-Yves Haberer à Michel Debré, 7 février 1967.

4. This had long been an objective of Debré. In June 1966, in an interview with *La Vie française* journalist Pierre Laurent, he had declared: "I believe that it is essential to our economic expansion that as many new investors as possible take an interest in the Bourse, and that the investor base be extended to new layers of the population. [. . .] Corporations, market intermediaries, entities which collect funds from investors, as well as the press must take part to the effort undertaken in order to improve the information of the population. I insist upon the role of the press, an objective, independent, well-informed press, capable of clearly explaining problems to non-professionals." Pierre Laurent, "Michel Debré s'explique," *La Vie française*, June 17, 1966.

5. Note No. 409/CAB8 from Jean-Yves Haberer to Michel Debré, February 7, 1967: "Adaptation de certains dispositifs américains destinés à "améliorer" la Bourse," CAEF, Archives Jean-Yves Haberer, 5A0000362.

6. Centre d'histoire de Sciences-Po, Fonds Michel Debré, Archives de Michel Debré, ministre de l'Économie et des Finances 1966–1968 4DE, Box 4DE35 (Déc. 1965–mai 1968): dossier rigide "Marché Financier–Epargne," dossier souple "Idées de réforme dans le domaine de l'épargne, du crédit et des institutions financières," Note No. 421/CAB8, April 1, 1967, signed by Jean-Yves Haberer.

7. Centre d'histoire de Sciences-Po, Fonds Michel Debré, Archives de Michel Debré, ministre de l'Économie et des Finances 1966–1968 4DE, Box 4DE35 (Déc. 1965–mai 1968).

8. Michael E. Parrish, *Securities Regulation and the New Deal* (New Haven: Yale University Press, 1970), 113–144.

9. Author's interview with Jean-Yves Haberer, April 12, 2014.

10. "Avant-projet d'ordonnance tendant à instituer une Commission de normalisation des opérations boursières," CAEF, Trésor–Marchés financiers: Box B-0051929/2.

11. "Ordonnance no. 67–du [. . .] 1967 relative à l'information des porteurs de valeurs mobilières et à la publicité de certaines opérations de bourse (projet non daté)," CAEF, Trésor–Marchés financiers: Box B-0051929/2.

12. Author's interview with Jean-Yves Haberer, April 12, 2014.

13. Note from René Larre, Directeur du Trésor, to Michel Debré, August 4, 1967, CAEF, Trésor–Marchés financiers: Box B-0051929/2.

14. Author's interview with Jean-Yves Haberer, April 12, 2014.

15. Jay Walz, "'Vive Quebec Libre!' De Gaulle Cries Out to Montreal Crowd," *New York Times*, July 25, 1967.

16. In the French original, the word *initié* is in quotation marks. Memorandum from Jacques Chabrun to Bernard Tricot, July 27, 1967, Archives nationales, Présidence de Charles de Gaulle, Dossiers AG/5(1)2318–2322.

17. Unsigned memorandum to Bernard Tricot, July 28, 1967, Archives nationales, Présidence de Charles de Gaulle, Dossiers AG/5(1)2318–2322.

18. Memorandum from Jean Dromer to Général de Gaulle, August 26, 1967, Archives nationales, Présidence de Charles de Gaulle, Dossiers AG/5(1)2318–2322.

19. "Communication au Conseil des Ministres du 31 juillet 1967." CAEF, Archives Jean-Yves Haberer, 5A0000362.

20. "Communication au Conseil des Ministres du 31 juillet 1967."

21. "Communication au Conseil des Ministres du 31 juillet 1967."

22. "Communication au Conseil des Ministres du 31 juillet 1967."

23. André Vene, "Les sociétés pourront acheter en Bourse leurs propres actions: Une commission de surveillance va être créée pour accroître la confiance des épargnants," *Le Monde*, August 9, 1967.

24. Letter of Léon Amar to Yves Meunier, April 26, 1967, CAEF–Compagnie des Agents de change–Secrétariat général: Box B-0067977/1 (*correspondance*, notes, articles, brochures, etc., 1972–1982). The first annual report of the COB analyzed the scenario—without disclosing the name of the company. Its conclusion—or lack thereof—was laced with ambiguity: "During the year 1968, the Commission also took an interest in the case of a company which had been criticized by the press for disclosing accounting losses shortly after publishing really optimistic forecasts about its turnover. It had been insinuated that individuals close to the company had benefited from this time lag and had sold some of their shares of the company. Information gathered during the investigation conducted by the commission, along with additional information obtained subsequently, have not allowed the commission, within the limits of its powers, to follow up on this case. It is true that the sequence of contradictory releases does not seem to have been organized artificially; it simply illustrates the insufficient attention paid to public information by many French companies." Commission des opérations de Bourse, "Rapport annuel 1968," *Journal Officiel de la République française* (April 7, 1969): 56–57.

25. John L. Hess, "French Cabinet Approves Wide-Ranging Economic Reforms," *New York Times*, August 31, 1967.

26. Rapport du Conseil d'État–Section des Finances No. 298.160, September 11, 1967 (rapporteur Mr. Weill), CAEF, Trésor–Marchés financiers: Box B-0051929/2.

27. A good example is the Conseil National du Crédit (CNC, National Council of Credit), an advisory body established by article 12 of the December 2, 1945, Banking Act nationalizing the Banque de France and other large banks (*Loi "relative à la nationalisation de la Banque de*

France et des grandes banques et à l'organisation du crédit"). In addition to members designated by the ministers in charge of economic and social affairs, the CNC included several representatives of the banking sector and of state-controlled financial institutions (*Caisse des Dépôts et Consignations, Crédit Foncier, Crédit National*, etc.), along with "active forces of the nation," a broad category comprised of representatives of farmers' organizations, professional organizations, chambers of commerce, trade unions, etc. See Pierre Besse, "Le Conseil National du Crédit," *Revue économique* 2, no. 5 (1951): 578–590.

28. Conac, *La régulation des marchés boursiers par la Commission des Opérations de Bourse (COB) et la Securities and Exchange Commission (SEC)*, 28–29.

29. Rapport du Conseil d'État–Section des Finances No. 298.160, September 11, 1967 (rapporteur Mr. Weill), CAEF, Trésor–Marchés financiers: Box B-0051929/2. Letter from René Larre, Directeur du Trésor, to Michel Debré, December 11, 1967, CAEF, Trésor–Marchés financiers: Box B-0051929/2.

30. Décret no. 68-30 du 3 janvier 1968 supprimant le comité des bourses de valeurs et fixant certaines attributions de la commission des opérations de bourse instituée par l'ordonnance no. 67-833 du 28 septembre 1967. *Journal Officiel de la République française*, 13 janvier 1968, 532.

31. Neither the report from the Conseil d'État nor the response from Debré's *cabinet* refer to the United States, where margin requirements were set by the central bank rather than by the SEC.

32. "Projet de décret concernant les pouvoirs de la COB," bordereau d'envoi, December 15, 1967, CAEF, Archives Jean-Yves Haberer, 5A000036211.

33. Communiqué du Bureau de Presse du Service de l'Information du Ministère de l'Économie et des Finances, January 13, 1968, CAEF, Archives Jean-Yves Haberer, 5A000036211.

34. Letter from Michel Debré to the chairman of the Comité des Bourses de Valeurs, December 22, 1967, CAEF, Trésor–Marchés financiers: Box B-0051929/2.

Chapter 6 · Takeoff

1. Antoine Dupont-Fauville, "Michel Debré, ministre de l'Économie et des Finances." *Michel Debré, un réformateur aux Finances 1966–1968* (Paris: Ministère de l'Économie, des Finances et de l'Industrie, Comité pour l'Histoire économique et financière de la France, 2005), 10.

2. Memorandum from Jean Dromer to Général de Gaulle, October 15, 1965. Archives nationales, Présidence de Charles de Gaulle, Dossiers AG/5(1)2318–2322.

3. Archives orales René Larre (1990 interviews conducted by Sophie Coeuré). Interview 5, track 5, June 27, 1990. Comité pour l'histoire économique et financière de la France / Institut de la gestion publique et du développement économique (IGPDE).

4. Letter from René Larre, Directeur du Trésor, to Michel Debré, September 15, 1967, CAEF, Archives Jean-Yves Haberer, 5A-0000357/2.

5. Letter from René Larre, Directeur du Trésor, to Michel Debré, September 15, 1967.

6. Author's interview with Jean-Yves Haberer, April 12, 2014.

7. Pierre Chatenet, *Décolonisation: Souvenirs et Réflexions* (Paris: Buchet-Chastel, 1988), 152.

8. Chatenet, *Décolonisation*, 13.

9. Chatenet, *Décolonisation*, 41.

10. Chatenet, *Décolonisation*, 37.

11. Chatenet, *Décolonisation*, 161.

12. Maurice Doublet, "Le Ministère de l'Intérieur," in *Pierre Chatenet: 1917–1997* (Paris: Mme Chatenet, 1999), 38–39.

13. See Brigitte Gaïti, "Les modernisateurs dans l'administration d'après-guerre: L'écriture d'une histoire héroïque," *Revue française d'administration publique* 2, no. 102 (2002): 295–306.

14. Luc Boltanski, *Les Cadres: La formation d'un groupe social* (Paris: Les Éditions de Minuit, 1982), 165.

15. Chatenet, *Décolonisation*, 15. The recordings of an interview he gave French historian Laure Quennouëlle-Corre in 1990, and in which he referred to several American individuals and institutions, indicate that his accent was reasonably good. Archives orales Pierre Chatenet (September 27 and October 12, 1990, interviews conducted by Laure Quenouëlle-Corre). Comité pour l'histoire économique et financière de la France / Institut de la gestion publique et du développement économique (IGPDE).

16. Georges Suffert, portrait de Georges Chatenet pour introduire l'émission *Le Club de la Presse* du 13 août 1971, Papiers de Jean-Jacques Burgard.

17. Archives orales Pierre Chatenet (September 27 and October 12, 1990, interviews conducted by Laure Quenouëlle-Corre). Interview 6, tape 8, September 27, 1990. Comité pour l'histoire économique et financière de la France / Institut de la gestion publique et du développement économique (IGPDE).

18. Debré, *Mémoires IV*, 109.

19. In 1967, the net average salary of a male senior executive (*cadre supérieur*) amounted to 45,045 French francs per year, i.e., approximately 3,750 French francs per month. Christian Baudelot and Anne Lebeaupin, "Les salaires de 1950 à 1975," *Économie et statistique* 113, no. 1 (1979): 16.

20. Note from Antoine Dupont-Fauville to Jean-Yves Haberer, December 5, 1967, CAEF, Archives Jean-Yves Haberer, 5A000036211.

21. Author's interview with Jean-Yves Haberer, April 12, 2014.

22. Letter from René Larre, Directeur du Trésor, to Michel Debré, September 15, 1967, CAEF, Archives Jean-Yves Haberer, 5A-0000357/2.

23. Note from Jean-Yves Haberer to Michel Debré, September 15, 1967, CAEF, Archives Jean-Yves Haberer, 5A-0000357/2.

24. Xavier Dupont, *Salut la compagnie! Mémoires d'un agent de change* (Paris: Albin Michel, 2002), 64.

25. Letter from René Larre, Directeur du Trésor, to Michel Debré, September 15, 1967. CAEF, Archives Jean-Yves Haberer, 5A-0000357/2.

26. Note from Jean-Yves Haberer to Michel Debré, September 15, 1967, CAEF, Archives Jean-Yves Haberer, 5A-0000357/2.

27. Note from Jean-Yves Haberer to Michel Debré, September 15, 1967.

28. Author's interview with Jean-Yves Haberer, April 12, 2014.

29. Jean-Jacques Burgard, "Pierre Chatenet et la Commission des opérations de bourse," papiers de Jean-Jacques Burgard.

30. "Ceux dont on parle: Jean-Jacques Burgard," *La Vie Française*, 12 janvier 1968, papiers Jean-Jacques Burgard.

31. Jean-Jacques Burgard, "Pierre Chatenet et la Commission des opérations de bourse," papiers de Jean-Jacques Burgard.

32. Jean-Jacques Burgard, "Pierre Chatenet et la Commission des opérations de bourse," papiers de Jean-Jacques Burgard.

33. Author's interview with Mrs Burgard, December 2, 2014.

34. Jean-Jacques Burgard, "Pierre Chatenet et la Commission des opérations de bourse," papiers de Jean-Jacques Burgard.

35. Note from Pierre Chatenet to Michel Debré, November 19, 1967, CAEF, Archives Jean-Yves Haberer, 5A000036211.

36. Pierre Chatenet, "L'information des actionnaires," Lecture at the University of Toulouse, December 4, 1969. Centre d'Histoire de Sciences Po, Fonds Pierre Chatenet (Box PCH8: "Com-

mission des opérations de bourse 1967–1972," Dossier 2–Dossiers de Pierre Chatenet, 1968–1971).

37. Note from Jean-Yves Haberer to Michel Debré, October 3, 1967, CAEF, Archives Jean-Yves Haberer, 5A000036211.

38. Note from Jean-Yves Haberer to Michel Debré, October 3, 1967.

39. Note from Jean-Yves Haberer to Michel Debré, October 3, 1967.

40. Note from Pierre Chatenet to Michel Debré, November 19, 1967, CAEF, Archives Jean-Yves Haberer, 5A000036211.

41. Archives orales Pierre Chatenet (September 27 and October 12, 1990, interviews conducted by Laure Quenouëlle-Corre). Interview 6, tape 8, September 27, 1990, Comité pour l'histoire économique et financière de la France / Institut de la gestion publique et du développement économique (IGPDE).

42. Note from Pierre Chatenet to Michel Debré, November 19, 1967, CAEF, Archives Jean-Yves Haberer, 5A000036211.

43. Note from the Secrétariat of the *Comité des Bourses de Valeurs*, October 4, 1967, CAEF, Trésor–Marchés financiers, Box B-0051919/2.

44. Note from the directeur du Trésor to the minister for the economy and finances, November 8, 1967, CAEF, Trésor–Marchés financiers, Box B-0051919/2.

45. Note from the directeur du Trésor to the minister of the economy and finances, November 8, 1967.

46. Note from the directeur du Trésor to the minister of the economy and finances, November 8, 1967.

47. Note from Pierre Chatenet to Michel Debré, December 27, 1967.

48. Note from Pierre Chatenet to Michel Debré, December 27, 1967.

49. Note from Pierre Chatenet to Michel Debré, December 27, 1967.

50. Note from Pierre Chatenet to Michel Debré, December 27, 1967.

51. "M. Debré installe la Commission des opérations de Bourse," *Les Échos*, 4 janvier 1968.

52. "Allocution de M. Michel Debré, Ministre de l'Économie et des Finances, à l'ouverture de la première séance de la Commission des Opérations de Bourse," CAEF, Archives Jean-Yves Haberer, 5A0000357/2.

Chapter 7 · The Red Flag over the "Temple of Gold"

1. Lloyd Garrison, "Hundreds Are Hurt in Clashes in Paris," *New York Times*, May 25, 1968.

2. Joseph Carroll, "Paris Gripped by Insurrection," *The Guardian*, May 25, 1968.

3. Xavier Dupont, *Salut la compagnie! Mémoires d'un agent de change* (Paris: Albin Michel, 2002), 74–75.

4. Laurent Joffrin, *Mai 68: Une histoire du mouvement* (1998; Paris: Éditions du Seuil, 2008), 269–271. See also Jean-François Sirinelli, *Mai 68* (2008; Paris: CNRS Éditions, 2013), 267–270.

5. Maurice Grimaud, *En Mai, fais ce qu'il te plait* (Paris: Stock, 1977), 242.

6. Dupont, *Salut la compagnie!*, 74. In June, an agreement was reached between the chambre syndicale and union representatives, resulting in an overall raise of 7.5 percent in salaries. CAEF, Compagnie des Agents de change–Secrétariat général: Box B-0069934/1. The 1970s were marked by a series of violent social conflicts at the Paris Bourse. Paul Lagneau-Ymonet and Angelo Riva, *Histoire de la Bourse* (Paris: Éditions La Découverte, 2012), 89.

7. "Approuvez-vous le projet de loi soumis au peuple français par le Président de la République pour la rénovation universitaire, sociale et économique ?," Décret no. 68-468 du 27 mai 1968 décidant de soumettre un projet de loi au referendum, *Journal Officiel*, 29 mai 1968, 5267.

8. "Text of French Proposal," *New York Times*, May 29, 1968.

9. "De Gaulle's Referendum," *New York Times*, May 26, 1968.

10. Jean Vigreux, *Croissance et contestations, 1958–1981* (Paris: Éditions du Seuil, 2014), 164.

11. Jérôme Perrier, *Michel Debré* (Paris: Ellipses, 2010), 374–376.

12. Michel Debré, *Trois républiques pour une France: Mémoires–IV. Gouverner autrement (1962–1970)* (Paris: Albin Michel, 1993), 223.

13. Antoine Dupont-Fauville, who had been Debré's directeur de cabinet at the Ministry of the Economy and Finances, was no longer available: he had been appointed directeur of the Crédit National, a parapublic banking entity. Debré *Mémoires–IV*, 236–237.

14. Henry Tanner, "Couve Reappoints Cabinet Leaders," *New York Times*, July 13, 1968.

15. Jean-Jacques Burgard, "Pierre Chatenet et la Commission des opérations de bourse," papiers de Jean-Jacques Burgard.

16. Marshall Hubert Lyautey (1854–1934), French resident general in Morocco (1912–1916 and 1917–1925) and minister of war (1916–1917), published his influential article, "On the Social Duty of the Officer" (*Du rôle social de l'officier*) in 1891.

17. Ordonnance no. 58-128 du 7 janvier 1959 tendant à favoriser l'association ou l'intéressement des travailleurs à l'entreprise, *Journal Officiel*, January 9, 1959, 641–642.

18. Loi no. 65–566 du 12 juillet 1965 modifiant l'imposition des entreprises et des revenus de capitaux mobiliers, *Journal Officiel*, July 13, 1965, 6003–6008.

19. John L. Hess, "Break in Paris Market Is Laid to de Gaulle Talk on Business," *New York Times*, October 12, 1966.

20. Marcel Loichot, *La réforme pancapitaliste* (Paris: Robert Laffont, 1966).

21. Henri Deniau, Note sur la participation des salariés à la marche de leur entreprise, October 3, 1966, Archives nationales, Présidence de Charles de Gaulle, Dossiers AG/5(1)2318–2322.

22. Henri Deniau, Note sur l'insertion des salariés dans l'économie, September 28, 1966, Archives nationales, Présidence de Charles de Gaulle, Dossiers AG/5(1)2318–2322.

23. "Communication faite au conseil d'administration de la B.N.P. du 3 août 1966 par M. Défossé," CAEF, Trésor–Marchés financiers: Box B-0051929/2.

24. Hess, "Break in Paris Market."

25. Ordonnance no. 67-693 du 17 août 1967 relative à la participation des salariés aux fruits de l'expansion des entreprises, *Journal Officiel*, August 18, 1967, 8288–8290.

26. Ordonnance no. 67-693 du 17 août 1967 relative à la participation des salariés aux fruits de l'expansion des entreprises, *Journal Officiel*, August 18, 1967, 8288–8290.

27. Ordonnance no. 67-693 du 17 août 1967 relative à la participation des salariés aux fruits de l'expansion des entreprises.

28. Bernard Ducamin, "La participation des travailleurs aux fruits de l'expansion: Souvenirs sur l'élaboration de l'ordonnance du 17 août 1967," online at the website of the Charles de Gaulle Foundation, http://www.charles-de-gaulle.org/pages/l-homme/dossiers-thematiques/1958-1970 -la-ve-republique/de-gaulle-et-la-participation/temoignages/bernard-ducamin-lrsquoelaboration -de-lrsquoordonnance-du-17-aout-1967.php, accessed November 13, 2014.

29. Author's interview with Jean-Yves Haberer, April 12, 2014.

30. "Note," datée de juin 1968, Centre d'Histoire de Sciences Po, Fonds Pierre Chatenet, Box PCH8: "Commission des opérations de bourse 1967–1972," Dossier 2–Dossiers de Pierre Chatenet, 1968–1971.

31. "Note remise à M. Tricot le 27 juin 1968," papiers de Jean-Jacques Burgard.

32. "Note remise à M. Tricot le 27 juin 1968," papiers de Jean-Jacques Burgard.

33. Other subjects, such as marketing, were considered "the boss's problem." According to the author(s), this was the sign of workers' suspicion of paternalism and of their reluctance to be dependent on their employer: they were more interested in participating in the benefits of macroeconomic growth than of their employer's growth. Union leaders pointed to the vulner-

ability of workers who might be penalized by the specific difficulties of their employer or the crisis of a particular business sector. "Note remise à M. Tricot le 5 juillet 1968," papiers de Jean-Jacques Burgard.

34. Alain Jourdan, "Le référendum comme procédure d'adoption du projet de réforme régionale," in Cahiers de l'Institut d'Études Politiques de Grenoble, *La réforme régionale et le référendum du 27 avril 1969* (Paris: Éditions Cujas, 1970), 197–275.

35. "Approuvez-vous le projet de loi soumis au peuple français par le Président de la République et relatif à la création de régions et à la rénovation du Sénat?," Décret no. 69-296 du 2 avril 1969 décidant de soumettre un projet de loi au referendum. *Journal Officiel*, 3 avril 1969, 3315.

36. "The Fifth Republic's Second President," *New York Times*, June 16, 1969.

37. Bernard Tricot, "De Gaulle et l'esprit de participation," *Espoir* 58, 1987. Online at the website of the Charles de Gaulle Foundation, http://www.charles-de-gaulle.org/pages/l-homme /dossiers-thematiques/1958-1970-la-ve-republique/de-gaulle-et-la-participation/analyses/de -gaulle-et-lrsquoesprit-de-participation.php, consulted November 13, 2014.

38. Pierre Chatenet, "Le marché des valeurs mobilières instrument d'évolution du capitalisme," January 1970, Centre d'Histoire de Sciences Po, Fonds Pierre Chatenet (Box PCH8: "Commission des opérations de bourse 1967–1972," Dossier 2–Dossiers de Pierre Chatenet, 1968–1971).

39. In a 1969 lecture at the University of Toulouse, Chatenet noted that the number of General Motors shareholders was equivalent to the population of Denmark. Pierre Chatenet, "L'information des actionnaires," lecture at the University of Toulouse, December 4, 1969, Centre d'Histoire de Sciences Po, Fonds Pierre Chatenet (Box PCH8: "Commission des opérations de bourse 1967–1972," Dossier 2–Dossiers de Pierre Chatenet, 1968–1971).

40. Chatenet, "Le marché des valeurs mobilières instrument d'évolution du capitalisme."

41. Chatenet, "Le marché des valeurs mobilières instrument d'évolution du capitalisme."

42. Julia C. Ott, *When Wall Street Met Main Street: The Quest for an Investors' Democracy* (Cambridge: Harvard University Press, 2011), 214–216.

43. The Rue du Quatre Septembre in Paris runs along the Palais Brongniart. Chatenet, "Le marché des valeurs mobilières instrument d'évolution du capitalisme."

44. Chatenet, "Le marché des valeurs mobilières instrument d'évolution du capitalisme."

Chapter 8 · *In Search of Legitimacy*

1. Note from Pierre Chatenet to Michel Debré, November 19, 1967, CAEF, Archives Jean-Yves Haberer, 5A000036211.

2. Author's interview with Jean-Yves Haberer, April 12, 2014.

3. Jean-Jacques Burgard, "Pierre Chatenet et la Commission des opérations de bourse," papiers de Jean-Jacques Burgard.

4. The SEC did maintain a regional office in New York, however.

5. Ada Louise Huxtable, "Paris's La Défense Cluster: Coup of Drawing-Board Style," *New York Times*, June 11, 1978.

6. Emphasis added. Note from Pierre Chatenet to Michel Debré, December 27, 1967, CAEF, Archives Jean-Yves Haberer, 5A000036211.

7. Note from Jean-Yves Haberer to Michel Debré, October 3, 1967, CAEF, Archives Jean-Yves Haberer, 5A000036211.

8. Michel Gentot, *Les autorités administratives indépendantes* (Paris: Montchrestien, 1994), 9.

9. Burgard, "Pierre Chatenet et la Commission des opérations de bourse."

10. Edgard Pisani, "Administration de gestion, administration de gestion," *Revue française de science politique*, 1956, 315–330. During his long and varied career as civil servant, minister of agriculture, member of the European Commission, etc., Pisani had many opportunities to practice the theory he had developed in his 1956 article. Ironically, he was the only member of

the French government to resign in protest when de Gaulle, upon Debré's suggestion, decided to activate article 38 of the Constitution in 1967 (see chapter 1).

11. Note from the Secrétariat of the Comité des Bourses de Valeurs, October 4, 1967, CAEF, Trésor–Marchés financiers, Box B-0051919/2.

12. Note from Pierre Chatenet to Michel Debré, November 19, 1967, CAEF, Archives Jean-Yves Haberer, 5A000036211.

13. "La commission des opérations de bourse, créée par l'ordonnance n° 67-833 du 28 septembre 1967, est une institution spécialisée de caractère public dont les frais de fonctionnement sont pris en charge par l'État." Décret no. 68-23 portant organisation administrative et financière de la commission des opérations de bourse, *Journal Officiel*, January 12, 1968, 476–477.

14. In the May–June 1980 edition of *La Revue administrative*, Jean Donnedieu de Vabres, then chairman of the COB (1974–1980), published an article entitled "La COB, une administration de mission." While Donnedieu de Vabres reiterated the distinction between *administrations de mission* and *administrations de gestion*, he also emphasized the fact that the ordonnance had not endowed the COB with an independent legal personality. Jean Donnedieu de Vabres, "La COB, une administration de mission," *La Revue administrative*, 33rd Year, no. 195 (May–June 1980): 237–241.

15. Letter from Michel Debré to Jacques Brunet, governor of the Banque de France, December 28, 1967, Archives de la Banque de France, Box No. 58, 1035200250/58, "Commission des opérations de bourse 1967–1972."

16. Letter from Pierre Chatenet to Jacques Brunet, governor of the Banque de France, January 25, 1968, Archives de la Banque de France, Box No. 58, 1035200250/58, "Commission des opérations de bourse 1967–1972."

17. Circulaire No. 10.909 du 12 février 1968 "Droit d'investigation des représentants de la "Commission des Opérations de Bourse," Archives de la Banque de France, Box No. 77, 1370198301, "La banque, la bourse, l'assurance 1959–1972," dossier 260/09, "Marché financier-COB."

18. Minutes of the meeting of the *Chambre syndicale*, December 8, 1967, CAEF, Compagnie des Agents de change–Secrétariat général: Box B-0069934/1.

19. Author's interview with Jean-Yves Haberer, April 12, 2014.

20. Minutes of the meeting of the Chambre syndicale, October 17, 1967, CAEF, Compagnie des Agents de change–Secrétariat général: Box B-0069934/1. Yves Meunier would be the first syndic to sit on the board of the COB.

21. Xavier L. Dupont, *Salut la compagnie! Mémoires d'un agent de change* (Paris: Albin Michel, 2002), 64–68.

22. Author's interview with Jean-Yves Haberer, April 12, 2014.

23. Author's interview with Jean-Yves Haberer, April 12, 2014.

24. Note from Pierre Chatenet to Michel Debré, November 19, 1967, CAEF, Archives Jean-Yves Haberer, 5A000036211.

25. Note from Pierre Chatenet to Michel Debré, November 19, 1967.

26. On the increasing role of French banks in the securities market, see Laure Quennouëlle-Corre, *La place financière de Paris au XXe siècle: Des ambitions contrariées* (Paris: Comité pour l'histoire économique et financière de la France, 2015), 233–280.

27. Note from Pierre Chatenet to Michel Debré, November 19, 1967, CAEF, Archives Jean-Yves Haberer, 5A000036211.

28. Jean-Jacques Burgard, "Pierre Chatenet et la Commission des opérations de bourse," papiers de Jean-Jacques Burgard.

29. Pierre Chatenet, "L'information des actionnaires," lecture at the University of Toulouse, December 4, 1969, Centre d'Histoire de Sciences Po, Fonds Pierre Chatenet, Box PCH8: "Com-

mission des opérations de bourse 1967–1972," Dossier 2–Dossiers de Pierre Chatenet, 1968–1971.

30. René Tendron, "La Commission des Opérations de Bourse: Un formalisme lourd et contraignant," *Les Échos*, December 31, 1968.

31. Tendron, "La Commission des Opérations de Bourse."

32. Décret no. 68-857 du 3 octobre 1968 modifiant et complétant le décret no. 67-236 du 23 mars 1967 sur les sociétés commerciales, *Journal Officiel*, October 4, 1968, 9391.

33. Tendron, "La Commission des Opérations de Bourse."

34. Burgard, "Pierre Chatenet et la Commission des opérations de bourse."

35. Commission des opérations de Bourse, "Rapport annuel 1969," *Journal Officiel de la République française* (March 11, 1970): 171.

36. Dominique Pons, "Ces incorruptibles qui surveillent votre épargne," *France Soir Magazine*, 25 octobre 1971 (Papiers Jean-Jacques Burgard).

37. Burgard, "Pierre Chatenet et la Commission des opérations de bourse."

38. Chatenet, "L'information des actionnaires."

39. Chatenet, "L'information des actionnaires."

40. Commission des opérations de Bourse, "Rapport annuel 1968." *Journal officiel de la République française* (April 7, 1969): 43.

41. Transcript of the interview between Pierre Chatenet and Georges Leroy on Europe 1, "Europe Soir," February 21, 1969, Centre d'Histoire de Sciences Po, Fonds Pierre Chatenet, Box PCH8: "Commission des opérations de bourse 1967–1972," Dossier 5–Interviews, 1968–1971.

42. Transcript of the interview between Pierre Chatenet and Georges Leroy on Europe 1.

43. Letter from Pierre Chatenet to Michel Drancourt, June 8, 1970, Centre d'Histoire de Sciences Po, Fonds Pierre Chatenet, Box PCH8: "Commission des opérations de bourse 1967–1972," Dossier 1–Correspondance 1970–1972.

44. A few weeks later, Chatenet did indeed write a confidential letter to Prime Minister Chaban-Delmas. Putting forward as a pretext the fact that he had completed the first half of his term as COB chairman, he reiterated the gist of the argument he had developed in his letter to Drancourt. He did not, however, request that a law or another ordonnance correct the situation by enlarging the powers of the COB. Instead, he rather sheepishly expressed his desire that "his action be judged on the basis of [how he actually fulfilled] his real responsibilities, which are important, but only the responsibilities that are his." Letter from Pierre Chatenet to Jacques Chaban-Delmas, Prime Minister, July 21, 1970, Centre d'Histoire de Sciences Po, Fonds Pierre Chatenet, Box PCH8: "Commission des opérations de bourse 1967–1972," Dossier 2–Dossiers de Pierre Chatenet, 1968–1971.

45. Commission des opérations de Bourse, "Rapport annuel 1968," *Journal officiel de la République française* (April 7, 1969): 63.

46. Commission des opérations de Bourse, "Rapport annuel 1969," *Journal officiel de la République française* (March 11, 1970): 163.

47. Synopsis of the COB report, prepared by Jean de Marcillac, sent to Michel Jobert, and annotated by Georges Pompidou, March 24, 1971, Archives nationales, Présidence de Georges Pompidou, Dossiers 540AP29.

48. Synopsis of the COB report, prepared by Jean de Marcillac, sent to Georges Pompidou, March 23, 1972, Archives nationales, Présidence de Georges Pompidou, Dossiers 540AP29.

49. Letter from Pierre Chatenet to René de Lestrade, March 27, 1972, Centre d'Histoire de Sciences Po, Fonds Pierre Chatenet, Box PCH8: "Commission des opérations de bourse 1967–1972," Dossier 1–Correspondance, 1969–1972.

50. Chatenet's letter provided no further indication about these "difficulties."

51. Pierre Chatenet, preface to Françoise Marnata, *La Bourse et le financement des investissements* (Paris: Armand Colin, 1973).

52. Wilfrid Baumgartner was the chairman of the board of French chemical and pharmaceutical company Rhône-Poulenc and a former minister of finance in Michel Debré's government (1960–1962). Established in March 1971, the committee issued a much-noted report on the modernization of the Paris stock market. Burgard was a member of the Committee. See Quennouëlle-Corre, *La place financière de Paris au XXe siècle*, 310–316.

53. Wilfrid Baumgartner, "Presentation to the Conseil Économique et social," February 8, 1972, Archives nationales, Présidence de Georges Pompidou, Dossiers 540AP29.

54. Letter of Georges Pompidou to Wilfrid Baumgartner, February 25, 1972, Archives nationales, Présidence de Georges Pompidou, Dossiers 540AP29.

Chapter 9 · Mr. Chatenet Goes to Washington

1. Securities and Exchange Commission, 35th Annual Report, For the Fiscal year Ended June 30th 1969, SEC Historical Society website.

2. Letter from Pierre Chatenet to Pierre Viénot, June 17, 1971, Centre d'Histoire de Sciences Po, Fonds Pierre Chatenet, Box PCH8: "Commission des opérations de bourse 1967–1972," Dossier 1–Correspondance 1970–1972.

3. Note from Jean-Yves Haberer to Michel Debré, October 3, 1967, CAEF, Archives Jean-Yves Haberer, 5A000036211; note from Pierre Chatenet to Michel Debré, November 19, 1967, CAEF, Archives Jean-Yves Haberer, 5A000036211.

4. No records have been found of Chatenet's visit(s) to Brussels. Apparently, the chairman of the COB did not feel it necessary to keep a written trace of the information he might have collected in Belgium in his personal archives.

5. Archives orales Pierre Chatenet, September 27 and October 12, 1990, interviews conducted by Laure Quenouëlle-Corre, Interview 6, tape 8, September 27, 1990, Comité pour l'histoire économique et financière de la France / Institut de la gestion publique et du développement économique (IGPDE).

6. Pierre Chatenet, "Entretiens à New York avec un certain nombre de personnalités," December 1969, Centre d'Histoire de Sciences Po, Fonds Pierre Chatenet, Box PCH8: "Commission des opérations de bourse 1967–1972," Dossier 2–Dossiers de Pierre Chatenet, 1968–1971.

7. Pierre Chatenet, *Décolonisation: Souvenirs et Réflexions* (Paris: Buchet-Chastel, 1988), 77.

8. Jean-Jacques Burgard, "Pierre Chatenet et la Commission des opérations de bourse," papiers de Jean-Jacques Burgard.

9. Pierre Chatenet, "L'information des actionnaires," lecture at the University of Toulouse, December 4, 1969, Centre d'Histoire de Sciences Po, Fonds Pierre Chatenet, Box PCH8: "Commission des opérations de bourse 1967–1972," Dossier 2–Dossiers de Pierre Chatenet, 1968–1971.

10. Pierre Chatenet, "Dynamisme et encadrement du marché des valeurs mobilières sur les places financières des Etats-Unis, de Grande-Bretagne et de France," December 10, 1970.

11. Chatenet, "Dynamisme et encadrement du marché des valeurs."

12. Chatenet, "Dynamisme et encadrement du marché des valeurs."

13. Chatenet, "Dynamisme et encadrement du marché des valeurs."

14. Airy-Edward Routier, "Le président de la COB pose le problème du statut des agents de change," *Les Échos*, December 14, 1970.

15. Letter from Pierre Chatenet to Marc Viénot, June 17, 1971, Centre d'Histoire de Sciences Po, Fonds Pierre Chatenet, Box PCH8: "Commission des opérations de bourse 1967–1972," Dossier 1–Correspondance 1970–1972.

16. As indicated in chapter 4, the Belgian securities regulator cannot be considered an inspiration for the creation of the COB. However, the fact that Chatenet viewed the French-Belgian reciprocity agreement as a model for a potential agreement with the SEC echoes political scientist Daniel W. Drezner's statement that "smaller states and nonstate actors in the international system

do not affect regulatory outcomes, but they do affect the processes through which coordination is attempted." Drezner, *All Politics Is Global: Explaining International Regulatory Regimes* (Princeton: Princeton University Press, 2007), 5.

17. Letter from Pierre Chatenet to Marc Viénot, June 17, 1971, Centre d'Histoire de Sciences Po, Fonds Pierre Chatenet, Box PCH8: "Commission des opérations de bourse 1967–1972," Dossier 1–Correspondance 1970–1972.

18. Letter from Pierre Chatenet to Marc Viénot, September 14, 1971, Centre d'Histoire de Sciences Po, Fonds Pierre Chatenet, Box PCH8: "Commission des opérations de bourse 1967–1972," Dossier 1–Correspondance 1970–1972.

19. Note from Pierre Chatenet to the members of the COB's collège, November 5, 1971, Centre d'Histoire de Sciences Po, Fonds Pierre Chatenet, Box PCH8: "Commission des opérations de bourse 1967–1972," Dossier 2–Dossiers de Pierre Chatenet, 1968–1971.

20. Letter from William J. Casey to Pierre Goodrich, May 3, 1972, Hoover Institution Archives, William J. Casey Papers, Box/Folder 144/3.

21. Commission des opérations de Bourse, "Rapport annuel 1971," *Journal officiel de la République française* (March 24, 1972): 243–245.

22. David Andrew Singer, *Regulating Capital: Setting Standards for the International Financial System* (Ithaca: Cornell University Press, 2007), 2–3.

23. Memorandum from Allan S. Mostoff to William J. Casey, June 3, 1971, Hoover Institution Archives, William J. Casey Papers, Box/Folder 147/3.

24. Memorandum from Allan S. Mostoff to William J. Casey, June 3, 1971, Hoover Institution Archives, William J. Casey Papers, Box/Folder 147/3.

25. "Off-shore funds–Recent Developments," Transcript of remarks of Allan S. Mostoff at the Third Trans-World Investment Company Seminar, October 27, 1971. Hoover Institution Archives, William J. Casey Papers, Box/Folder 147/2.

26. Memorandum from Allan S. Mostoff to William J. Casey, January 30, 1973. Hoover Institution Archives, William J. Casey Papers, Box/Folder 147/3.

27. William J. Casey, "The Internationalization of the Capital Markets," Address at the First International Meeting of Stock Exchanges, Milan, Italy, March 15, 1972. Hoover Institution Archives, William J. Casey Papers, Box/Folder 141/20.

28. William J. Casey, "The Internationalization of the Capital Markets," Address at the First International Meeting of Stock Exchanges, Milan, Italy, March 15, 1972. Hoover Institution Archives, William J. Casey Papers, Box/Folder 141/20.

29. William J. Casey, "The Internationalization of the Capital Markets," Address at the First International Meeting of Stock Exchanges, Milan, Italy, March 15, 1972. Hoover Institution Archives, William J. Casey Papers, Box/Folder 141/20.

30. William J. Casey, "The Internationalization of the Capital Markets," Address at the First International Meeting of Stock Exchanges, Milan, Italy, March 15, 1972. Hoover Institution Archives, William J. Casey Papers, Box/Folder 141/20.

31. William J. Casey, "The Internationalization of the Capital Markets," Address at the First International Meeting of Stock Exchanges, Milan, Italy, March 15, 1972. Hoover Institution Archives, William J. Casey Papers, Box/Folder 141/20.

32. Memorandum from Allan S. Mostoff to William J. Casey, May 10, 1972, Hoover Institution Archives, William J. Casey Papers, Box/Folder 147/1.

33. William J. Casey, "Toward Common Accounting Standards," address at the Conference on Financial Reporting, Paris, France, May 19, 1972, Hoover Institution Archives, William J. Casey Papers, Box/Folder 142/1.

34. William J. Casey, "Toward Common Accounting Standards," address at the Conference on Financial Reporting, Paris, France, May 19, 1972. Hoover Institution Archives, William J. Casey Papers, Box/Folder 142/1.

35. Paul Lewis, "The Paris Bourse Watchdog: Kiss of Life Still Needed," *Financial Times*, December 5, 1968.

36. Lewis, "The Paris Bourse Watchdog."

37. "French Version of S.E.C. Unexpectedly Effective," *New York Times*, November 27, 1971. The first occurrence of the COB in the *New York Times* was dated March 29, 1970 ("Bourse Penalties Urged," Reuters, *New York Times*, March 29 1970). It was actually a fifteen-line dispatch from Reuters explaining that the annual COB report to the French President had suggested the introduction "legal penalties for certain Bourse activities." Less than a year later, on January 15, 1971, the *New York Times* informed its readers that foreign exchanges had not fared better than Wall Street ("Bears Trample Over the Bourses," *New York Times*, January 25, 1971). A brief mention of the 6.5 percent decline in French stock prices in 1970 was accompanied by a tentative explanation: "The National Assembly voted the Commission des Operations de Bourse powers to exact civil and criminal penalties for takeovers that might strip a company of its assets. The new powers may force companies to supply more accurate and timely information to brokers and the public."

Chapter 10 · Mission Accomplished?

1. Commission des opérations de Bourse, "Rapport annuel 1968," *Journal officiel de la République française* (April 7, 1969): 43.

2. Commission des opérations de Bourse, "Rapport annuel 1968."

3. Franklin D. Roosevelt, "Government and Modern Capitalism," Fireside Chat, September 30, 1934, in Russel D. Buhite and David W. Levy, *FDR's Fireside Chats* (Norman: University of Oklahoma Press, 1992), 56.

4. Commission des opérations de Bourse, "Rapport annuel 1968," 45.

5. Pierre Chatenet, "L'information des actionnaires," lecture at the University of Toulouse, December 4, 1969, Centre d'Histoire de Sciences Po, Fonds Pierre Chatenet, Box PCH8: "Commission des opérations de bourse 1967–1972," Dossier 2–Dossiers de Pierre Chatenet, 1968–1971.

6. Commission des opérations de Bourse, "Rapport annuel 1970," *Journal officiel de la République française* (March 26, 1971): 65.

7. Commission des opérations de Bourse, "Rapport annuel 1968," *Journal officiel de la République française* (April 7, 1969): 50.

8. Commission des opérations de Bourse, "Rapport annuel 1968," 51.

9. Commission des opérations de Bourse, "Rapport annuel 1971," *Journal officiel de la République française* (March 24, 1972): 274; Commission des opérations de Bourse, "Rapport annuel 1972," *Journal officiel de la République française* (April 26, 1973): 229.

10. Commission des opérations de Bourse, "Rapport annuel 1970," *Journal officiel de la République française* (March 26, 1971): 68.

11. Commission des opérations de Bourse, "Rapport annuel 1971," *Journal officiel de la République française* (March 24, 1972): 259

12. Archives orales Pierre Chatenet, September 27, and October 12, 1990, interviews conducted by Laure Quenouëlle-Corre. Interview 7, tape 10, October 12, 1990, Comité pour l'histoire économique et financière de la France / Institut de la gestion publique et du développement économique (IGPDE). Jean-Jacques Burgard, "Pierre Chatenet et la Commission des opérations de bourse," papiers de Jean-Jacques Burgard.

13. "French Scandal Brings New Rules for Legislators," *New York Times*, November 28, 1971. André Rives-Henrÿs was a Gaullist *député* (1962–1967, 1968–1972). In 1974, he was sentenced to several months in jail for his involvement in the Garantie Foncière scandal. Bertrand Le Gendre, "La Garantie foncière: le premier scandale politico-financier du régime," *Le Monde*, July 19, 2006.

14. Dominique Pons, "Ces incorruptibles qui surveillent votre épargne," *France Soir Magazine*, October 25 1971.

15. Loi no. 70-1300 du 31 décembre 1970 fixant le régime applicable aux sociétés civiles autorisées à faire publiquement appel à l'épargne, *Journal Officiel*, December 31, 1970, 9–12.

16. Dominique Pons, "Ces incorruptibles qui surveillent votre épargne," *France Soir Magazine*, October 25 1971.

17. Burgard, "Pierre Chatenet et la Commission des opérations de bourse," papiers de Jean-Jacques Burgard.

18. "French Scandal Brings New Rules for Legislators," *New York Times*, November 28, 1971.

19. Commission des opérations de Bourse, "Rapport annuel 1968," *Journal Officiel de la République française* (April 7, 1969): 62.

20. The act provided for the retroactive modification of several paragraphs of the September 28, 1967, ordonnance. Loi no. 70-128 du 23 décembre 1970 portant modification de la loi no. 66-537 du 24 juillet 1966 sur les sociétés commerciales et de l'ordonnance no. 67-833 du 28 septembre 1967 instituant une commission des opérations de bourse et relative à l'information des porteurs de valeurs mobilières et à la publicité de certaines opérations de bourse, *Journal Officiel*, December 24, 11891–11892.

21. Commission des opérations de Bourse, "Rapport annuel 1970," *Journal Officiel de la République française* (March 26, 1971): 96.

22. Letter from Pierre Chatenet to René Pleven, Garde des Sceaux (Minister of Justice), July 28, 1971, Centre d'Histoire de Sciences Po, Fonds Pierre Chatenet, Box PCH8: "Commission des opérations de bourse 1967–1972," Dossier 1–Correspondance, 1979–1972.

23. Memorandum from Jean de Marcillac to Michel Jobert, January 21, 1971, Archives nationales, Présidence de Georges Pompidou, Dossiers 540AP29.

24. Commission des opérations de Bourse, "Rapport annuel 1971," *Journal Officiel de la République française* (March 24, 1972): 219.

25. Letter from Pierre Chatenet to François Bloch-Lainé, April 7, 1972, Centre d'Histoire de Sciences Po, Fonds Pierre Chatenet, Box PCH8: "Commission des opérations de bourse 1967–1972," Dossier 1–Correspondance 1970–1972.

26. Loi de finances rectificative pour 1970 (no. 70-1283). *Journal Officiel de la République française* (December 31, 1970): 12275–12280.

27. Letter from Pierre Chatenet to Edgar Faure, Ministre d'État chargé des Affaires sociales (Minister for Social Affairs), October 24, 1972, Centre d'Histoire de Sciences Po, Fonds Pierre Chatenet, Box PCH8: "Commission des opérations de bourse 1967–1972," Dossier 1–Correspondance, 1969–1972.

28. Letter from Pierre Chatenet to Edgar Faure, Ministre d'État chargé des Affaires sociales (Minister for Social Affairs), October 24, 1972, Centre d'Histoire de Sciences Po, Fonds Pierre Chatenet, Box PCH8: "Commission des opérations de bourse 1967–1972," Dossier 1–Correspondance, 1969–1972).

29. Memorandum from Jean-René Bernard to Michel Jobert, April 8, 1972, Archives nationales, Présidence de Georges Pompidou, Dossiers 540AP29.

30. Letter from Michel Debré to Pierre Chatenet, January 15, 1973. Burgard, "Pierre Chatenet et la Commission des opérations de bourse," papiers de Jean-Jacques Burgard.

31. André Passeron, "M. de La Malène soutient la candidature de M. Debré," *Le Monde*, December 22, 1980.

32. Michel Debré, *Trois républiques pour une France: Mémoires—IV: Gouverner autrement (1962–1970)* (Paris: Albin Michel, 1993), 203.

33. On the paradoxical turn taken by the French socialists in the 1980s, see Rawi Abdelal, *Capital Rules: The Construction of Global Finance* (Cambridge: Harvard University Press, 2007), 58–65.

34. Debré, *Mémoires IV*, 109.

35. Debré, *Mémoires IV*, 109.

36. Loi no. 89-531 du 2 août 1989 relative à la sécurité et à la transparence du marché financier, *Journal Officiel*, August 4, 1989, 9822–9827.

37. Loi no. 96-597 du 2 juillet 1996 de modernisation des activités financières, *Journal Officiel*, July 4, 1996.

38. Jean-Jacques Burgard, "Pierre Chatenet et la Commission des opérations de bourse," papiers de Jean-Jacques Burgard.

39. Loi no. 88-70 du 22 janvier sur les bourses de valeurs, *Journal Officiel*, January 23, 1988.

40. Xavier Dupont, *Salut la compagnie! Mémoires d'un agent de change* (Paris: Albin Michel, 2002), 172–183.

41. Paul Lagneau-Ymonet and Angelo Riva, *Histoire de la Bourse* (Paris: Éditions La Découverte, 2012), 96.

42. Lagneau-Ymonet and Riva, *Histoire de la Bourse*, 102.

43. Loi no. 85-321 du 14 décembre 1985 modifiant diverses dispositions du droit des valeurs mobilières, des titres de créances négociables, des sociétés et des opérations de bourse, *Journal Officiel*, December 15, 1985, 14598–14604.

44. Loi no. 89-531 du 2 août 1989 relative à la sécurité et à la transparence du marché financier, *Journal Officiel*, August 4, 1989, 9822–9827.

45. Yves Guyon, foreword to Pierre-Henri Conac, *La régulation des marchés boursiers par la Commission des Opérations de Bourse (COB) et la Securities and Exchange Commission (SEC)*, Librairie Générale de Droit et de Jurisprudence, Paris, 2002, vii.

46. Loi no. 96-597 du 2 juillet 1996 de modernisation des activités financières, *Journal Officiel*, July 4, 1996. A 2006 report prepared by French senator Patrice Gélard listed thirty-nine autorités administratives indépendantes. Among them the Agence française de lute contre le dopage (French Anti-Doping Agency, established in 2006), the Autorité de régulation des communications électroniques et des postes (Agency in Charge of Regulating Telecommunications and Postal Services, established in 2005), the Conseil Supérieur de l'Audiovisuel (Superior Council of Audiovisual, established in 1989), the Médiateur du cinéma (Movie industry ombudsman, established in 1982), the Autorité de sûreté nucléaire (Nuclear Safety Authority, established in 2006), the Comité consultatif national d'éthique pour les sciences de la vie et de la santé (National Advisory Council on Bioethics Issues, established in 2004), etc. Quoted in "Les autorités administratives indépendantes," *La documentation française*, no. 330, April 2007, 17.

47. Author's interview with Jean-Yves Haberer, April 12, 2014. Interestingly, though, the preamble of the first annual report of the CONSOB, while mentioning the United States and Belgium, was silent about France. Commissione Nazionale per le Società e la Borsa, "Relazione Sull'Attività Svolta Nell'Anno 1975," document transmitted by CONSOB–Public Relation Office on May 13, 2016.

48. Tony Porter, *Globalization and Finance* (Cambridge: Polity Press, 2005), 69.

49. David Andrew Singer, *Regulating Capital: Setting Standards for the International Financial System* (Ithaca: Cornell University Press, 2007), 72.

50. France joined IOSCO in 1984.

51. Daniel W. Drezner, *All Politics Is Global: Explaining International Regulatory Regimes* (Princeton: Princeton University Press, 2007), 138.

52. On the limits of democratization in multilateral organizations, see Jan Aart Scholte, "Global Capitalism and the State," *International Affairs (Royal Institute of International Affairs 1944–)*, 73, no. 3; *Globalization and International Relations* (July 1997), 427–452.

53. Such memoranda of understanding (MOU) were to become a priority of IOSCO. Porter, *Globalization and Finance*, 80–81.

54. Understanding Regarding the Establishment of a Framework for Consultations and

Administrative Agreement, December 14, 1989. https://www.sec.gov/about/offices/oia/oia_bi
lateral/france.pdf (Accessed June 17, 2016).

55. Loi no. 2003-706 du 1er août 2003 de sécurité financière, *Journal Officiel*, August 2, 2003.

56. Nathalie Boschat and Philippe Guillaume, "La COB à l'âge adulte," *Les Échos*, September
26 and 27, 1997.

Conclusion

1. Louis Uchitelle, "Volcker Pushes for Reform, Regretting Past Silence," *New York Times*,
July 9, 2010.

2. Beyond the creation of the SEC in 1934, East Asia's adoption of international regulatory
standards in the wake of the financial crisis of the late 1990s offers another case in point: "Faced
with a crisis that destabilized some of the world's most rapidly growing countries, governments
in the major developed countries responded by launching one of the most ambitious governance
reform projects in living memory. Its main objective was to transform domestic financial governance in emerging market countries and, in particular, to eradicate the 'cronyism, corruption,
and nepotism' assumed to lie at the heart of Asia's (and by extension most of the developing
world's) financial vulnerability." Andrew Walter, *Governing Finance: East Asia's Adoption of International Standards* (Ithaca: Cornell University Press, 2008), 1. On how American lawmakers
reacted to the 2007/2008 financial crisis by passing the 2010 Dodd-Frank Act, see Robert G.
Kaiser, *Act of Congress: How America's Essential Institution Works, and How It Doesn't* (New York:
Alfred A. Knopf, 2013).

3. On the political influence of the " 'race-to-the-bottom' imagery," see Daniel W. Drezner,
All Politics Is Global: Explaining International Regulatory Regimes (Princeton: Princeton University Press, 2007), 14–15. See also Beth A. Simmons, "The International Politics of Harmonization:
The Case of Capital Market Regulation," *International Organization* 55, no. 3 (Summer 2001):
589–620.

4. According to legal scholar Alain Supiot, for example, the influence of "governance by
numbers" on corporate and financial law originated in the "ultra-liberal turn of the 1980s, with
the substitution of *régulation* by market authorities to the *réglementation* by the state [. . .]."
Supiot, *La Gouvernance par les nombres: Cours au Collège de France (2012–2014)* (Paris: Fayard / I
nstitut d'Études avancées de Nantes, 2015), 224.

5. A similar observation has been made by Éric Monnet about the Banque de France's attempt
to reform French monetary policy in the early 1970s. Monnet, "La politique de la France au
sortir des Trente Glorieuses: un tournant monétariste?," *Revue d'histoire moderne et contemporaine* 1, no. 62-1 (2015): 147–174.

6. On the role of global civil society in global finance, see Tony Porter, *Globalization and
Finance* (Cambridge: Polity Press, 2005), 138–202.

7. Elliott Posner, *The Origins of Europe's New Stock Markets* (Cambridge: Harvard University
Press, 2009), 73. The Second Marché was a smaller-company stock market.

8. From the 1980s on, French policy makers were to become adept at playing the rules of
financial cooperation in a global environment, advocating at the same time complete freedom
for capital movements and more regulation—with a varying degree of success. Rawi Abdelal,
Capital Rules: The Construction of Global Finance (Cambridge: Harvard University Press, 2007),
220–221.

9. David Andrew Singer, *Regulating Capital: Setting Standards for the International Financial
System* (Ithaca: Cornell University Press, 2007), 1.

10. Posner, *Origins of Europe's New Stock Markets*, 73.

11. In the epilogue of her book on the historical foundations of shareholder democracy,
historian Julia C. Ott stresses the paradox that "the most enduring legacy of the New Deal may
be the Securities and Exchange Commission (SEC), which aims to safeguard retail investment,

not to sustain aggregate demand or to protect producers as in other New Deal–era programs and agencies." Ott, *When Wall Street Met Main Street: The Quest for an Investors' Democracy* (Cambridge: Harvard University Press, 2011), 214–215.

12. The social and economic legacy of the 1944–1946 provisional government, while impressive and durable, can hardly be called Gaullist—or at least not exclusively so.

13. Michel Foucault, "Leçon du 5 avril 1978," in *Sécurité, territoire, population: Cours au Collège de France. 1977–1978* (Paris: Seuil/Gallimard, 2004), 341–370.

14. Robert J. Shiller, *Irrational Exuberance* (Princeton: Princeton University Press, 2015), 60–61.

15. By 2015, however, that number had gone down to 3.3 million. Autorité des Marchés Financiers, "Étude 2015 sur les dispositifs de communication des sociétés cotées à destination de leurs actionnaires individuels," November 26, 2015.

16. Michel Debré, *Trois républiques pour une France: Mémoires—IV: Gouverner autrement (1962–1970)* (Paris: Albin Michel, 1993), 110. Emphasis added.

Sources

Archives

Paris, France: Archives de la Banque de France

Box 1035200250/58: "Commission des opérations de bourse, création, détachement du personnel de l'ancien comité des Bourses de Valeurs de la Banque de France, demandes d'information entre les deux, correspondance, bulletin. 1967–1972."

Box 1307198301/77: "Commission des opérations de bourse."

Box 1135200516/95: "Chronologie COB 1967–1977."

Paris, France: Archives personnelles de Jean-Jacques Burgard

Paris, France: Centre d'histoire de Sciences Po

Fonds Michel Debré. Archives de Michel Debré, ministre de l'Économie et des Finances 1966–1968 4DE. Box 4DE29, 4DE31, 4DE33, 4DE35.

Fonds Pierre Chatenet. Box PCH8: "Commission des opérations de bourse 1967–1972."

Paris, France: Archives historiques du Crédit Agricole

Box DAF 3343-1: "Comité des Bourses de Valeurs. Lettres des bourses, cotation province, examen de nouvelles valeurs, annexes aux séances des 9 juin et 25 octobre 1966."

Box DAF 3343-2: "Comité des Bourses de Valeurs. Dossier général: correspondance, décisions, procès-verbaux et ordres du jour."

Box DAF 3343-1: "Comité des Bourses de Valeurs. Annexes des séances des 4 octobre et 22 novembre 1966."

Box DAF 3343-2: "Comité des Bourses de Valeurs. Annexes des séances des 28 février et 9 mai 1966."

Paris, France: Archives historiques de BNP Paribas

Box IND/3316: "Pechiney Ugine Kuhlmann / Notes."

Box IND/3317: "Pechiney Ugine Kuhlmann / Documentation."

Pierrefitte-sur-Seine, France, Archives nationales

Présidence Charles de Gaulle

Box AG/5/(1)2318 to AG/5/(1)2322: "Notes des conseillers économiques."

Présidence Georges Pompidou

File 540AP29: "Dossiers de Jean Daney de Marcillac, chargé de mission au secrétariat général de la Présidence de la République."

La Courneuve, France: Centre des archives diplomatiques (Ministère des Affaires étrangères)

File FRMAE91QO/668: "Relations économiques, financières et commerciales des États-Unis avec la France (janvier 1964–décembre 1966)."

File FRMAE91QO/669: "Relations économiques, financières et commerciales des États-Unis avec la France (janvier 1967–décembre 1968)."

Savigny-le-Temple, France: Centre des archives économiques et financières (CAEF)
Archives Jean-Yves Haberer: Box 5A-0000326, 5A-0000362, 5A-0000357, 5A-0000350
Trésor–Marchés financiers: Box B-0051929, B-0068017, B-0068014, B-68050, B-68052, B-0068019

Compagnie des Agents de change de Paris
Box B-0069433/1 to B-0069437/1: "Procès-verbaux des séances, 1965–1974."

Compagnie des Agents de change–Secrétariat général
Box B-0067977/1: "Correspondance, notes, articles, brochures, etc., 1972–1982."
Box B-0067782/1 to B-0067784/1: "Registre des décisions et avis de la chambre syndicale, 1966–1968."
Box B-0067815/1 to B-0067816/1: "Circulaires de la chambre syndicale, 1966–1970."
Box B-0068589/1 to B-0068590/1: "Notes et circulaires de la chambre syndicale, 1966–1973."

Comité des Bourses de valeurs
Box B-0069180/1 and B-0069181/1: "Procès-verbaux 1965–1967."
Box B-0069181/2: "Comptes rendus d'activité, 1942–1968."

Clichy, France: Institut pour l'Histoire de l'aluminium

Rio Tinto France, Archives Pechiney–Collection historique, Direction générale
Box 200-6-55024 / 55025: Fusion Pechiney-Ugine-Kuhlmann (1971).

Rio Tinto France, Archives Pechiney–Collection historique, Secrétariat général
Box 072-2-22052: Sté d'Électro-Chimie–Métallurgie et Aciéries Électrique d'Ugine (1965–1966).
Box 072-2-22054/ 22055: Ugine Kuhlmann (1967–1971).
Box 072-2-24929 / 24913: SECEM et AEU (1965–1966).
Box 072-2-24914/ 24915: Ugine Kuhlmann–Fusion UK/SPA (1966).
Box 072-2-27714: Ugine Kuhlmann (1969–1971).
Box 072-2-24974: Société des Produits Azotés–Fusion Ugine Kuhlmann / SPA (1966).

Stanford University, Palo Alto, California, United States: Hoover Institution Archives, William J. Casey Papers, 1928–1996
Box/Folder 142/1: Conference on Financial Reporting, Paris, France, 1972 May 19.
Box/Folder 141/20: International Meeting on Stock Exchanges, Milan, Italy, 1972 March 15.
Box/Folder 147/1–2: Foreign Capital Markets.
Box/Folder 148/1: International Economic Relations.
Box/Folder 147/3: Foreign Participation in U.S. Securities Markets.
Box/Folder 144/3, A–F: Casey Correspondence.

Printed Primary Sources

Cinquième Plan de développement économique et social, 1966–1970, Tomes I et II.
Sixième Plan de développement économique et social, 1971–1975.
Commission des opérations de Bourse. "Rapport annuel 1968." *Journal officiel de la République française* April 7, 1969: 41–63.
Commission des opérations de Bourse. "Rapport annuel 1969." *Journal officiel de la République française* March 21, 1970: 125–171.
Commission des opérations de Bourse. "Rapport annuel 1970." *Journal officiel de la République française* April 2, 1971: 46–115.
Commission des opérations de Bourse. "Rapport annuel 1971." *Journal officiel de la République française* April 6, 1972: 218–306.
Commission des opérations de Bourse. "Rapport annuel 1972." *Journal officiel de la République française* May 9, 1969: 186–279.

Rapports du Conseil économique et social:
   Georges Lutfalla, "Étude du marché financier," *Journal officiel de la République française*, November 14, 1952: 409–468.
   Robert Pelletier, "Le Financement des investissements," *Journal officiel de la République française*, March 2, 1965: 261–292.
   Wilfrid Baumgartner, "Le marché financier et l'information des actionnaires," *Journal officiel de la République française*, April 2, 1972: 232–259.

Interviews

Author's interview with Jean-Yves Haberer, April 12, 2014.

Montreuil, France: Comité pour l'histoire économique et financière de la France / Institut de la gestion publique et du développement économique (IGPDE)
Archives orales Pierre Chatenet (1990 interviews conducted by Laure Quenouëlle-Corre).
Archives orales Jean-Yves Haberer (1995 interviews conducted by Laure Quenouëlle-Corre).
Archives orales René Larre (1990 interviews conducted by Sophie Coeuré).

Selected Works Cited
General Works and Global Perspectives on Financial Regulation

Abdelal, Rawi. *Capital Rules: The Construction of Global Finance*. Cambridge: Harvard University Press, 2007.
Bastidon Gilles, Cécile, Jacques Brasseul, and Philippe Gilles. *Histoire de la globalisation financière*. Paris: Armand Colin, 2010.
Belze, Loïc, and Philippe Spieser. *Histoire de la finance. Le temps, le calcul et les promesses*. Paris: Vuibert, 2007.
Bonin, Hubert, and Jean-Marc Figuet (eds.). *Crise et régulation bancaires. Les cheminements de l'instabilité et de la stabilité bancaires*. Genève: Droz, 2016.
Cassis, Youssef, and Éric Bussière. *London and Paris as International Financial Centres in the Twentieth Century*. Oxford: Oxford University Press, 2005.
Drezner, Daniel W. *All Politics Is Global: Explaining International Regulatory Regimes*. Princeton: Princeton University Press, 2007.
Feiertag, Olivier, and Michel Margairaz (eds.). *Les banques centrales à l'échelle du monde. Central Banks at World Scale*. Paris: Presses de Sciences Po, 2012.
Kindleberger, Charles P. *A Financial History of Western Europe*. New York: Oxford University Press, 1993.
Kindleberger, Charles P., and Robert Aliber. *Manias, Panics, and Crises: A History of Financial Crises*. 1978. Hoboken: Wiley, 2005.
Klaus, Ian. *Forging Capitalism: Rogues, Swindlers, Frauds, and the Rise of Modern Finance*. New Haven: Yale University Press, 2014.
Lepetit, Jean-François. *Dysfonctionnements des marchés financiers*. Paris: Economica, 2014.
Plender, John. *Capitalism: Money, Morals and Markets*. London: Biteback, 2015.
Porter, Tony. *Globalization and Finance*. Cambridge: Polity Press, 2005.
Posner, Elliott. *The Origins of Europe's New Stock Markets*. Cambridge, MA: Harvard University Press, 2009.
Reinhart, Carmen M., and Kenneth S. Rogoff. *This Time Is Different: Eight Centuries of Financial Folly*. Princeton: Princeton University Press, 2009.
Rhee, Changyong, and Adam S. Posen (eds.). *Responding to Financial Crisis: Lessons from Asia Then, the United States and Europe Now*. Washington, DC: A Copublication of the Asian Development Bank and Peterson Institute for International Economics, 2013.
Shiller, Robert J. *Irrational Exuberance*. Princeton: Princeton University Press, 2015.

Singer, David Andrew. *Regulating Capital: Setting Standards for the International Financial System.* Ithaca: Cornell University Press, 2007.

Walter, Andrew. *Governing Finance: East Asia's Adoption of International Standards.* Ithaca: Cornell University Press, 2008.

Yergin, Daniel, and Joseph Stanislaw. *The Commanding Heights: The Battle between Government and the Marketplace That Is Remaking the Modern World.* New York: Simon and Schuster, 1998.

Zumello, Christine. *L'intermédiation en question.* Paris: Presses Sorbonne Nouvelle, 2011.

Zysman, John. *Governments, Markets, and Growth: Financial Systems and the Politics of Industrial Change.* Oxford: Martin Robertson, 1983.

French Political Background

Cahiers de l'Institut d'Études Politiques de Grenoble. *La réforme régionale et le référendum du 27 avril 1969.* Paris: Éditions Cujas, 1970.

Jankowski, Paul F. *Stavisky: A Confidence Man in the Republic of Virtue.* Ithaca: Cornell University Press, 2002.

Joffrin, Laurent. *Mai 68. Une histoire du mouvement.* 1998. Paris: Éditions du Seuil, 2008.

Lacouture, Jean. *De Gaulle. 1-Le rebelle, 1890–1944.* Paris: Éditions du Seuil, 1984.

Margairaz, Michel, and Danielle Tartakowsky. *1968 entre libération et libéralisation. La grande bifurcation.* Rennes: Presses universitaires de Rennes, 2010.

Mouré, Kenneth, and Martin S. Alexander. *Crisis and Renewal in France, 1918–1962.* New York: Berghahn Books, 2002.

Nord, Philip. *Le New Deal français.* Paris: Perrin, 2016.

Perrier, Jérôme. *Michel Debré.* Paris: Ellipses, 2010.

Roussel, Éric. *Georges Pompidou, 1911–1974.* Paris: Jean-Claude Lattès, 1994.

———. *Pierre Mendès France.* Paris: Gallimard, 2007.

Saint-Geours, Jean. *Pouvoir et Finance.* Paris: Fayard, 1979.

Sirinelli, Jean-François. *Mai 68.* 2008. Paris: CNRS Éditions, 2013.

Valence, Georges. *VGE: Une vie.* Paris: Flammarion, 2011.

Vigreux, Jean. *Croissance et contestations, 1958–1981.* Paris: Éditions du Seuil, 2014.

Historical Perspectives on the French Economy

Andrieu, Claire. *La Banque sous l'occupation. Paradoxes de l'histoire d'une profession.* Paris: Presses de la Fondation nationale des sciences politiques, 1990.

Asselain, Jean-Charles. *Histoire économique de la France du XVIIIe siècle à nos jours. 2- Depuis 1918.* 1984. Paris: Seuil, 2011.

Beaud, Michel, Pierre Danjou, and Jean David. *Une multinationale française. Pechiney Ugine Kuhlmann.* Paris: Éditions du Seuil, 1975.

Buat, Nicolas. *John Law. La dette ou comment s'en débarrasser.* Paris: Les belles lettres, 2015.

Bussière, Éric. *Georges Pompidou face à la mutation économique de l'Occident, 1969–1974.* Paris: Presses Universitaires de France, 2003.

Chaussinand-Nogaret, Guy. *Gens de Finance au XVIIIe siècle.* 1972. Paris: Éditions Complexe, 1993.

Effosse, Sabine. *Le crédit à la consommation en France, 1947–1965. De la stigmatisation à la réglementation.* Paris: Comité pour l'histoire économique et financière de la France–IGPDE, 2014.

Esambert, Bernard. *Pompidou capitaine d'industries.* Paris: Éditions Odile Jacob, 1994.

Feiertag, Olivier. *Wilfrid Baumgartner. Un grand commis des finances à la croisée des pouvoirs (1902–1978).* Paris: Comité pour l'histoire économique et financière de la France–IGPDE, 2006.

Lagneau-Ymonet, Paul, and Angelo Riva. *Histoire de la Bourse*. Paris: Éditions La Découverte, 2012.

Lazarus, Jeanne. *L'épreuve de l'argent. Banques, banquiers, clients*. Paris: Calmann-Lévy, 2012.

Lemoine, Benjamin. *L'ordre de la dette. Enquête sur les infortunes de l'État et la prospérité du marché*. Paris: Éditions de la découverte, 2016.

Loriaux, Michael. *France after Hegemony: International Change and Financial Reform*. Ithaca: Cornell, 1991.

Marnata, Françoise. *La Bourse et le financement des investissements*. Paris: Armand Colin, 1973.

Patat, Jean-Pierre. *Monnaie, institutions financières et politique monétaire*. Paris: Economica, 1986.

Quennouëlle-Corre, Laure. *La place financière de Paris au XXe siècle. Des ambitions contrariées*. Paris: Comité pour l'histoire économique et financière de la France, 2015.

Thaure Philippe. *Pechiney ? . . . vendu!* Paris: Presses des Mines, 2007.

Warlouzet, Laurent. *Le choix de la CEE par la France. L'Europe économique en débat de Mendès France à de Gaulle (1955–1969)*. Paris: Comité pour l'histoire économique et financière de la France–IGPDE, 2011.

Accounting, Law, and Regulation in France

Colasse, Bernard. *Les fondements de la comptabilité*. Paris: La Découverte, 2012.

Conac, Pierre-Henri. *La régulation des marchés boursiers par la Commission des Opérations de Bourse (C.O.B.) et la Securities and Exchange Commission (S.E.C.)*. Paris: Librairie Générale de Droit et de Jurisprudence, 2002.

Gentot, Michel. *Les autorités administratives indépendantes* (2nd ed.). Paris: Montchrestien, 1994.

Merville, Anne-Dominique. *Droit financier*. Paris: Gualino éditeur, 2014.

Robert, Marie-Claude, and Béatrice Labboz. *La Commission des Opérations de Bourse*. Paris: Presse Universitaires de France, 1991.

Szramkiewicz, Romuald, and Olivier Descamps. *Histoire du droit des affaires*. Paris: Librairie Générale de Droit et de Jurisprudence, 2013.

Valette, Jean-Paul. *Régulation des marchés financiers*. Paris: Ellipses, 2013.

Véron, Nicolas. *Le grand dérèglement. Chroniques du capitalisme financier*. Paris: Lignes de repères, 2009.

"Les autorités administratives indépendantes." *La documentation française*, no. 330, April 2007, 89 pp.

Historical Perspectives on US Regulation

Brandeis, Louis D. *Other People's Money and How the Bankers Use It*. New York: Frederick A. Stockes, 1914.

Dolan, Chris J., John Frendreis, and Raymond Tatalovich. *The Presidency and Economic Policy*. New York: Rowman & Littlefield, 2008.

Eichengreen, Barry. *Hall of Mirrors: The Great Depression, the Great Recession, and the Uses—and Misuses—of History*. Oxford: Oxford University Press, 2015.

Fuller, Robert Lynn. *"Phantom of Fear": The Banking Panic of 1933*. Jefferson: McFarland, 2012.

Hawley, Ellis W. *The New Deal and the Problem of Monopoly*. Princeton: Princeton University Press, 1966.

Kaiser, Robert G. *Act of Congress: How America's Essential Institution Works, and How It Doesn't*. New York: Alfred A. Knopf, 2013.

Khoury, Sarkis J. *U.S. Banking and Its Regulation in the Political Context*. Lanham: University Press of America, 1997.

Krippner, Greta R. *Capitalizing on Crisis: The Political Origins of the Rise of Finance*. Cambridge: Harvard University Press, 2011.

Levine, Lawrence W., and Cornelia R. Levine, *The People and the President: America's Conversation with FDR*. Boston: Beacon Press.

Levitt, Arthur, with Paula Dwyer. *Take on the Street: How to Fight for Your Financial Future*. New York: Random House, 2003.

Lind, Michael. *Land of Promise: An Economic History of the United States*. New York: Harper, 2013.

Meiners, Roger E., and Bruce Yandle (eds.). *Regulation and the Reagan Era*. New York: Holmes & Meier, 1989.

Ott, Julia C. *When Wall Street Met Main Street: The Quest for an Investors' Democracy*. Cambridge: Harvard University Press, 2011.

Parrish, Michael E. *Securities Regulation and the New Deal*. New Haven: Yale University Press, 1970.

Perino, Michael. *The Hellhound of Wall Street: How Ferdinand Pecora's Investigation of the Great Crash Forever Changed American Finance*. New York: Penguin Press, 2010.

Rosen, Jeffrey. *Louis D. Brandeis: American Prophet*. New Haven: Yale University Press, 2016.

Schwarz, Jordan A. *The New Dealers: Power Politics in the Age of Roosevelt*. New York: Alfred A. Knopf, 1993.

Seligman, Joel. *The Transformation of Wall Street: A History of the Securities and Exchange Commission and Modern Corporate Finance*. Boston: Houghton Mifflin, 1982.

Stein, Herbert. *Presidential Economics: The Making of Economic Policy from Roosevelt to Clinton*. Washington, DC: American Enterprise Institute for Public Policy Research, 1994.

Stigler, George J. *The Citizen and the State: Essays on Regulation*. Chicago: University of Chicago Press, 1975.

Van der Yeught, Michel. *Une histoire de Wall Street*. Paris: Éditions Eska, 2009.

Zinn, Howard. *New Deal Thought*. 1966 Indianapolis: Hacket, 2003.

France and the United States

Cogan, Charles G. *Oldest Allies, Guarded Friends: The United States and France since 1940*. Westport: Praeger, 1994.

Costigliola, Frank. *France and the United States: The Cold Alliance since World War II*. New York: Twayne, 1992.

Kuisel, Richard. *The French Way: How France Embraced and Rejected American Values and Power*. Princeton: Princeton University Press, 2012.

Kuisel, Richard. *Seducing the French: The Dilemma of Americanization*. Berkeley: University of California Press, 1993.

Rodgers, Daniel T. *Atlantic Crossings: Social Politics in a Progressive Age*. Cambridge: Belknap Press of Harvard University Press, 1998.

Roger, Philippe. *L'ennemi américain. Généalogie de l'antiaméricanisme français*. Paris: Éditions du Seuil, 2002.

Tournès, Ludovic. *Les fondations philanthropiques américaines en France au XXe siècle*. Paris: Classiques Garnier Poche, 2013.

Autobiographies, Memoirs, Testimonies

Baruch, Bernard. *The Public Years*. New York: Holt, Rinehart and Winston, 1960.

Bloch-Lainé, François. *Ce que je crois*. Paris: Grasset, 1995.

Bouthillier, Yves. *Le drame de Vichy: II. Finances sous la contrainte*. Paris: Librairie Plon, 1951.

Chatenet, Pierre. *Décolonisation. Souvenirs et Réflexions*. Paris: Buchet-Chastel, 1988.

Debré, Michel. *Trois républiques pour une France: Mémoires—I: Combattre*. Paris: Albin Michel, 1984.

Debré, Michel. *Trois républiques pour une France: Mémoires—IV: Gouverner autrement (1962–1970)*. Paris: Albin Michel, 1993.

Douglas, William O. *Go East, Young Man: The Early Years; The Autobiography of William O. Douglas*. New York: Random House, 1974.

Dupont, Xavier. *Salut la compagnie! Mémoires d'un agent de change*. Paris: Albin Michel, 2002.

Geismar, Alain. *Mon mai 1968*. Paris: Perrin, 2008.

Grimaud, Maurice. *En Mai, fais ce qu'il te plait*. Paris: Stock, 1977.

Hoover, Herbert. *The Memoirs of Herbert Hoover: The Great Depression, 1929–1941*. New York: Macmillan, 1952.

Ickes, Harold L. *The Secret Diary of Harold L. Ickes: The First Thousand Days, 1933–1936*. New York: Simon and Schuster, 1953.

Mauriac, François. *Bloc-notes. Tome IV, 1965–1967*. Paris: Éditions du Seuil, 1993.

Murphy, Robert. *Diplomat among Warriors*. Garden City: Doubleday, 1964.

Peyrefitte, Alain. *C'était de Gaulle* (vol. 3). Paris: Éditions de Fallois, Fayard, 2000.

Pierre Chatenet: 1917–1997. Paris: Mme Chatenet, 1999.

Pisani, Edgard. *Persiste et signe*. Paris: Éditions Odile Jacob, 1992.

Pompidou, Georges. *Pour rétablir une vérité*. Paris: Flammarion, 1982.

Tricot, Bernard. *Mémoires*. Paris: Quai Voltaire, 1994.

Articles

Baudelot, Christian, and Anne Lebeaupin. "Les salaires de 1950 à 1975." *Économie et statistique* 113, no. 1 (1979): 15–22.

Berger, Karine. "La régulation bancaire et financière face aux crises. Roosevelt et aujourd'hui." *Franklin D. Roosevelt aujourd'hui, Pouvoirs*, no. 150 (September 2014): 77–91.

Besse, Pierre. "Le Conseil National du Crédit." *Revue économique* 2, no. 5 (1951): 578–590.

Blancheton, Bertrand, Hubert Bonin, and David Le Bris, "The French Paradox: A Financial Crisis during the Golden Age of the 1960s." *Business History* 56, no. 3 (2014): 391–413.

Burgard, Jean-Jacques. "La Commission des opérations de bourse." *Banque*, no. 311 (October 1972): 861–870.

Casanova, Jean-Claude. "L'amendement Vallon." *Revue française de science politique*, no. 1 (1967): 97–109.

Donnedieu de Vabres, Jean. "La C.O.B., une administration de mission." *La Revue administrative* 33, no. 195 (May–June 1980): 237–241.

Douvreleur, Olivier. "L'indépendance de l'autorité des marchés financiers." *Revue française d'administration publique* 3, no. 143 (2013): 747–758.

Dupont-Fauville, Antoine. "Michel Debré, ministre de l'Économie et des Finances." *Michel Debré, un réformateur aux Finances 1966–1968* (5–12). Conference held at the Ministère de l'Économie, des Finances et de l'Industrie on January 8, 2004. Paris: Ministère de l'Économie, des Finances et de l'Industrie, Comité pour l'Histoire économique et financière de la France, 2005.

Fournier, H. "La Commission de Contrôle des Banques." *Revue économique*, 2, no. 5 (1951): 591–599.

Gaïti, Brigitte. "Les modernisateurs dans l'administration d'après-guerre. L'écriture d'une histoire héroïque." *Revue française d'administration publique*, 2, no. 102 (2002): 295–306.

Grabar, Nicolas. "La Commission des opérations de Bourse à la lumière de l'expérience américaine." *Le Débat* 5, no. 52 (1988): 67–75.

Guillaume, Marc. "Les ordonnances. Tuer ou sauver la loi?" *Pouvoirs*, no. 114 (3rd Quarter 2005): 117–129.

Hautcoeur, Pierre-Cyrille. "Marchés financiers et développement économique. Une approche historique." *Regards croisés sur l'économie*, 1, no. 3 (2008): 159–172.

Helleiner, Eric, and Stefano Pagliari. "The End of an Era in International Regulation? A Postcrisis Research Agenda." *International Organization* 65 (Winter 2011): 169–200.

Kovar, Jean-Philippe. "L'indépendance des autorités de régulation financière à l'égard du pouvoir politique." *Revue française d'administration publique* 3, no. 143 (2013): 655–666.

Kuisel, Richard. "L'*American Way of Life* et les missions françaises de productivité." *Vingtième Siècle, revue d'histoire* 17, no. 1 (1988): 21–38.

Le Bris, David. "Les krachs boursiers en France depuis 1854." *Revue économique* 61, no. 3 (2010): 421–430.

Le Bris, David, and Pierre-Cyrille Hautcoeur. "A Challenge to Triumphant Optimists? A Blue Chips Index for the Paris Stock Exchange (1854–2007)." *Financial History Review* 17, no. 2 (2010): 141–183.

Monnet, Éric. "La politique de la France au sortir des Trente Glorieuses. Un tournant monétariste?" *Revue d'histoire moderne et contemporaine* 1, no. 62-1 (2015): 147–174.

Montricher, Nicole de. "A National Pattern of Policy Transfer: The Regulation of Insider Trading in France." *French Politics* 3, no. 1 (March 2005): 28–48.

———. "Norme légale et internationalisation des marchés boursiers. La délinquance financière en liberté surveillée." *Droit et société* 1, no. 71 (2009): 133–160.

Morsel, Henri. "La mission de productivité aux États-Unis de l'industrie française de l'aluminium." *Histoire, économie et société* 18, no. 2 (1999): 413–417.

Newman, Abraham, and Elliott Posner. "Transnational Feedbacks, Soft Law, and Preferences in Global Financial Regulation." *Review of International Political Economy* 23, no. 1 (2016): 123–152.

Pisani, Edgard. "Administration de gestion, administration de gestion." *Revue française de science politique*, no. 2 (1956): 315–330.

Quennouëlle-Corre, Laure. "Les réformes bancaires et financières de 1966–1967." *Michel Debré, un réformateur aux Finances 1966–1968* (85–117). Conference held at the Ministère de l'Économie, des Finances et de l'Industrie on January 8, 2004. Paris: Ministère de l'Économie, des Finances et de l'Industrie, Comité pour l'Histoire économique et financière de la France, 2005.

Rajan, Raghuram G., and Luigi Zingales. "The Great Reversals: The Politics of Financial Development in the 20th Century." *Journal of Financial Economics* 69 (2003): 5–20.

Scholte, Jan Aart. "Global Capitalism and the State." *International Affairs (Royal Institute of International Affairs 1944–)* 73, no. 3; *Globalization and International Relations* (July 1997): 427–452.

Simmons, Beth A. "The International Politics of Harmonization: The Case of Capital Market Regulation." *International Organization* 55, no. 3 (Summer 2001): 589–620.

Simmons, Beth A., and Zachary Elkins. "Globalization and Policy Diffusion," in Miles Kahler and David A. Lake (eds.), *Governance in a Global Economy: Political Authority in Transition* (275–304). Princeton: Princeton University Press, 2003.

Vasseur, Pierre. "La Commission des opérations de bourse." *Banque*, no. 271 (February 1969): 83–93.

Verteneuil, Jacques H. "La Commission bancaire a vingt-cinq ans." *La Revue de la banque*, no. 9–10 (1960): 607–618.

Wang, Jessica. "Imagining the Administrative State: Legal Pragmatism, Securities Regulation, and New Deal Liberalism." *Journal of Policy History* 17, no. 3 (2005): 257–293.

———. "Neo-Brandeisianism and the New Deal: Adolf A. Berle, Jr., William O. Douglas, and the Problem of Corporate Finance in the 1930s." *Seattle University Law Review* 33, no. 4 (2010): 1221–1246.

Other Works Cited or Consulted

Boltanski, Luc. *Les Cadres. La formation d'un groupe social*. Paris: Les Éditions de Minuit, 1982.

Boris, Georges. *La Révolution Roosevelt*. Paris: Gallimard, 1934.

Boyer, Robert. *Économie politique des capitalismes. Théorie de la régulation et des crises.* Paris: La Découverte, 2015.

———. *La théorie de la régulation. Une analyse critique.* Paris: Éditions La Découverte, 1986.

Fontaine, Laurence. *Le marché. Histoire et usages d'une conquête sociale.* Paris: Gallimard, 2014.

Foucault, Michel. *Sécurité, territoire, population. Cours au Collège de France. 1977–1978.* Paris: Seuil/Gallimard, 2004.

Loichot, Marcel. *La réforme pancapitaliste.* Paris: Robert Laffont, 1966.

Servan-Schreiber, Jean-Louis. *Le défi américain.* Paris: Denoël, 1967.

Supiot, Alain. *La Gouvernance par les nombres. Cours au Collège de France (2012–2014).* Paris: Fayard / Institut d'Études avancées de Nantes, 2015.